Capitalism and its Challenges Across Borders

Perspectives from the Asian, African, and American Continents

Bahaudin G. Mujtaba
Editor

ILEAD Academy, LLC
Davie, Florida. United States of America
www.ileadacademy.com

Bahaudin G. Mujtaba, 2014. *Capitalism and its Challenges Across Borders*

Cover Design by: Cagri Tanyar

ISBN-13: 978-1-936237-08-1
ISBN-10: 1-936237-08-3

Subject Code & Description

BUS029000   Business & Economics : Free Enterprise
BUS000000   Business & Economics : General
BUS072000   Business & Economics : Development - Sustainable Development

Printed in the United States of America by ILEAD Academy, LLC. Davie, Florida.

☆ International ☆
ILEAD ACADEMY
Leadership Education and Associate Development Academy

Dedication

We dedicate this book to students, researchers, business owners, managers, entrepreneurs, and policy-makers who are cognizant of cross-cultural knowledge and differing economic systems and who effectively apply this knowledge in their decision-making every day. A special appreciation goes to educators who help learners think expansively and critically and who inculcate cultural competency, so that learners can be responsible and successful future leaders in today's global society.

Knowing is not enough,
We must APPLY.
Willing is not enough,
We must DO.

-Bruce Lee

You reap what you sow. "Don't plant anything but love." - Rumi

Table of Contents

Acknowledgements

There are many individuals that have contributed to this volume; *first,* I would like to thank the following colleagues for their contributions to the content of this book:

- Acheraporn Plangmarn
- Albert Williams
- Belal A. Kaifi
- Belay Seyoum
- Bob McClelland
- Cagri Tanyar
- Donovan A. McFarlane
- Frank J. Cavico
- Guillermo Gibens
- Han Ping
- Ikwukananne I. Udechukwu
- Isaac Wasswa Katono
- Jackson David
- Jatuporn Sungkhawan
- Kazuhito Isomura

- Lam D. Nguyen
- Mahmoud Bodla
- María I. Méndez
- Mario E. Delgado
- Naseem Habib
- Noel Fernandez
- Osman Masahudu
- Pedro F. Pellet
- Peter Williamson
- Ramón J Venero
- Ruth Torres
- Talat Afza
- Terrell G. Manyak
- Yunshan Lian
- Warren Byabashaija

Second, I would like to thank all those professional organizations, such as the Academy of Management, and our family members who have helped us get to this point.

Third, I would like to extend special thanks to my dear colleagues, Dr. Frank Cavico and Dr. Pedro Pellet, for their review, editing and suggestions on the final draft of this book.

Fourth, the authors and I would like to thank you for reading this material; and we trust you will find this book interesting, thought-provoking, useful, and beneficial. You can always contact the editor at: *mujtaba@nova.edu.*

Overall, the content of this book is diverse, as it covers many countries in four different continents across the globe. As such, some of the content might be culture specific. Each author is responsible for his/her own writing and the copyright ownership for their submission. This book is based on the papers prepared for, and presented at, the annual Academy of Management (AoM) conference in Orlando, Florida on August 11, 2013. The following is the conference citation:

- Mujtaba, B.G., Afza, T., Byabashaija, W., Cavico, F.J., David, J., Delgado, M.E., Fernandez, N., Habib, N., Isomura, K., Katono, I.W., Manyak, T.G., Masahudu, O., McFarlane, D.A., Mendez, M.I., Nguyen, L.D., Pellet, P.F., Plangmarn, A., Ping, H., Torres, R., and Udechukwu, I. (August 2013). *Capitalism and Corruption across the African, Asian, and North American Economies.* Professional Development Workshop, Academy of Management Conference, *Orlando,* Florida. Sunday, August 11, 2013.

Bahaudin

Preface

The editor and contributors of this book believe that knowledge and application of diverse and relevant economic ideas, concepts, and philosophies is important to business leaders; and also they must act in a socially responsible manner in order for society to become progressively better. As such, business leaders in pursuing profits must obey the law, act for the greater good, treat all stakeholders with dignity and respect, and be socially responsible by supporting the community in civic and philanthropic efforts. Acting in a responsible way will require business leaders to be cognizant of all stakeholder interests and values as well as to attempt to balance them in a fair and just way.

Capitalism and free markets must stand on a foundation of morality and justice for all. The economy needs to be free to function, but the economy also needs rules to function correctly and effectively. The idea is to create sustainable forms of economic systems, whereby acting in a socially responsible manner will produce profits for the shareholders but also long-term value for all the other stakeholders of the company and community in a fair manner. The task of business leaders, therefore, is to incorporate not only legal rules but also social responsibility, ethics, and stakeholder considerations into corporate strategy. Transparency, truthfulness, and trustworthiness should be the hallmarks of successful business. A true business leader must be keenly aware and foresee the consequences of his or her company's actions on all the firm's stakeholders, including society as a whole. Business leaders must be aware that law, ethics, and social responsibility are all interconnected and underpin the economy and the free market system.

This book provides a great deal of relevant cross-cultural knowledge for students, academicians, business owners, entrepreneurs, and policy-makers. However, as once emphasized by the actor and martial artist, Bruce Lee, "knowing is not enough, we must apply…willing is not enough, we must do"; and following this advice is the socially responsible thing to do in order to make our society a little better every single day.

The authors hope that this book serves as a tool for true business success, stakeholder responsibility, and organizational and societal sustainability.

Bahaudin!

CHAPTER 1
Introduction to Economic Systems

Capitalism has had a great economic impact on Western culture. This book brings together researchers with extensive research and personal experience to examine and to discuss the challenges of capitalism and corruption from cross-cultural perspectives. We emphasize that capitalism, which can be an excellent system for progress under the right conditions, can also lead to increased levels of corruption in some economies, where the collective nature of the culture and the paternalistic expectations from the government are the societal norms. As such, corruption can be a by-product of capitalism; and when it is coupled with bad governance, it can have a direct negative impact on the economy. This chapter begins by discussing capitalism and economic systems while laying out the theme of the book with a paradigm from across borders.

Capitalism
Capitalism, which primarily has been a Western economic system, is about the personal or private ownership of relevant tools along with the financial and human resources for the acquisition and production of products that are sold for a profit. A major element of capitalism is the creation of market-based, management practices where the best products and services which are produced at lowest average total costs will be the most competitive in the industry and thereby will be earning the most profits. The nature of competitive workplace, along with a lack of proper governance and/or the absence of a strong public sector, can lead to unethical and corrupt practices in business.

The profit motive coupled with the temptation of continuously increasing total profits can also lead or tempt some individuals to take "shortcuts" in order to satisfy the demands and expectations of their shareholders. Furthermore, a mixture of violence, lack of trust, and incompetence on the part of some public officials can easily lead to a corrupt business environment in a country. A corrupt business culture not only leads to inefficiencies, along with a rising gap between the rich and poor, but it also leads to lack of trust between the citizens of a country and the government, which can serve as fuel for crime and violence (Kelman, 2000).

The unfortunate result of corruption is that it hurts people, cities, countries, and societies overall. While some governments have specific rules and enforceable policies in place to combat bribery and other forms of corruption, others allow some forms of payments to government officials, or do not enforce their stated laws prohibiting bribery. What is clear is that in a collective culture it is even more difficult to quickly detect bribery, in particular because the total group norm might mistakenly approve of such practices due to embedded customs, cronyism, pluralistic ignorance, and/or other tribal and paternalistic paradigms along with overall group conformity. The unfortunate externality associated with group conformity is that it can legitimize inappropriate and highly unethical behaviors that are commonly practiced among some greedy entrepreneurs and corporations.

Figure 1.1 – Becoming Rich by Taking from the Poor

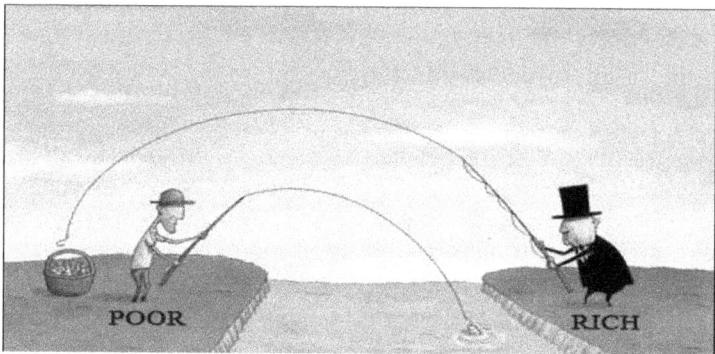

Source unknown: taken from Facebook posting, October 2012.

In a gathering when politics and business topics were being discussed in a bad economy, a colleague mentioned that in the western world there are two kinds of thieves that steal from others. The first kind of a thief is the one who steals by taking something from you, runs away with your property, and usually stays away from you due to shame. This thief knows that what he/she is doing is illegal and unethical. The second kind is the person who takes care of you as the customer, offers you free coffee and donuts while you wait at their office for service, sells you their products or services at "outrageous levels of profit", and you happily go back to them again and again because you see them as a trusted friend or because you don't have many other options. This thief knows that what he/she is doing is not illegal but can be highly unethical. The colleague went on to say that the second type is the worst thief, because this person would usually see himself/herself as a capitalist. Sadly, this example, at times, is not too far from the truth in a free market economy.

One example of the second kind of thief is an actual quotation of $4,800 for painting a car at a South Florida car dealership in 2012. The paint job would take about four days and the dealership would be offering a loaner car for free to the customer during the four days when the car is being painted. Since the price seemed a little high, other companies and entrepreneurs were contacted to see how much they would charge for the same job of painting the car. This car was eventually painted during a four-day period with the best quality paint through a private entrepreneur for $650. The entrepreneur, who owned his own auto repair and paint shop, was referred by a colleague – he did not paint the car for free but rather did it for a fair price as he had his employees spend time doing the work and they obviously paid for the cost of the paint. As a result of this transaction, this entrepreneur made some profit for his shop and kept his employees busy working on this paint job. This transaction demonstrates that the big company employees were trying to earn an outrageously huge profit for a job that should cost less than one-sixth of their estimated quotation from this corporately-owned dealership. Sadly, if this was an emergency repair work that needed to be done on the engine, then many people would not have had the option of searching other shops to find a better price. Even though most people are aware of the "buyer beware" proclamation in a free market economy, many end up paying the $4,800 estimated cost even though they cannot necessarily afford it and might have to finance this loan through a bank – which then keeps causing this family to become poorer as a result of paying more fees for the loan and high interest rates that the bank will keep charging for the financing services. What is even more disappointing is that the dealership is usually highly trusted since their firm owns the car brand. Yet, some of these businesses take advantage of their customers by charging them enormous prices for little service. It is basically the same as stealing money from the hard working men and women without giving them an equivalent value. This type of "stealing" is almost always legal but often highly unethical in any economic system or country. Ultimately, because of these types of situations where people only focus on maximizing their profits at any cost, the rich tends to become richer and the poor becomes poorer thereby widening the gap between them on a continuous basis.

Capitalism is not necessarily bad, but when greedy people and businesses are fattening their personal profits through highly unethical means or other "get rich quick fixes", everyone in society suffers in the long-term as a result. Let us hope that a thief is not operating under any economic system so we can see more socially responsible corporations and entrepreneurs in the modern workplace.

Economic Systems

Capitalism is one form of an economic system for doing business in a market-oriented context. While there are many economic systems being practiced across the globe, the content of this book is focused on capitalism, its challenges, opportunities, and the consequences, which are being demonstrated in various countries. We can start by reviewing some basic content on economic systems and market orientation.

There are many economic systems today; and they are very diverse around the globe. Three of the major types of economic systems currently in existence are the market economy, the command economy, and the mixed economy. Each type of economic system has its advantages and disadvantages for each country's unique circumstances. Generally, a market economy is known as a free-market run by the citizens of the country. In the next type, the government leaders and officials in the country run a command system of economy. Thirdly, a mixed economy is run partially by private ownership, where the government officials operate the remaining parts.

State-Directed or the Command Economy

A command economy has been known to stifle the growth of the economy in a country. In a stated-directed Economy, the government has full control of what is to be produced and provided to its citizens. Citizens do not have much of a choice in what they will have; and consequently quality in production is often sacrificed for quantity.

      Having certain businesses being state owned allows the state to direct how investments are made. These investments are usually made for the collective benefit of the nation and not the individual. The biggest problem with a command economy is that there is no control over costs or efficiency (Gable and Ellig, 1993). This situation occurs because the state knows that it cannot "go out of business." One of the challenges about the command economy is that there is little to no incentive for innovation, which practice is often associated with capitalism and free market economies. Businesses do not necessarily "go out of their way" to look for better ways to serve customer needs; yet some exceptional companies, despite the fact that they are owned and operated by the government, have become very good at serving their customers – an example is Thai Airways which has over 27,000 employees and is fully operated by the government in Thailand. Another example of a mixed economy system is the Virtual University of Pakistan (VUP) which is now serving over 100,000 students across the sixth largest populated country in the world. Nonetheless, it is generally agreed that state-directed economies usually stifle growth because resources are often funneled to a central agency within the government. It is then left up to the government to allocate finances back into programs that the government officials and politicians deem important, based on their vision and not necessarily competitive necessity. If companies are not productive, they are not profitable; and therefore this negative fact can stifle economic growth. State-directed economies usually are meant to serve the collective needs of the community and country instead of the needs of a specific individual or a group of shareholders (Free Market Economy, 2010).

Free Market Benefits

Free market economies usually stimulate greater economic growth, as there is a balance between supply and demand. As such, the right quantity of relevant goods and services that are desired are produced in a timely manner, and thus consumers would pay a premium for them. The free market allows money and resources to go to the projects that provide the most economic benefit for the company's owners, managers, and other shareholders (Free Market Economy vs. State Driven Economy, 2010). In a market economy, most of the businesses are privately owned and are "just" regulated by the state. Competition exists to produce a better product or service; and this competition is what stimulates creativity, innovation, and ultimately, the economy. In such an environment, companies are more likely to produce goods and services with the highest standards possible in order to make sure customers pay well for them.

Overall, the free market economy is based in the basic economic principle of demand and supply without intervention by the government. Free market economy allows business to earn money and profits by providing goods and services that people demand and are willing to pay a fair price for it. A free market can distribute resources much more efficiently than can a state-run economy (Gable and Ellig, 1993). Free market economies tend to stimulate economic growth because they rely on people to buy and sell things or services proactively and based on their desires and values. A free market economy stimulates growth because businesses and entrepreneurs want to keep up with the latest trends in order to make a profit from initiating and successfully continuing the venture. Making money and growing one's business allow companies to purchase more goods and services, which in turn can stimulate the economy. Supply and demand drive a free market economy. If the demand is high and the supply is low, then the price of a commodity will go up (Free Market Economy, 2010).

By enabling a free market society to exist, people continue on with not only political freedom, but also the freedom of economic enterprise and entrepreneurship. The United States of America was meant to be a nation of free choice; not one ruled by tyrannical political elites, which can distort freedom and abrige rights (Quinn, Mujtaba and Cavico, 2011). Yet serious issues regarding capitalism and social responsibility of our free market system have recently emerged in the American culture. In particular, today all companies are expected to conduct international business and trade in not only a legal manne,r but also a moral and ethical as well as in a socially responsible manner. That is, what they are expected to do is to "combine ethical conduct with the bottom line" (Sanyal, 2010, p. 448).

Of course, economic developments should not be limited just to a government structure. The Nobel prize-winning economist, Amartya Sen, argues that the concept of development should be broadened to include more than just economic development processes. Sen (2010) believes that personal freedom is what is important; and accordingly the key to growth requires the removal of major roadblocks to gain that freedom in any given country or market. These roadblocks can include poverty, oppression, and lack of economic opportunities, systematic social deprivation, and neglect of public facilities, as well as the intolerance of repressive states. Sen (2010) believes that "development is not just an economic process, but it is a political one too, and to succeed requires the "democratization" of political communities to give citizens a voice in the important decisions made for the community" (p. 61). Sen encourages the rights of basic health care and education, especially for all minorities, women, and children. These rights are paramount in order to build a nation that is fair for all. A person cannot reach his/her full potential if he or she is ill or uneducated. Evidence suggests that governments that have adopted Sen's policy on education have had significant economic development in the past three decades compared to those that have not used Sen's recommendations. Some of these countries that have made significant improvements are China, South Korea, Taiwan, Singapore, and Hong Kong, China.

In general, we can all agree that a democratic political system is an essential condition for sustained economic progress in the modern era. Today's democratic systems are representative systems of various people groups and their desires. Unlike those "pure" democratic systems used by some cities in ancient Greece, where each individual citizen had a say in each decision made by the government, today's modern republic systems use representatives of the citizens to make government decisions on everyone's behalf. In other words, the citizens of the country or state do not directly take part in the decisions that are made in government. Instead the citizens of the community elect officials to represent them in the various levels or branches of government. The elected officials in turn are trusted to do what is best for the citizens that elected them.

One of the major advantages of a democratic political system is the freedom that it gives to the people to pursue new business ventures based on an idea or vision that they have from personal experiences or the perceived needs of the community. A true democracy is defined by those freedoms, which include individual's rights of free speech, free media, regular and fair elections, limited terms in office for the elected officials, fair legal and court systems, non-political police officers, and access to accurate information.

An open democratic system usually allows for competition to enter the market and take advantage of the opportunities. Moreover, today we are seeing even the command economies moving toward a mixed economy. As a result, some non-democratic system countries are able to achieve a relatively high economy; but the fear is that eventually they may stagnate and stop growing. This is primarily due to central planning or central decision-making at the top of the organization or institution, which often lacks political as well as economic competition. Without free and fair competition in the market, we know that monopolistic institutions are created, which do not have a great need to find better and more efficient ways of doing business. Essentially, if innovation and creativity are not rewarded through monetary means, then they will probably cease to exist. As such, many believe that a capitalistic economic system best encourages innovation, risk-taking, and creativity in business and development for the economy. Today, amid a capitalistic structure, business must deal with another value – the expectation that business, as it grows and especially once it attains a certain size, wealth, and prominence, not only be free of corruption and other illegalities, but also act in an ethical and a "socially responsible" manner in all their dealings.

Book Overview: Countries and Authors
This book brings together researchers with extensive research and personal experience in the African, Asian, Latin American, and North American countries to discuss the challenges of capitalism and corruption in markedly diverse economies

and cultures. It is emphasized that capitalism can lead to increased challenges for policy-makers in some economies where people's expectations from the government are merely paternalistic. Furthermore, capitalism can result in increased corruption when the government is not able to create and enforce the right policies and/or implement laws. As such, we can see corruption as a by-product of capitalism coupled with bad governance. Hence any discussion of economy ought to incorporate an understanding of the causes of corruption and its role in the informal as well as formal sectors. We draw examples from several countries across continents, where bribery can be a commonly accepted business practice in some areas. Some of these countries are considered to be world's most corrupt nations. While capitalism might be practiced in each of these countries to some extent, we argue that capitalism combined with a lack of proper governance are partially responsible for such negative externalities or unintended consequences.

The book is a forum for researchers and practitioners to discuss existing business strategies and market-based management practices across the selected countries. We discuss the causes and role of corruption in the business environment and offer strategies to address deeply-embedded corrupt practices in different cultures. We also highlight business and managerial implications in each economy. In particular, we discuss business ethics education and development as an emerging local and global challenge for public officials and private sector entrepreneurs who want to take full advantage of capitalism for their personal and community growth. The book begins by exploring the theme of capitalism and its challenges along with the difficulties of capitalism in the war ravaged environments, such as Afghanistan, where the government might be weak and corruption high. This is followed by colleagues' noteworthy writings associated with the following countries in several continents: Asia (Afghanistan, Pakistan, India, China, Japan, Thailand, Vietnam, and Singapore), Africa (Uganda, Nigeria, and Ghana), Latin America (Venezuela), and North America (the United States, Jamaica, Haiti, and Cuba).

So, this book brings together researchers with extensive research and personal experience in fourteen countries who explore some of the challenges related to capitalism and corruption across cultures. The first three chapters provide a discussion on the foundational concepts related to economic systems, such as capitalism, along with an emphasis on the need for good governance. The remaining chapters are focused on specific countries along with the continuing discussion of capitalism and/or corruption. The book provides literature, examples, and information regarding economic systems focused on the following countries:

1. *Afghanistan*. Belal Kaifi explores capitalism and its consequences in Afghanistan. Widespread corruption is increasing as capitalism is allowing some entrepreneurs to become very rich and others are pushed toward poverty. The findings are then related to the challenges faced by local public sector government officials in working to reduce radicalization and violence as they rebuild this country after years of war.

2. ***China***. This chapter by Han Ping focuses on how the medical corruption of China has already aroused great concern from society. This study analyzes the medical corruption expression, influence of China's medical corruption to trust relationship between doctors and patients, as well as the down-side of reduced doctor-patient trust. Then it analyzes the fundamental cause of medical corruption, which results from the macro-economic system outside the medical system as well as current complicated social factors. Corruption also is directly related to the problems of morality inside the medical system and the supervisory institutions. It can also be attributed to people's psychological state, value orientation, and cultural background. Based on the analysis, the author offers some countermeasures to prevent medical corruption.

3. ***Cuba***. Pedro F. Pellet, Mario E. Delgado, and María I. Méndez argue that economic growth for its own sake is a very shortsighted, and ultimately a self-defeating, goal. Human progress requires effort, but of the type that allows one to enjoy the fruits of his or her labor. Progress must occur in an environment that prevents one from becoming an expendable "cog" in an endless production-consumption "wheel." We must strive to enhance the Wealth of Nations, and not to surrender their potential for the Wealth of Industries by continually benefiting relatively narrow elites. Finally, let's remember that cultural as well as economic progress requires ethical and moral development.

4. ***Ghana***. Osman Masahudu states that Ghana, which is located on the West Coast of Africa, is a country with flourishing democracy; and it appears to be an "envy" of the continent. Ghana is often referred to as an "island of peace" in a most troubling region of the continent. Investors around the world may soon have greater interest in Ghana because of the recent discovery of oil coupled with its "teething" democracy. Ghana has ten states and 110 counties. A former British colony, and the first country in the Sub-Sahara Africa to gain independence in 1957, Ghana practices parliamentary democracy. In the past decade or so, a series of events have enfolded to confirm Ghana's place as a "beacon of hope" for democracy and progress in Africa.

5. ***Haiti***. Ruth Torres and David Jackson explore the impact of capitalism in Haiti, which is a small, beautiful Caribbean Island of just 360km bordering the Dominican Republic and occupying 1/3rd of the island of Hispaniola, which is is right in the middle of "hurricane alley". Haiti has been plagued by political violence for most of its history. During the three-decade reign of François "Papa Doc" Duvalier and his son Baby Doc, the clan terrorized Haiti — 30,000 opponents were abducted, kidnapped and killed by their Gestapo-like secret police, the Tonton Macoutes — and Baby Doc alone,

according to recent Haitian judicial investigations, allegedly stole some $300 million, including, in one case, funds appropriated for a major railroad that was never built. Their dynasty is a key reason why Haiti is still the Western hemisphere's poorest and most dysfunctional country today.

6. ***India.*** Mohammed Ahmed, while focusing on examples from the country of his birth and culture of India, emphasizes that capitalism is the process of achieving personal, social, political, technological, and economic growth, with fewer constraints and boundaries, in order to provide opportunities for everyone in the society to participate in that growth. Capitalism is understood in Eastern societies as a belief or process for the exploitation of markets and sowing the seeds of corruption. It is sometimes difficult to define or explain capitalism to the people of Eastern countries because for decades it was labeled as a process to get rich at the expense of the poor. The growth in monetary value, or getting rich, is one of the outcomes of capitalism, and if we focus on only one of the outcomes of capitalism, it becomes an unattractive alternative in South Asian countries for managing growth.

7. ***Jamaica.*** Donovan McFarlane discusses how, in August 2012, Jamaica celebrated its 50th year of independence from British colonial governance, along with the insufficiency of economic and social progress that has been made, particularly with regards to the development of economy, wealth of the nation, the standard of living of the people and their overall prosperity and well-being. Jamaica has not progressed much in 50 years, and this view is held by many given the nation's current economic standing: declined currency value, high crime rate, high unemployment rate, high rate of poverty, and other developmental issues.

8. ***Japan.*** In this chapter, Kazuhito Isomura points out several varieties of capitalism, and provides an overview of the Japanese economy. When the Soviet Union and other socialist regimes began to collapse at the end of the 1980s, the victory of capitalism was proclaimed. However, this does not mean that the entire world now is dominated by one type of capitalism. Several researchers argue that there are several varieties of capitalism; they suggest that capitalism takes different forms as a result of being combined with the socio-cultural factors of each country and region.

9. ***Nigeria.*** Ikwukananne I. Udechukwu explores corruption in Nigeria and states that the basis for it has not yet been fully studied. Some studies have approached corruption in Nigeria from a judiciary, executive, labor, law enforcement, and legislative perspective. This paper attempts to use the institutional and architectural perspectives to glean into the nature and

consequences of corruption in Nigeria. It is hoped that other developing economies with abundant natural resources, as is the case in Nigeria, using the matrix provided in the chapter, can study the nature of the formal and informal institutions that exist within their boundaries.

10. *Pakistan*. Talat Afza and Naseem Habib argue that capitalism is often seen as an economic system where individuals own the means of production and thus they are free to control the means of production in accord with their interests. Such system confers the responsibility of providing peace and justice upon government. Government also imposes "tolerable" taxes but does not intervene in price mechanism of market, which is adjusted in the best interests of society through coordination of the forces of supply and demand. They discuss Pakistan as a case which the country fell prey to moves of nationalization and new liberal economies in alternative periods; and consequently in more than sixty years it could not devise an effective economic policy which best suits its circumstances. Pakistan is the clear example of a system which lacks proper control and which allows the small group of people comprised of politicians, military higher-ups, civil bureaucrats, feudalists and industrialists to control the fate and wealth of the country and make accessibility to political, human and physical rights very cumbersome. Advocates of the free market contend that free market will generate bourgeoisies who will pressurize government for more freedom, human rights, and political participation, but in Pakistan's case the bourgeoisies has induced a system of bribes and misappropriation of state assets. Political power is vested in feudalists and industrialists who have purloined the state assets.

11. *Singapore*. Noel Fernandez mentions how Singapore is an island country in Southeast Asia located in a major sea route between India and China. Singapore has a population of approximately 4.8 million made up by the three official ethnic groups of Chinese, Malay, and Indian origins. Due to its ethnic diversity, the country has four official languages: English, Chinese, Malay, and Tamil. Singapore is governed on the basis of a strong state and prioritizing collective welfare over individual rights like freedom of speech. This form of governance has been criticised by many people and organisations like the Freedom House, which ranks Singapore as only "partly free." The Singaporean economy relies on exports and the refining of imported goods, especially in its manufacturing sector, and has one of the busiest ports in the world. It has a highly developed market-based economy characterised by free, innovative, competitive and friendly business practices. It was one of the original Asian "tigers" along with Taiwan, Hong Kong, and South Korea. Singapore is the only Asian country with a credit rating of AAA from the three major credit rating

agencies; and the country was ranked the second freest economy in the world in 2011.

12. ***Thailand***. Acheraporn Plangmarn states that we live in the age of markets, using examples from the Kingdom of Thailand. While markets have been around for thousands of years, we are just beginning to understand their power for organizing society and creating value. In the last 200 years, markets have unleashed a tremendous amount of innovation and progress in the West. Capitalism and markets have also notoriously increased the divide between the rich and the poor, both within and across nations. In the pursuit of innovation, we have become blind to some of the harmful consequences of our actions on others, such as environmental degradation, dominance of less privileged groups, and the inequitable distribution of opportunities. The "seeds" of these deeply troubling issues are beginning to germinate.

13. ***United States***. Frank Cavico, Pedro Pellet, Mario Delgado and other contributors in various chapters discuss how capitalism as an economic system is premised largely on the theoretical foundation of Adam Smith's "invisible hand," that is, by advancing one's own self-interest, the interests of society are often advanced as well, and thereby the individual's welfare and the general welfare are enhanced. They emphasize that competition in a free market economy can create personal wealth and societal prosperity. However, , capitalism can create many challenges, as demonstrated by the presence of materialism, greed, Conspicuous consumption," and healthcare challenges in the United States. It is further mentioned that capitalism will not be sustainable as an economic system if entrepreneurs and policymakers do not act in a legal, ethical, and socially responsible manner, since, most likely, the long-term consequence will be a systemic breakdown and societal ruin, which obviously no one desires.

14. ***Uganda***. Based on intensive research with respondents in Uganda, Terrell Manyak, Isaac Wasswa Katono, and Warren Byabashaija examine the influence of contextual factors on educators and their entrepreneurial intentions. The chapter is based on the conflicts that confront local government leaders in Uganda. These conflicts are traced to the "jockeying" for political power by national politicians, local corruption, illiteracy, ethnic differences, and serious structural inefficiencies which inhibit the development of effective governance. Despite these daunting challenges, local government leaders remain committed to building an effective system of local government.

15. ***Vietnam***. Lam Nguyen examines the impact of capitalism on Vietnamese workers and businesses. The Socialist Republic of Vietnam, or Vietnam in

short, is one of the ten members of the Association of Southeast Asian Nations (ASEAN). Vietnam has a population of about 90.5 million people, of which almost 70% are in the age range of 15-64 years. There are 58 provinces and 5 municipalities (major cities) including Ho Chi Minh City and Can Tho in the South, Hanoi (the capital), Hai Phong in the North, and Da Nang in the Central. Vietnamese is the official language, while English is increasingly referred to as the "second language." Other commonly spoken languages include French, Chinese, Khmer, and "mountain area" languages (Mon-Khmer and Malayo-Polynesian). The Vietnamese government is considered a Communist political state.

16. *Venezuela.* Guillermo Gibens, an American citizen who was born in Venezuela and who is currently teaching in the United Arab Emirates (UAE), explores Venezuela's transformation, which has dramatically changed the economic environment of the country from its inception as an independent nation to the current state of affairs. The advent of Hugo Chavez in 1999 under the promise of wiping out corruption infused new hopes for a new kind of "clean" democracy among Venezuelans. Nevertheless, the late Chavez's administration has fallen into the same corruption pattern.

The broad range of research topics reflected in these chapters provides a foundation for an open discussion as to where capitalism and corruption studies might proceed so as to extend the theories and methodologies which have been developed in the Western world. For instance, very little is said in Western research about the impact of cultural norms, religious practices, ethnic customs, and social status differences on capitalistic practices because these issues are typically less intense than in developing countries.

From a methodological perspective, researchers in developing countries face far more difficulty in developing empirical data bases for statistical analysis. People in some of these countries have little exposure to completing survey questionnaires and are often suspicious about revealing personal information to anonymous researchers. Another concern is that corruption research in developing countries focuses on urban centers, while rural, less educated populations remain unstudied.

This book will be of interest to a broad range of researchers, policy-makers, business people, and academicians. The book will be of direct concern to entrepreneurs, management practitioners and researchers, and public officials. For example, this work will be especially of interest to the public administration field, because the public sector role is of critical importance in bringing social and economic progress to the developing world, while minimizing corruption. The book will also be of particular interest to those from developing countries, because the focus of the discussion is to look at capitalism and corruption research from diverse and non-Western perspectives. We believe that much needed progress can be made in theory-building by expanding research into the developing world, but this expansion is only possible by developing new ideas and methodologies that meet the research challenges and practical needs for policy-makers across the globe.

Summary
This chapter provided an introduction to economic systems; and also has briefly presented the main components for business leaders and policy-makers that will be explored in this book.

Global business leaders are likely to face many decisions that will impact themselves, their companies, employees, and colleagues, as well as their family members, local communities, and society in general. As such, it is incumbent upon academics, business and corporate leaders, community leaders, policy-makers, and government regulators to help business people to understand capitalism and particularly its challenges so that they can act accordingly in best interest of the all relevant stakeholders in society through socially responsible and efficacious approaches.

CHAPTER 2

Globalization and the Demise of the Market Economy

Pedro F. Pellet, Nova Southeastern University, Florida, USA
Mario E. Delgado, Rural Development Specialist/USDA
María I. Méndez, Ramkhamhaeng University, Thailand

This chapter focuses on the "unchecked globalization" and the demise of the market economy, as the authors reflect on the thought of twenty-first century capitalism and the debasing and betrayal of nationhood. *An Inquiry into the Nature and Causes of the Wealth of Nations*, written by Adam Smith and published in 1776, is considered the theoretical basis of Industrial Capitalism.

The concept of the "Invisible Hand", as a metaphysical allocating device, rooted in competition and self-interest, was supposed to provide the best possible outcome or welfare for the majority or the common good. Reality, however, shows that the globalization strategies as implemented by multinational corporations and, in particular, by the relatively new Globally Integrated Enterprises (GIE), do not embody the logical or constructive expression of the framework of the market-oriented economic system. It appears to be doing so by aggressively promoting the free and competitive elements of the theory, but these two components are not the core principles. Although the freedom of market entry and exit by informed competitors does serve to improve the quality of the output, increase supply, and reduce its price to the ultimate consumers, these characteristics are only enhancements to the fundamental tenets of the theory. The cornerstones tenets of the model are specialization and exchange or trade between individuals within their respective nation-states and between nations in accordance to the comparative advantage efficiency principle. The Wealth of Nations, expected to be promoted by open market economies, becomes replaced under the current globalization paradigm by the Wealth of Industries. This inadvertent shift in results is taking place at the expense not only of the national welfare but of the structure of the market economy itself. What we are seeing is a direct product of the fact that comparative advantage and product specialization and trade are being supplanted by the hunt for mega-profits under the GIEs' global supply-chain operational design. Also the additional independence gained by the GIEs from the fortunes of individual nations, enhance like never before their influence over politicians and citizens alike.

Entrepreneurs not subject to regulation were once valuable to their nations, and their patriotism rhetoric was practical. Such was the case when the geo-political realities limited their geographical reach towards profits and when national support safeguarded their overseas investments. However under the current globalization paradigm such limitations have been significantly weakened and entrepreneurs are showing their true original colors. They are demonstrating that they have no sense of patriotism or national allegiance, only narrow minded opportunism. Unfettered market capitalism has been dominating all other economic systems because of its superior opportunities to individuals and its overall positive national economic growth. However under today's evolving global framework it has not only been faltering, but delivering detrimental results to many of the participating nations. Ironically, the nations that have benefited thus far are the ones under a quasi-state regulated environment that limits the reach of its entrepreneurs with global ambitions.

It makes sense for members of a society to forego some individual preferences in exchange for the security and synergy secured as participants in a larger and cohesive community. However, it does not make sense for a society to in turn condition its members to respond like cogs in a production-consumption boundless vortex. Neither to coerce them to support the economic arrangements of a system set up for the benefit of a self-serving sub-group. A sub-group that is insensitive to the point of disregarding how their actions are debasing and betraying their own nations and population.

Economic growth for its own sake is a very shortsighted and ultimately a self-defeating goal. Human progress requires effort, but of the type that allows man to enjoy the fruits of his labor in a milieu that promotes the enjoyment of both and of life in general. Progress must occur in an environment that prevents human beings from becoming an expendable cog in a production-consumption endless vortex. We must strive to enhance the Wealth of Nations and not to surrender their potential for the Wealth of Industries benefiting as always relatively narrow elites. Finally, let's remember that cultural progress requires ethical and moral development.

Introduction

"Man is the measure of all things: of things which are, that they are, and of things which are not, that they are not"--Protagoras of Abdera.

The globalization strategies as implemented by multinational corporations and in particular by the relatively new Globally Integrated Enterprises (GIE) do not embody the logical or constructive expression of the framework of the capitalist economic system. It appears to be doing so by aggressively promoting the free and competitive elements of the theory, but these two components are not the core principles. Although the freedom of market entry and exit by informed competitors does serve to improve the quality of the output, increase supply and reduce its price to the ultimate consumers, these characteristics are only enhancements to the fundamental tenets of the theory. The cornerstone tenets of the model are specialization and exchange or trade between individuals within their respective nation-states and between nations in accordance to the comparative advantage efficiency principle.

The *Wealth of Nations* expected to be promoted by open market economies, becomes replaced under the current globalization paradigm by the *Wealth of Industries*. This inadvertent shift in results is taking place at the expense not only of the national welfare but of the structure of the market economy itself. What we are seeing is a direct product of the fact that comparative advantage and product specialization and trade are being supplanted by the "hunt" for "mega-profits" under the GIEs' global supply-chain operational design. Also the additional independence gained by the GIEs from the fortunes of individual nations, enhance like never before their influence over politicians and citizens alike.

Unregulated entrepreneurs were once valuable to their nations, and their patriotism rhetoric was practical. Such was the case when the geo-political realities limited their geographical reach towards profits and when national support safeguarded their overseas investments. However, under the current globalization paradigm such limitations have been significantly weakened and entrepreneurs are showing their true original colors. They are demonstrating that they have no sense of patriotism or national allegiance, only narrow minded opportunism.

Unfettered market capitalism has been dominating all other economic systems because of its superior opportunities to individuals and its overall positive national economic growth. However under today's evolving global framework it has not only been faltering, but delivering detrimental results to many of the participating nations. Ironically, the nations that have benefited thus far are the ones under a quasi-state regulated environment that limits the reach of its entrepreneurs with global ambitions.

It makes sense for members of a society to forego some individual preferences in exchange for the security and synergy secured as participants in a larger and cohesive community. However, it does not make sense for a society to in turn condition its members to respond like cogs in a production-consumption boundless vortex. Neither to coerce them to support the economic arrangements of a system set up for the benefit of a self-serving sub-group. A sub-group that is insensitive to the point of disregarding how their actions are debasing and betraying their own nations and population.

Globally Integrated Enterprises (GIEs)

What went wrong, or better, what unrecognized dimensions of the free market model were by-passed in its original design and in later modifications? Although excluded factors could be lumped under the label of negative externalities or other catch-all category, the omitted underlying dynamics go well beyond mere exceptions or minor omissions. They have surfaced from out the opportunities brought by the ongoing rapid globalization of markets. They originate from structural/conceptual flaws in the original model as far as the fundamental intentions and roles played by the entrepreneur-rial class and the concept of nation-state.

In the conventional free markets model, *the invisible hand* intervenes for the benefit of the final consumer, the national economy and at the expense of inefficient suppliers and industries. In today's global market the "invisible hand" works again at the expense of weaker producers and industries, but unlike before, also at the expense of the national economies and the final consumers.

How does the modern expression of globalization, under the leadership of the Globally Integrated Enterprises (GIEs) violate the original foundation of market economies? It does so by destroying the primacy of the production of completed products within each trading nation, as well as diluting the relevance of supporting economic, social and cultural institutions. It does so in particular by dispersing the product "development-production processes-chain" across national boundaries. It does so in efforts not just to remain profitable and competitive, but to ultra-maximize profitability at any social cost. The GIE persists regardless of the negative consequences its actions bring to the impacted economies including their birthing ones. The modern GIE does not settle with the gains derived from the comparative advantage attained by operating in any one nation, but aims instead to secure an absolute advantage from exploiting globally wide resource mixes. GIEs focus on gaining not just adequate but maximum profitability by outsourcing and offshoring each sub-operation to locations that can minimize operating average costs, and maximize the penetration of global markets.

For a national economic system to thrive, it needs an effective overseeing institutional framework, capable of channeling its creative energies and limiting destructive excesses, also called or defined as diseconomies of scale. The global paradigm of today does not offer such a controlling regime, on the contrary. It is polluted with incongruent if non-existing regulations and gaps in oversight that vested interests exploit constantly. Furthermore, a politico-economic system, domestic or global, to be sound needs to be the product of a permeating free-willed morality from the majority of its members and not just from superimposed laws and rules. Unfortunately, the globally expanding callous materialism and its compulsive consumerism do not comply with the basic assumptions of economic efficiency.

Why would not economic globalization with some adjustments capture if not surpass the socio-economic benefits and overall superior efficiency ascribed to nations under the market economy model?

Globalization and Economic Efficiency
Globalization with its far flung interdependencies and requirements for cooperation elicits results counter to its touted superior economic effectiveness and efficiency. Its results are not only inferior but systemically deleterious to many of the participating nation-states and populations. This reality is not hard to recognize if we review the theoretical underpinnings of economic efficiency. Economic efficiency is achieved with the extension of all possible unambiguous increase in self-defined welfare with a *Pareto Optimal (Optimum optimorum)* framework in the

society under review. It represents an achievement in which individuals increase their welfare rationally and without making anyone else worse off. The prerequisites to attain such an estate are:

1. The incentives reflected in prices - as Pareto famous or infamous dictum: the price mechanism should reflect individual differences - and driving the rational individual, represent all the costs and benefits to society that result from the individual choice.
2. Each diseconomy, at the margin, must be accurately compensated.
3. Each gain, at the margin, must be appropriately priced.
4. Individual and property rights must be clearly defined.
5. Information must be complete, true and readily and easily accessible.
6. Promises must be kept.

Reality, even under a simpler separate individual nation circumstances, is far from, if not in opposition to, the above prerequisites. More often than not what occurs is:

1. We may not understand or care to grasp the true and full consequences of our actions, in other words the capitalist fundamental assumption of perfect rationality, does not prevail.
2. We may voluntarily choose actions that make us worse off.
3. People lie about their intentions.
4. People break their promises.
5. Rights may be ambiguous, not fully assigned or not fully protected.

Therefore, individual rational choices can make someone else including the originator worse off. Imagine the results when the choices are not only irrational, but intentionally malicious. Even under a simpler national socio-political framework, the above failures continuously take place. Imagine how much more frequent is the case across divergent cultures and where some of them promote mistrust and corruption, and others want in earnest to defraud and even destroy the interest of others, including those of entire nation-states.

But why not would established forces such as the entrepreneurial class, benefiting from national economic stability and growth, serve as an antidote? Why would not engaged entrepreneurs attempt to minimize if not eradicate all emerging destructive circumstances jeopardizing their political and economic foundations?

"Entrap-preneurship"

The entrepreneurial class and, in particular, its segment with international business interest, has never been fundamentally patriotic. It displays its allegiance to any one country just as long as its political and military support needs are being met, but not much beyond it. It has always been profit oriented above all else and in today's expanding global markets, it has become even more ruthless and rootless in the absence of well-defined regulatory boundaries. Entrepreneurs in their outreach for the much larger market shares and profit margins available globally are betraying even the national economies that facilitated their birth and nurtured their growth.

They are doing so through the unconstrained transfers of technologies, production processes, employment, assets and even elements of national security. They do so even with known dictators, oligarchies and even terrorist regimes.

The entrepreneurial class will remain detached from national concerns for as long as it can secure superior profits from such mercenary behavior. It will justify its conduct even under the guise of patriotic concerns. It will invoke the banner of the modern global paradigm with its purported superior economic benefits to the world. It will get away with it by vocally extrapolating the theoretical benefits from the market capitalism model to an uncharted, very complex and generally undefined global scheme. It's true intentions are to rationalize and paper over its rapidly expanding concentration of wealth and political influence. It aims to assuage the doubts of the general population through propaganda, reinforcing a materialistic ideology and by increasing the dependency of the labor force on highly specialized occupations and production networks. The ultimate implications are a roundabout return to a modern version of mercantilism and concentration but based on global industries and not on national boundaries.

What the entrepreneurial class is doing from a national sovereignty standpoint, is nothing but treasonous. It has been strengthening asymmetrical and unregulated competing economies as well as ideological enemy regimes. Its members are so obsessed with the ultra-profits available that they don't consider the fact that in the long run they will become victims of their own greed. They are de-stabilizing and weakening the socio-economic foundations that provided them with the political and regulatory national platforms that saw to their safe emergence. It is well known that the theoretical premises and determinants of a free and competitive economic system do not exist and hence, the full realization of its benefits. This is the case even within supportive democracies; imagine how much less across mixtures of less complementary economic systems. Add to this equation participating centrally planned economies with imperialistic agendas, and the global landscape will end up littered with socioeconomic casualties.

There is no valid justification for establishing global economic alliances at the expense of the national well-being. This is the case under any pretense, but much more so under the false pretense of capturing benefits that will never materialize. Nations will do much better by adapting within their respective geographical boundaries the technologies, processes, products and cost structures that will allow them to compete from within their borders even if at a more limited basis. Unless of course the true underlying motivation of the entrepreneurial class is to strengthen their global networks laid out to "entrap" resources and dominate markets above all else.

Factor Mobility and Application

In any economy, it is costly and time-consuming for the labor force to relocate in search of employment within its immediate regions and localities. How much more difficult it would be to find jobs overseas for want of replacement employment at home. Imagine the long delays in economic recovery as well as trauma to the labor force and society in general. Is labor under the globalization scheme expected to take out roots entirely and move anywhere including overseas without delay? How could labor in general do so when typically it has not been ready so domestically under more favorable circumstances? But it is not only labor the affected resource, land also becomes unemployed or underutilized and for extended periods of time.

Once upon the time, developed economies, and in particular the U.S. economy had a global monopoly in products and production processes. Their multinationals could move overseas to locations with a more favorable factor mix because the production and employment voids they left behind could be easily closed with new products or more sophisticated versions. There were few other sources of meaningful competition, if any. However, today under globalization the US and other developed nations have been losing segments or entire production processes to new profitable industries and without ready replacements at hand. This widespread industrial erosion makes the re-allocation of resources very difficult as the lack of replacement employment opportunities increase with each downturn and by labor- substituting technological advances.

Furthermore, globalization's negative impact extends beyond labor and land markets into the balance of trade as well. The demand-supply chains create the necessity for the developed nations to have to import the products they once exported, even while retaining their comparative advantage over the new exporting nation. How so? Simply because the end process in a production chain is often labor intensive of the low skills variety. As labor costs and productivity advantages are the hallmark of emerging nations, they become the assemblers of the final product.

Therefore globalization dilutes the economic wealth and stability of nations in general and of developed ones in particular by:

1. Simultaneously and widely displacing the land and labor resources from many of their established industries.
2. Weakening the national tax base as the assembly of intermediate component and final products are transferred abroad.
3. Having to innovate to replace lost products, while emerging competing ones have only to replicate existing ones.
4. Making importers out of previous exporting nations, even of the nations that originated, designed and introduced to the markets the subject products.
5. Replacing each trading nation's comparative advantage with the absolute advantages generated individually by each participating GIE's globally distributed supply-chains and networks.
6. Delaying, if not truncating the economic rebound of developed economies by transferring technologies, physical and financial capital, production processes and managerial and entrepreneurial skills to competing nations.
7. Financial stimulus efforts by developed nations, without widely accessible sources of domestic market intelligence, end up diverting the ensuing liquidity to established growth markets abroad.

Case in Point: The USA Experience

The economic strength of the U.S.A. does not rest on its middle class. It rests instead on the abundance of business opportunities available to the entrepreneurial class under free and competitive market structures. Historically, market opportunities supported by a robust entrepreneurial class have been a sure antidote to monarchies and other sundry statist regimes much more so than structures based on socio-political ideologies.

But as important as the above perspective is the realization that unlike the middle-class, the entrepreneurial class is as a whole un-patriotic. Its ultimate focus is maximum self-gain independent of national interests; the latter invoked when it helps to maximize the former. In addition, the entrepreneurial class with global ambitions is also very mercurial and without borders. It reaches out for business opportunities wherever they may be, and with whoever can facilitate the venture, without concerns over their democratic and/or human rights credentials. Entrepreneurs play up accepted clichés on patriotism to secure preferential public treatment and resources. Ironically such conduct betrays the same transparent, honest and competitive practices that provided the environment for them to succeed in the first place.

For example, the foundations of the U.S.A.'s economic strength took a firm hold towards the end of the 19th Century. It did so responding to the technological innovations and free markets model provided by the English Industrial Revolution of the 18th Century. The opportunities and model were applied to a rapidly expanding national territory, resource base and markets. Its economic strength sprung from developing and interconnecting its domestic markets in the production of quality products for domestic consumption first and exports second. It was energized by the emphasis on individual liberty, encouragement of entrepreneurship, expansion of the physical infrastructure and support for public institutions. Global competition at the same time was narrow and limited to a relatively small number of manufactured products. The USA's entrepreneurial class was in turn very protective of the national reputation and physical strength that helped guarantee international political power and access to cheap resources worldwide. It helped that during the same period competing nations were concerned with perpetuating their status-quo benefiting entrenched elites. Their elites, and to the USA advantage, favored limiting entrepreneurship and access to opportunities for their respective general population.

Nowadays, the traditional USA entrepreneurial class's observed nationalism is "turning on its head" and displaying its "true colors." Entrepreneurs invested globally are not claiming protectionism for their domestic businesses as before; they are instead re-locating much of their operations and assets overseas, where the resource mix and markets are more profitable. They are also entering into strategic economic alliances with foreign private and public businesses and institutions without compunction with their political color, ideology or practices. Since approximately the 1970s, the USA began losing its post WWII global economic monopoly as more and more able and willing competitors emerged overseas. The primer for this shift can be attributed to the lessons provided to foreign competitors and economies by US multinationals (developers of comparative advantage of nations), economic change-agents at the forefront of the onset of the ongoing globalization and parents of the modern Globally Integrated Enterprises (GIEs) (destroyers of comparative advantage of nations for the benefit of their private absolute advantages).

Governments and Economic Policies

What happens to national economies when domestic policies are implemented within a porous global landscape? What happens where there is more interdependence and connectivity between economic agents and markets from different nations than from within their respective national boundaries? Well, simply that their beneficial impacts could be more readily felt anywhere else in the world than in the intended locality. Under today's global environment neither expansionary fiscal nor loose monetary policies promote economic growth in nations where a significant proportion of their consumer and investment products are being imported and when both capital and financial investments are taking place overseas. On the contrary, such policies mostly benefit growing foreign producing economies and the participating GEIs.

For example, the ongoing expansionary monetary policy of the US Federal Reserve to inflate the supply of dollars in circulation and to support a policy of negative real interest rates will not help the US economy to recover. Instead it will weaken its industrial foundations even more by strengthening its foreign competitors. It will not help to increment and/or diversify its industrial composition either. On the contrary, it will continue hollowing its industrial base while increasing the domestic supply of unemployed and underemployed labor. It will generate imported consumer and producer goods price inflation by depreciating the exchange rate value of the dollar. It will promote the exodus of financial capital towards stronger currencies. GIEs will borrow "cheap" dollars in the USA to continue strengthening their global networks and market shares overseas.

This expanded liquidity will also not benefit the purported target of existing and potential small and mid-size enterprises. What these target groups need and much more than financial capital is digested and readily accessible strategic markets intelligence. They need the type intelligence that would help them decide on effective and sustainable investments. Small and mid-size enterprises as well as start-ups are at a loss on what and where to invest in an increasingly complex and competitive global market. They desperately need sets of academically derived objective investment alternatives to select from and accompanied with effective industrial support policies. These conclusions are based on the following premises:

1. The ubiquitous Financial Services Industry and in particular its investment bankers and private equity sub-set, do not care at all where their profits come from, go to and at what country (ies) expense; including their national security or ideology. They will acquire and apply capital anywhere in the world as long as it strengthens their networks and bottom line.

2. GIEs operating under widely distributed manufacturing and services networks, invest so as to strengthen their individual sub-operations with disregard for the fate of host nations inside their networks. GIEs will also move their resources worldwide as needed and independently of the economic needs or geopolitical concerns of their host nations including their parent nations.
3. US politicians have purposefully neglected the application of strategic industrial intelligence concepts in support of average businesses. They prefer to continue subsidizing by default their entrenched political pork beneficiaries. They do not want to limit their pandering largesse with constraining academic parameters and concerns for less influential or wealthy businesses.

In essence, the misguided US economic policies are weakening the national economy and its labor markets. They are also promoting a rise in the cost of living, the depreciation of the value of the dollar, and the exodus of its skilled labor force.

Nationhood: a Valid Construct or Fool's Gold?
If we peel off the recorded demagoguery in the evolution of market capitalism and perhaps in the history of mankind as well, it should be safe to postulate that there has never been such thing as a nation. Not a nation in the sense of being an extension of the cohesiveness found in families or clans. We may realize instead that nation has been and is but an emotional cover-up for the self-serving machinations of powerful economic interest and their supporting political allies. These interests shape the true functional framework labeled nations and impingements over "patriotism".

Nationhood is most of all a construct emotionally colored with deep hues of motherhood and fidelity sponsored by the powerful to keep the general population in a compliant and aspiring mood. Its validity disappeared when groups expanded beyond the clan structure or perhaps the extended family. During the Medieval period the survival needs of the populations, the coercive power of the kings and their literal ownership of the territory and its assets provided the internal glue to support the strength of the nation-states. However, under the modern market system, with its extreme dependency on specialization and the division of labor, large and anonymous urbanizations, diluted ownership of assets, greed and materialistic cultural values all have contributed in debasing all vestiges of nationhood.

In the current global economic environment, we can observe the above reality as the entrepreneurial class across the world replaces the fundamental interests of their respective nations for their own and their business networks. They unhesitant dismember national endowments under justifications of market prerequisites, consumer needs, and global competition. For example, the ongoing global economic meltdown exposes a systemic lack of respect for ethical behavior, laws and even for the achieved global industrial interdependence. Examples provided from within the food. financial, oil, mining, defense and pharmaceutical industries as well as the Government sector prove the above points many times over. To top it all, the political caste led by Congress and the Executive blames everyone else except their own complicity, negligence and incompetence. Their oversight (mostly out-of-sight) committees and inspectors general limit their response to after- the-facts finger pointing and not to the development of sound preventive methodologies and their execution. What family would allow any its members or from other related families to do likewise? None would, or last long if they did.

The globalization of today's markets is an inferior if not an implosive approach to the economic development of individual nations. Any approach to sustainable economic growth and balanced development requires limits on the entrepreneurial class and political caste's self-serving excesses. Limits could jeopardize some of the benefits from open markets, but in a fragmented and unregulated global environment there are many unaccounted for destructive interests lurking within empty regulatory spaces that would make conditions worse. The principles of open markets were not framed under today's erratic, if not anarchic, global milieu.

Summary

Globalization dominated by Globally Integrated Enterprises (GIEs) displaces the comparative advantages of the participating nations and replaces them with the absolute advantages from resource-dominant GIEs. These economic agents roam the globe in search of superior geographical locations for their demand-supply links (sub-operations) and alliances. The fact that often no one nation can provide the most profitable location for all the sub-operations of anyone GIE, and being that each sub-operation by design is readily re-locatable, leaves the nations at the will of foot-loose GIEs.

GIEs by the nature of their independence from any geographical location and their ability to capture absolute advantage, leads them to amass significant industrial concentration without much public accountability. Such dynamics eliminate existing competition and destroy the foundations of free markets. These mega-enterprises also end-up manipulating almost at will the global factors of production. The GEIs have two major sources of power; one source is their amassed wealth, also available to the traditional multinational; the second and more current source is the independence and mobility of their demand-supply chains.

Therefore, to ensure the well-being of nations the forces of globalization and the activities of GIEs should be carefully regulated. In addition, regions and not the entire globe should be made the optimal economic configuration for integration. Participating nations must compromise and combine their resources and rules into cohesive growth regions. Integration through regionalization with specialization and trade within and between regions is the only sustainable economic and political design. However, to capture the benefits from this vision, we must first grasp other more fundamental premises. First and foremost, the vision of an "entrepreneur" as an economic agent contributing to the stability and growth of nations has never been valid. Neither has been the image of "nationhood" as a protecting and nurturing family-like entity operating for the benefit of its citizens.

What does exist at the roots of nationhood is a romantic image used as cover for the exploitation of wealth and populations, by influential special economic interests. These interests in turn have been patronized by a political caste manipulating the public institutions and resources for their combined enrichment. The entrepreneurial class and in particular the globally connected sub-set, have shown more allegiance to their economic networks and cohorts, than to their nations of birth. They represent a class of individuals that is patriotic just as long as such approach secures the expansion of their resources, markets and profits. Beyond that, they are ready to take flight to more profitable geographies wherever they may be and at whomever expense it may fall.

How should nations respond to these debilitating forces? Both the state and value structure of the culture play fundamental roles, although inversely related. One the one hand, the state must retain its essential regulatory and protective activities, although as minimal as possible. On the other hand, a minimalistic involvement is tenable only if internalized moral values and conduct by all involved fills the vacant spaces. The state has to play an active role in preventing the usurpation of the national endowment by special interests. Its involvement must by necessity be more precise and disciplined the more complex and large its national and global environments become. Moreover, it's compact with society must be structured to prevent the exploitation of its authority while promoting voluntary mechanisms strengthening the moral character of the culture.

To accomplish these ends, governance must be structured around processes under the direct oversight of its citizens with the authority to change course and leadership rapidly. Governance must not be based on systems favoring the leadership of political parties or with guaranteed periods of leadership to any public servant independent of performance. Today's global interdependence is too strong and too explosive and impacts too immediate to allow otherwise.

Finally, there is nothing soft or disadvantageous about being moral first and foremost. On the contrary, being moral is synonymous with being consistent, dedicated as well as effective in the long run. Morality does not trump materialism on the contrary it brings quality of life to the fore while magnifying the pleasure of acquisition. These characteristics of morality in turn reduce the need for compulsive consumerism and the waste of resources it engenders. Ultimately, as their internalization progresses, the contributing states will be able to relinquish most of their external controls without sacrificing national cohesiveness and regional cooperation.

In closing, the markets must be allowed to function freely, but only within bounds clearly delimiting any conduct detrimental to the national interests and the general population. The national sovereignty and well-being must take precedence over pure economic growth under any socio-political regime, but in particular in the divided and divergent current global landscape. Today's global economy lacks cohesive or coherent structures that could bring sense and stability to sprawling direct investments and trade networks. If it's undefined and hap-hazard context is allow to prevail only state controlled capitalism and not open economic systems would benefit. In the meantime, if entrepreneurs remain determined to betray their original home grounds in search for more profitable soils, let the gaining economy be their sole supporter. A nation should not tolerate with impunity such betrayal, and especially when it leads to strengthening enemy ideologies and political systems.

Economic growth for its own sake is a very shortsighted and ultimately a self- defeating goal. Human progress requires effort, but of the type that allows man to enjoy the fruits of his labor in a milieu that promotes the enjoyment of both and of life, in general. Progress must occur in an environment that prevents man from becoming an expendable cog in a production-consumption endless vortex. We must strive to enhance the Wealth of Nations and thus not to surrender the potential of the Wealth of Industries by benefiting as always relatively narrow elites. Finally, let us remember that cultural progress requires ethical and moral development which is more comprehensively highlighted in the next chapter.

CHAPTER 3

Capitalism and Responsible Governance

Frank J. Cavico
Nova Southeastern University

Capitalism as an economic system is premised largely on the theoretical foundation of Adam Smith's "invisible hand," that is, by advancing one's own self-interest, the interests of society are often advanced as well, and thereby the individual's welfare and the general welfare are enhanced. This "invisible hand" to work efficaciously works in a free market economy where self-interest and competition produce growth, prosperity, and well-being. Competition in a free market economy, as opposed to a governmental, centrally planned system, efficiently and efficaciously creates personal wealth and societal prosperity. However, Adam Smith also stated that self-interest should be "enlightened" self-interest, and thus be tempered by rationality, prudence, and the taking of a long-term perspective, and most importantly that, ultimately, capitalism and free enterprise are built on a foundation of morality. Otherwise, narrow, short-term, excessive self-interest, in the form of greed and avarice, exacerbated by illegal, "border-line" legal, unethical, and immoral behavior, will seriously undermine a capitalistic system. Consequently, capitalism will no longer be sustainable as an economic system or as the underpinning of a democratic political system; the horrible result will be a systemic breakdown and societal ruin.

Introduction

The "sustainability" of capitalism has emerged as a critical topic for debate in today's political, economic, and philosophical spheres. As such, longer-term stakeholder considerations, above and beyond the "mere" interests of the shareholders of the corporation, have been raised, interpreted, and examined under the concept of "corporate social responsibility." The concepts of corporate social responsibility[1] (CSR), together with "sustainability," have become central issues for business leaders today. Moreover, stakeholder analysis as well as CSR and sustainability are converging with the notion of "corporate governance," which traditionally has had mainly legal, especially regulatory, connotations. The

---

[1] Some of the concepts in this chapter come from coauthored publications with Bahaudin G. Mujtaba, Nova Southeastern University.

imperative today of governing the corporation is not 'just" a profitable and legal manner, but also in a moral, and socially responsible way is underscored as the only true course to sustain a capitalistic "free market" system. The objective is for the corporation to achieve sustainable economic growth and development and also produce positive value for all stakeholders of the corporation, including betterment for society as a whole.

Initially, it is very important for a business leader, academician, and manager to look for, ascertain, and pay special attention to definitions and terms. When one initially encounters the fields of governance, social responsibility, and stakeholder analysis in a business context, one is confronted with some confusion due to a lack of an agreed-upon terminology and set of definitions. What is social responsibility? How does it differ from the law, ethics, and morality? What exactly do "corporate social responsibility," "stakeholder values," "sustainability," "people, planet, and profits," "going green," and "socially responsible investing" mean? What is a corporate "constituency" statute and how does it compare and contrast to a "social benefit" corporation? As such, if one is going to understand what social responsibility is and how it works in a modern global business environment, there must be some agreement on, and some insight into, the meaning and nature of the value of social responsibility especially when juxtaposed with the values of legality, based on the law, and the value of morality, based on ethics. There is, therefore, a need for words, terms, and definitions with precise meaning. In order to arrive at a precise meaning of the term "social responsibility," it is first necessary to define some fundamental terms and concepts. A value is something that possesses worth. Values can be intrinsic (also called terminal), meaning that they possess value and worth in and of themselves, for example, happiness; whereas values that are "merely" extrinsic (also called instrumental) possess worth and are valuable because they are the means to produce something else of value, for example, money (which can buy happiness). The value of legality is, of course, based on the law. The value of morality stems from ethics; yet the terms are not synonymous. Morality is the conclusion of what is right or wrong or good or bad; whereas ethics is the philosophical framework, consisting of ethical theories and principles that one uses to reason toward reaching moral conclusions. Whether morality is an intrinsic value or merely and instrumental one is an issue which the authors will leave to the philosophers. Social responsibility too is a value, related to, but distinct from law and ethics.

Social Responsibility

What exactly is a corporation's "social responsibility"? Does a corporation have a social obligation to take care of the poor, educate the public, give to charity, and fund cultural programs? Social projects and social welfare in the United States traditionally have been viewed as the appropriate domain of government, not of business. Business, of course, is taxed and such taxes may be used for social purposes. The traditional purpose of business as viewed in the U.S., moreover, is the profitable production and distribution of goods and services, not social welfare. Yet by raising the issue of social responsibility, business is forced to concern itself with the "social" dimension of its activities. Accordingly, what is the "social responsibility" of business today? The term at a basic philanthropic level may be defined as a business taking an active part in the social causes, charities, and civic life of one's community and society. However, corporate social responsibility (CSR) certainly can be more than "mere" philanthropy. The social responsibility of business can also be thought of in a broader constituency or stakeholder sense, that is, by the corporation considering the values and needs of employees, suppliers, consumers, local communities, and society as a whole. One can also take a "strategic" as well as stakeholder approach to corporate social responsibility by integrating stakeholder, social, environmental, as well as economic concerns into the organization's values, culture, governance, strategy, and decision-making.

The sustainability approach to capitalism and corporate social responsibility is premised on the idea that a company must remain economically viable in the long-term, and that in order to be viable the company must take into consideration other stakeholders beyond the shareholders. The objective is to simultaneously produce economic value for the company, but also value for society as a whole by helping to solve societal needs, particularly by improving the lives of the people (and potential consumers) who live in the communities where the company does business. "Sustainability" is often used when discussing such concepts as corporate citizenship, social responsibility, stakeholder analysis, and social enterprise. The topics of sustainability, social responsibility, and stakeholder analysis have emerged as critical ones for global business leaders who wish to preserve and prosper in a capitalistic system.

Stakeholder theory considers the business as a community with a number of stakeholders, that is, constituent groups that are directly and indirectly connected to the enterprise, affected by its activities, and may be dependent on its success and prosperity. These groups include employees, customers, suppliers, the state and especially the communities and society in which the enterprise is engaged in business. These stakeholder groups typically include shareholders and owners, employees, customers and consumers, suppliers and distributors, creditors, community, government, competition, and society. Shareholders as the owners are always listed first. Obviously, a corporation cannot survive unless it serves and benefits its shareholders in a financial sense. However, today, shareholders may view their investment as one that benefits society too and perhaps in a direct manner by means of the social benefit corporation. Regardless, all shareholders are entitled to the honest and efficient management of their investment as well as a fair return on their investment. Employees are of course interested in obtaining and maintaining employment. They value a just wage, fair employment practices and working conditions, and job security. They also may value working for a company that is regarded as a "socially responsible" one. Customers and consumers want access to goods and services that are of good quality, at a fair price, and that come with good customer service. Suppliers and distributors want financially rewarding, long-term contractual relationships with the company. Local communities want to see the corporation located in their cities and towns so as to provide employment for the citizens and residents and to support the local tax-base. The local community also values, and very well may expect, that the corporations in its presence participate in civic, charitable, philanthropic, and socially responsible activities. Creditors naturally value being repaid and also expect a fair rate of return as well as adequate assurances of security for the obligation. Government values legal compliance with business laws and business regulations. Government also values business as an important component of its tax-base. Government also values and thus desires to promote entrepreneurship and competition. As to the competition, the competitor values its own market share, yet expects in a capitalistic model "tough" and "hard-hitting" competition, but the competition also values completion that is legal and ethical. Society values its survival, of course, and also growth, prosperity for its members, and the sustainability of business and society. Members of society also value, and thus expect, that the corporation will be a socially responsible one, particularly regarding its stewardship of the environment and efforts to improve the environment. The goal of the business leader today, therefore, is to balance and harmonize these values and thus attempt to devise corporate governance policies that maximize these values in a legal, moral, socially responsible, and practically efficacious manner, thereby resulting in "win-win" scenarios for the business and all its stakeholders and attaining a level of continual sustainable business success.

Corporate and Self-Governance
Corporate governance today has emerged as significant subject for business; and the topic of social responsibility also arises in the context of corporate governance. Initially, one may think of "corporate governance" as having strictly legal components, especially business law and regulatory law. In the traditional governance models, the corporation's primary focus is on shareholder rights, and the primary governance rule is based on maximizing shareholder value. Directors, therefore, have a duty to ensure that companies fulfill their legal obligations, protect shareholder interests, and provide accurate and timely information to investors, markets, and government regulators. Yet corporate governance also has social responsibility as well as ethical ramifications. That is, corporate governance, in the expansive meaning that the authors wish to give to this concept, means the legal, ethical/moral, and social responsibility considerations for regulating business today. Business decision-making cannot be decoupled from the responsibility – legal, ethical, and social - of business leaders for their own risk-taking; otherwise, the whole business and entrepreneurial system will be undermined.

The idea is not "just" to maximize profits by "merely" obeying the law, for example, SEC regulations, but rather to also include ethical, moral, and social responsibility concerns into corporate decision-making. Making profits in a legal manner is obviously an essential component to corporate governance; but the focus on "just" the law is too narrow. The idea is that the corporation will engage in self-governance; and thus regulate, not only by the strictures of the law, but also by morality and ethics, as well as stakeholder and societal concerns, the manner by which it generates profits. In essence, corporations will act legally, morally, and in a socially responsible manner only if those people who exercise control over the corporation, whether directly or indirectly; that is, the directors, officers, and shareholders together, have the vision to see that the collective future of the business, its stakeholders, and society as a whole is inextricably tied to the sustainability of the entity and the society in which it operates and flourishes, as well as the strength of character and leadership ability to implement and act on that vision.

In order to sustain a capitalistic system, corporate governance guidelines for social responsibility should be premised on fundamental principles. First the company should formulate a corporate social responsibility policy to guide its strategic planning and provide a roadmap for its CSR initiatives. Second, that policy should be an integral part of the organization's overall business policy and aligned with the company's business goals. Third, the policy should be created and framed with the participation of various executives as well as representatives of other stakeholder groups, and the policy must be approved and overseen by the board and implemented by top management. The corporate social responsibility policy should cover the following core elements: (1) adherence to the law; (2) acting in an ethical, honest, and transparent manner; (3) consideration of the values and interests of all stakeholders, including shareholders, employees, customers, suppliers, local communities, society at large, and the environment; (4) treating all stakeholders with dignity and respect and as worthwhile means and not as mere means; (5) charitable and philanthropic activities; and (6) activities that promote social and economic development.

Another problem confronting corporate social responsibility, especially in the "sustainability" sense, is resistance from shareholders, who may be more interested in short-term profits than long-term sustainable outcomes. Today's shareholders may prefer immediate maximization of share value over a more long-term approach that is willing to wait for potentially greater returns in the future. This preference may lead management to prioritize short-term profits over longer-term considerations. This narrow approach will discourage corporate social responsibility and stakeholder analysis because benefits to stakeholders other than shareholders will reduce short-term profits. Nonetheless, it is the important "job" of the business leader to educate the shareholders, and perhaps corporate management as well, of the benefits that will accrue to the company and the shareholders by the company acting in a smart, shrewd, and strategic socially responsible manner. Corporate social responsibility, as such, should be treated as an investment, not a cost, comparable to quality improvement and employee training. Business leaders, executives, and managers, therefore, must be cognizant of and appreciate the instrumental strategic value of social responsibility in its constituency and sustainability formulations. Business leaders, executives, and managers today surely are well aware of societal expectations regarding the social responsibility of their companies.

Sustainability, Governance and CSR

The term "sustainability" has emerged, along with social responsibility and corporate governance, as important subject matters for business today. A sustainable business is one that governs itself in a long-term, stakeholder centered, and environmentally conscious manner (Mujtaba, 2014). Sustainability has legal and ethical components, and as such should result in moral decision-making by companies. In order to better illustrate as well as explicate the values of practicality, legality, morality, social responsibility, and stakeholder interests, and their relationship to sustainability, the authors have developed the model presented in Figure 3.1 (Mujtaba and Cavico, 2013), called The Business Sustainability Continuum (BSC).

Figure 3.1 – The Business Sustainability Continuum

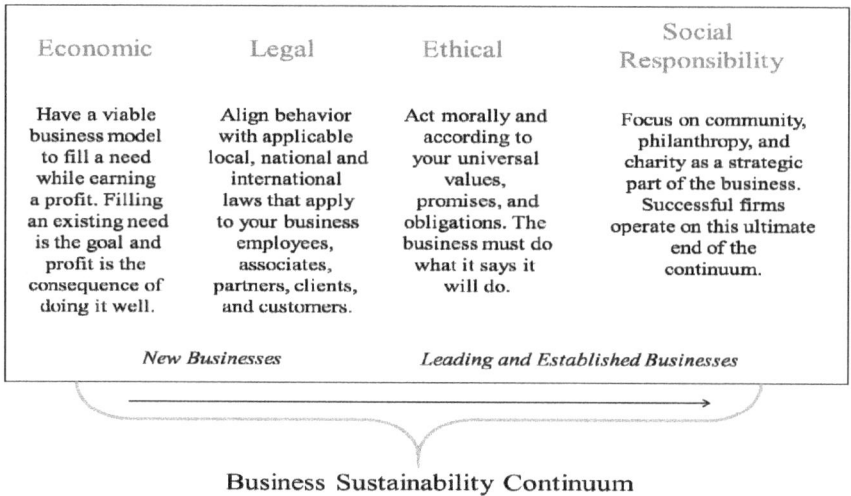

Economic	Legal	Ethical	Social Responsibility
Have a viable business model to fill a need while earning a profit. Filling an existing need is the goal and profit is the consequence of doing it well.	Align behavior with applicable local, national and international laws that apply to your business employees, associates, partners, clients, and customers.	Act morally and according to your universal values, promises, and obligations. The business must do what it says it will do.	Focus on community, philanthropy, and charity as a strategic part of the business. Successful firms operate on this ultimate end of the continuum.
New Businesses		*Leading and Established Businesses*	

Business Sustainability Continuum

The BSC illustrates that the continual success and "sustainability" of the business can only be achieved by an adherence to four core values (Mujtaba, Cavico and Plangmarn, 2012): *Economic*, indicating that a business obviously must have a viable business model which fulfills a need and enables the business to make a profit; *Legal*, indicating that this profit must be achieved in a legal manner by aligning the conduct of the business with all applicable local, national, and international laws; *Ethical*, indicating that since there may be no law or "gaps" in the law nonetheless the business must act in a moral manner and also must act in conformity with its values, promises, and obligations; and *Social Responsibility*, indicating that the business must focus on the community and engage in civic, philanthropic, and charitable endeavors as part of their overall strategic plan. Sustainability will help the business; but also help the business help governments solve pressing social problems; and, as such, sustainability provides a means to rebuild trust in the economic and political systems, which naturally is good for business and good for society. Accordingly, corporate governance policies must be devised to give credence and implementation to these "sustainable" values; and thereby will enable the business to achieve success and to sustain that success in a continual manner, thus benefiting the business, its shareholders, the communities where it does business, and all the stakeholders affected by the business, including society as a whole.

One can argue philosophically whether values are real intrinsically; yet it would seem beyond reasonable dispute that values possess instrumental worth. Values today increasingly drive consumer and also employee behavior. Consumers want to do business with, and employees want to work for, employers whose values are compatible. Legality, ethics, and morality are very important values; and today social responsibility is such a value too. Business leaders must be cognizant of these values. Furthermore, the emphasis on stakeholders or constituency groups is an essential component of business leadership and corporate governance. The business leader must take an enlightened approach to satisfying the values of stakeholders in order to achieve long-term sustainable success. As emphasized, the ultimate goal is to attain "win-win" resolutions where all the company's stakeholders receive value and thus the capitalistic system is preserved, prolonged, and produces wide benefits. Social responsibility emerges as a key element in achieving stakeholder symmetry and success and thus business sustainability. Furthermore, given the apparent positive relationship between successful financial performance and social responsibility, there is a critical need of both these values for society and a flourishing capitalistic economic system. Accordingly, corporate social responsibility, stakeholder analysis, and corporate governance have emerged as most relevant and profound topics for business today.

Social responsibility and sustainability, moreover, are now not only an "academic" matter for business school students and academics, or "merely" issues for "social activists"; rather, social responsibility and sustainability are also very real and practical concerns for the global business leader, executive, manager, and entrepreneur. Admittedly, in certain cases, social responsibility concerns may be more difficult for business people, who are primarily focused on economic issues, to discern and to handle. Moreover, there may be conflict as various constituencies make conflicting demands. Nonetheless, business leaders in fulfilling their corporate governance function are expected to recognize competing stakeholder interests, to provide balance among legitimate competing claims, and, as emphasized, to devise practical, legal, ethical, socially responsible, and mutually beneficial solutions. Business leaders very well may have to convince certain stakeholders, such as the shareholders, that it is in their long-term self-interest to accept some short-term financial sacrifices, say in the form of company's socially responsible efforts in the local community, in order to produce longer-term greater financial gains. Fundamentally, therefore, business leaders are expected to lead and to lead by values, encompassing legal values, moral values, and socially responsible values. Consequently, cognizance of, adherence to, and successfully dealing with the value of social responsibility have become imperatives for business leaders today. Business leaders must recognize that social responsibility and sustainability are now essential aspects of business; and thus these values must have a prominent place on the corporate vision, mission, and agenda. The view today is that business should pursue profits, of course, but also that business should strive to achieve social objectives too in a sustainable manner. Business leaders should, and actually are expected to, know and understand the rationales for corporate social responsibility and business sustainability as well as to create and implement corporate governance policies and business strategies to be a socially responsible and sustainable business. Social responsibility as well as sustainability, therefore, should now be incorporated into business values, missions, and models. Social responsibility is now the modern way, and truly the only sustainable way, to do business and to continue to do business in a capitalistic system. Social responsibility clearly possesses instrumental value because it can be used in a smart, shrewd, and strategic sense to help the business achieve and sustain successful performance. Social responsibility, therefore, is more than just "mere" "pure" charity; rather, in modern business sense social responsibility is an integral strategic component in a company's endeavor to achieve larger "pure" business objectives; and concomitantly, and also propitiously, society as whole is benefitted too by these social responsibility activities. Business, therefore, needs a formal, coherent, transparent, strategic, stakeholder-based, and sustainable policy to social responsibility. The goal is to make a positive, beneficial, and sustainable contribution to the company's growth, economic growth, societal growth, and the betterment of the environment. So, corporate social responsibility and sustainability are "smart business" and "good business" – for business, the capitalistic economic system, and society. The old maxim is true: one can do well by doing "good"!

Business leaders, whether an entrepreneur, employee, executive, officer, or a manager, must all act in a legal, ethical, and socially responsible manner. As such, business leaders in pursing profits must obey the law, act for the greater good, treat all stakeholders with dignity and respect, and in a prudent manner be socially responsible by contributing to charities and participating in and supporting community and civic activities. Acting in such a responsible way will require business leaders being cognizant of various stakeholder interests as well as seeking to balance these at times of conflicting constituencies in a fair and efficacious manner. This objective is a challenging one, indeed, but also a noble one. Yet the result will be the creation of long-term, sustainable value, not "merely" for the shareholders but for the employees, customers, communities, and all the stakeholders of the organization, including the capitalistic economic system and society as a whole.

The recent real estate, mortgage, and banking crisis in the United States, resulting in the still recessionary U.S. as well as global economy, was in main part created by so-called business "leaders" abandoning common sense, good sense, and ethics, as well as abdicating their corporate governance obligations; and consequently acting in a short-term, solely profit-centered, immoral, if not downright illegal, manner. Instead of earning rewards fairly, the prevailing mentality was a "get-rich-quick" mindset, one exacerbated by the false belief that price of real estate would go up – forever! Consequently, people with "NINJA" loans, that is, with no income and no jobs or assets, were borrowing money that they realistically could never repay to buy over-appraised houses. Then, the so-called, "sub-prime" mortgages, guaranteed in main part by the U.S. government, were "securitized" into basically fraudulent securities, though securities rated as "safe" ones. Next, this essentially worthless "paper" was sold to many, many unsuspecting buyers, all the way to Iceland. This series of events resulted in a financial disaster and economic "meltdown." Throughout the political, economic, business, banking, real estate, and mortgage fields, short-sighted, if not immoral, business people tolerated undue risks, illegal, "borderline" illegal, and clearly unethical conduct. Individualistic, risky, short-term profit-seeking – from real estate agents, mortgage brokers, and bankers - was the "moral" norm; and the deleterious effect on society of this misbehavior apparently did not even register. The result was a massive destruction of value – short- and long-term – the ruination of businesses, business and personal assets, and people's lives, necessitating massive government (that is, taxpayer) "bailouts," and engendering a serious undermining of confidence in economic and political systems as well as business and political "leaders."

Summary
Capitalism and free markets are built on, as Adam Smith wisely stated long ago, a foundation of morality. The economy needs to be free to function, but the economy also needs rules to function correctly and effectively. And when the legal rules are not present or they are not clear, there is all the more need for ethics and socially responsible behavior. The idea is to create a sustainable form of capitalism, whereby acting in a legal, ethical, and socially responsible manner, as well as taking a long-term perspective, will produce profits for the shareholders and long-term value for all the other stakeholders of the company. The answer is not necessarily more government regulation but more self-regulation. The task of business leaders, therefore, is to incorporate not only legal rules but also ethical, social responsibility, and stakeholder considerations into corporate values, mission statements, governance policy, and strategy, and to do so not "just" nationally but globally.

Transparency, truthfulness, and trustworthiness have been, are, should be, and must be the hallmarks of successful and sustainable business; business leaders have a moral obligation to be trustees of all the stakeholders of the organization; yet, sadly, these moral lessons now must be learned once again. A true business leader must be keenly aware and engaged, must look ahead, and must foresee the consequences of his or her company's actions on all the firm's stakeholders, including the economic system and society as a whole. Business leaders must be aware that law, ethics, and social responsibility are all interconnected and underpin the economy and the free market system. The goal is capitalism, yes; but a sustainable capitalism "regulated" and tempered by law, ethics, morality, and social responsibility, and thus capitalism with a "communitarian spirit".

Nevertheless, it should be noted that the full implementation of a capitalistic economic structure may not be suitable for every culture or country without a strong infrastructure to properly regulate and support it. As such, business leaders and policy-makers are advised to carefully consider whether capitalism without proper government regulation and/or sufficient self-regulation is appropriate for a specific country and culture at a given time. Once again, the ultimate goal is to have a sustainable capitalism, where people and businesses obey the law, act ethically, and people and particularly corporations take social responsibility seriously.

CHAPTER 4

Afghanistan's Conundrum: Capitalism in a Dependent Nation

Belal A. Kaifi, Trident University

Over the years, capitalism has spread throughout the world causing many conundrums for the citizens of each nation. Karl Marx (1818-1883) was one of the first opponents of capitalism and declared that in a capitalist society, a worker's meaning changes—becoming a productive tool rather than a human being. Furthermore, the CEO and Chairman of Microsoft, Bill Gates, said that capitalism's "systemic" problems are not doing enough for research and "the needs of the poorest." Klein (2007) explains how capitalism came to dominate the world, from Chile to Russia, China to Iraq, South Africa to Canada, with the help of violent "shock tactics" in times of natural disaster or tragedy.

The reality is that capitalism is a contemporary version of the Doctrine of Thrasymachus, also known as Survival of the Fittest or Social Darwinism. "One of its basic tenets is that the most secure avenue to development is provided by supply-side economic strategies that encourage and facilitate the accumulation of capital by the able and adept" (Weatherby et al., 2009, p. 54). As capitalism made its way to Afghanistan, the disparity between the rich and poor widened—resulting in widespread conflict, devious corruption, unnecessary competition, and de-culturalization.

Background of Afghanistan

The history of Afghanistan can be traced back to many cultures that have traveled throughout the country. Afghanistan's strategic location (Central Asia) has always connected the rest of the world to Afghanistan, dating back to the Silk Road. According to Ewans (2002), "Afghanistan has also over its long history been a highway of conquest between west, central and southern Asia" (p. 10). Different empires have traveled throughout Afghanistan, from China in the East to Italy in the West. Thus, Afghans have truly been exposed to the world of cultures and traditions. Throughout Afghanistan, there are different traditions, languages, and even physical characteristics because of the different empires that have traveled throughout the country (Kaifi, 2009, p. 6). For example, Afghans from the northeast usually have lighter features than Afghans in the south. Ewans (2002) explains, "Many of them have light skins and aquiline features, often combined with blue eyes and blond or red hair" (p. 8).

Afghanistan is located in the heart of Central Asia. Afghanistan, approximately the size of Texas is a landlocked country, bordered by Turkmenistan in the north, Uzbekistan, and Tajikistan, on the northeast by China, on the east and south by Pakistan, and by Iran on the west (Mujtaba, 2007). According to Tapper (2001), "The mountain ranges of the region run from east to west. The principal rivers carve deep gorges through them as they flow northwards into Turkistan" (p. 165). The country is divided east to west by the famous Hindu Kush mountain range and "several of its mountains are among the highest in the world" (Ewans, 2002, p. 1). The majority of the country is covered by mountains and valleys, which are natural barriers that have assisted Afghanistan during wars. According to Ewans (2002), "Some two-thirds of it lie above 5,000 feet, and several mountains are among the highest in the world" (p. 1).

The two main languages of Afghanistan are Farsi and Pashto. According to Ewans (2002), "In human terms, Afghanistan is one of the poorest and most miserable countries in the world" (p. 191). According to U.S. Department of State (2008), "the population of Afghanistan is 31,056,997. More than 3 million Afghans live outside the country, mainly in Pakistan and Iran, although over 5 million have returned" home in the post-Taliban era. Simonson (2004) reports, "Current attempts to estimate the relative proportion of ethnic groups put the Pashtuns at 44% of the population, while Tajiks, the Hazara and the Uzbeks, represents 25%, 10%, and 8% respectively" (p. 708).

Over the years, the struggle for a unified Afghanistan has been an arduous situation because of belligerent neighbors, dependency on Western empires, sub-optimal leadership, and "tribalocracy." One main reason is that Afghanistan is located in a strategic location in Central Asia which has caused many conflicts. In fact, throughout Afghanistan's history, there has been involuntary conflict. Ewans (2002) explains, "Although never colonized, Afghanistan is part of the colonial history of Tsarist Russia and British India" (p. 9). Throughout the late 1800s and early 1900s, the British attempted to colonize Afghanistan on three different occasions and were unsuccessful. Throughout the late 1970s and 1980s, the Russians invaded Afghanistan hoping to spread Communism, and were also defeated by the Afghan resistance. Afghans have never surrendered to an outside invader. "Uniquely among the nations of Eurasia, Afghanistan has steadfastly resisted conquest, despite being a crossroads for ambitious empires throughout ancient and medieval times and a battleground in the modern age during the Great Game and Cold War" (Tanner, 2009, p. 26). In 1996, the Pakistani backed Taliban aggressively invaded and controlled parts of the country. After the Taliban were defeated in 2001, a liberal democratic Afghanistan emerged where capitalism played a central role in the future of this nation.

Afghanistan: Pre-Capitalism (1900s-1970s)

Living off the fruits of the land and their own labors, indigenous Afghans were self-sufficient and unaffected by the demands of the global economy. For Afghans, *iman* (faith), *nang* (pride), and *namoos* (honor) played a major role in the society. The citizens lived in harmony with one another and shared the work of the harvest. They provided emotional and material support in times of crisis and transition. Children were raised in extended families surrounded by relatives and friends of all ages and sexes. When an issue emerged, they were abruptly defused with humility, patience, respect, and poise. The people had plenty of time to do as they wished and at their own pace. In Afghanistan, interactions were based primarily on barter and mutual aid. Money played a minimal role in the economy that was based primarily on Islamic principles. True wealth was determined by the quality of family and community relations. Afghans traditionally recycled everything and were super-environmentalists.

Impact of Capitalism on Afghanistan's Society

Afghanistan is comprised of 99.9% Muslims (Younos, 2008, p. 135). Islam is a complete way of life (Qur'an, 5:3); but one which clashes with capitalism. The root tenet of capitalism is self-interest, while the root tenet of Islam is benevolence. Furthermore, Muslims are taught to be compassionate and merciful in their daily interactions. From a social perspective, capitalism equates to a loss of culture, religion, and value system for Afghans. Capitalism has promoted dishonorable Machiavellian behaviors that revolve around illicit and precarious capitalistic endeavors, such as drug trafficking, prostitution, and exploitation throughout Afghanistan. Machiavellianism can be simply defined as doing whatever it takes to get one's way. Hence, those with authority and wealth are capitalizing on the less fortunate because of their inability to challenge those with wealth and power.

Drug trafficking in Afghanistan has become the norm for a small, wealthy group of individuals who are willing to contribute to a harmful global phenomenon that has destroyed so many lives. The drug traffickers have only one objective—to become extremely wealthy. "Central Asia is a major transit for drug traffickers moving their products from Afghanistan to markets in Russia and the West" (Weatherby et al., 2009, p. 322). The reality is that capitalism and corruption go hand-in-hand because they both have the same common denominator—self-interest. That is precisely why Muslims are instructed in the Qur'an to stay away from intoxicants in order to prosper (5:90) and to not contribute to destruction (2: 195). Furthermore, in Islam, Muslims learn: A time will come upon the people when one will not care how one gains one's money, legally or illegally. Unfortunately, the drug traffickers continue to take extreme measures that impact the entire society (i.e., production and distribution of opium) to accomplish their own selfish objectives. Figure 4.1 highlights opium production in Afghanistan. It should be mentioned that one metric ton equates to 1,000 kilograms.

Figure 4.1: Afghanistan: Opium Production (1970-2007)

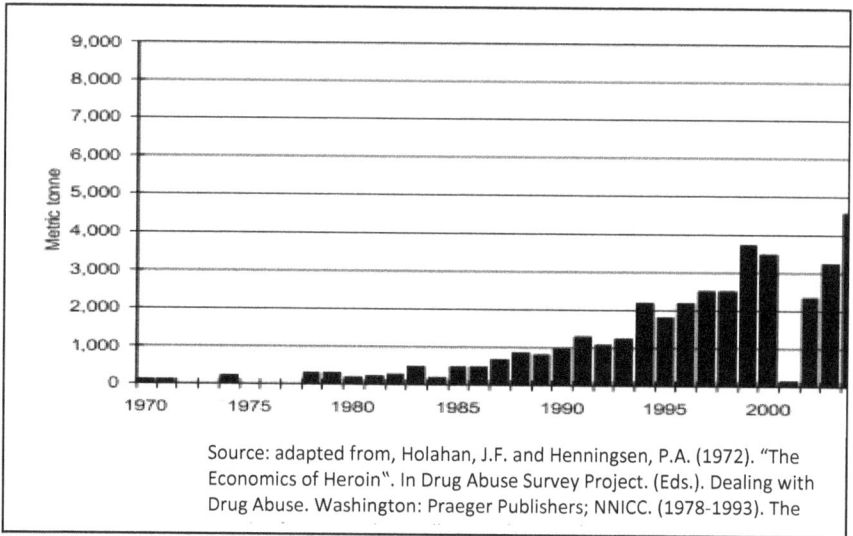

Source: adapted from, Holahan, J.F. and Henningsen, P.A. (1972). "The Economics of Heroin". In Drug Abuse Survey Project. (Eds.). Dealing with Drug Abuse. Washington: Praeger Publishers; NNICC. (1978-1993). The

As can be seen from the data, opium production has skyrocketed since 1970 and, more specifically, after 2001 when a liberal democratic Afghanistan emerged where capitalism has played a central role.

As a result of capitalism, brothels and prostitution have emerged in Afghanistan. According to Tang (2008A), "Sex is sold most obviously at brothels full of women from China who serve both Afghans and foreigners. Far more controversial are Afghan prostitutes, who stay underground in a society that pretends they don't exist." These prostitutes are managed by individuals who exploit these women in order to become wealthier. According to an article that appeared in the Los Angeles Times by Tang (2008B), "Paradise is a brothel in an unmarked residential compound in an upscale Kabul neighborhood." For any Muslim country, brothels and prostitution are against Islamic principles. The Qur'an has made it very clear that unlawful sex is prohibited (17:32, 24:2). Some of the prostitution that occurs in Afghanistan is due to a lack of opportunity for the poor, because in a capitalistic society, the "rich get richer and the poor get poorer." This results in women who have no means of financial support to take extreme and unlawful measures to provide for their children. Those with wealth are capitalizing on this unfortunate situation by providing immoral opportunities for women to make a dreadful living. Afghanistan is one of the world's most conservative countries, yet its sex trade appears to be thriving.

A different adverse trend that has gained significant media attention in the past couple of years involves children and sexual abuse. According to Londoño

(2012), "A growing number of Afghan children are being coerced into a life of sexual abuse. The practice of wealthy or prominent Afghans exploiting underage boys as sexual partners who are often dressed up as women to dance at gatherings is on the rise in post-Taliban Afghanistan." Many of the young boys are either orphans or come from a family who have no financial means and have no choice but to sell their young son to a wealthy businessman so they can use those funds to take care of the rest of the family. Wealthy businessmen capitalize on the opportunity of purchasing these young boys, training them, sexually abusing them, and also having them dance at parties for a financial profit. This conduct is against Islamic principles. The Qur'an clearly states: "Give unto orphans their wealth. Exchange not the good for the bad (in your management thereof) nor absorb their wealth into your own wealth. Lo! That would be a great sin" (4:2).

The examples highlighted above (drug trafficking, the emergence of brothels and prostitution, and the purchase of young boys) delineate the negative impact of capitalism on a society such as Afghanistan. Capitalism eliminates the middle-class resulting in a tiny upper-class and a substantial lower-class. Capitalism is not for the people, of the people, and/or by the people; it is for a select few with wealth and authority. According to Younos (2008), "Capitalism, as one may think, is not the business of free trade, proper investment, and constructive production for the sake of its people" (p. 64). The next section will highlight the negative impact of capitalism on Afghanistan's economy.

Afghanistan's Economy

When a developing nation embraces capitalism, the implications on the economy are vast. Ultimately, there is a loss of philanthropic endeavors because of self-interest and greed. In the case of Afghanistan, where the majority of the population is illiterate and live below the poverty line, capitalism is not a feasible solution. As mentioned above, Afghanistan is a Muslim country and Islamic principles should become the way of life in all matters and situations. That is precisely why Islam emphasized the importance of waqf, sadaqah, and zakah over 1,400 years ago:

- *Waqf* - welfare or charity foundations to aid the poor,
- *Sadaqah* - voluntary charity,
- *Zakah* - an annual tax where a Muslim donates to the needy.

The following verses from the Qur'an also delineate the importance of helping the needy: "And be steadfast in prayer; practice regular charity; and bow down your heads with those who bow down (in worship)" (2:43); "And be steadfast in prayer and regular in charity: And whatever good ye send forth for your souls before you, ye shall find it with God: for God sees Well all that ye do" (2:110); "They ask thee what they should spend (In charity). Say: Whatever ye spend that is good, is for parents and kindred and orphans and those in want and for wayfarers. And whatever ye do that is good, - God knoweth it well" (2:215). Thus, it can be concluded that Islam preaches benevolence with a balance for altruistic behaviors, and not the motivation for "extreme" profits at all costs.

In a capitalistic economy, usury is used to its fullest capacity to exploit and control the citizens of the society. Individuals pay high levels of interest when they purchase a house (i.e. mortgage), go to college (i.e., school loan), purchase a car (i.e., car note), use a credit card (i.e., purchase necessities), and this is only the tip of the iceberg. It is no wonder that most citizens in capitalistic economies feel as if they are underpaid, undervalued, and overworked. The concept of "living paycheck to paycheck" has become the norm for the majority in most capitalistic economies. On the contrary, Islam protects mainstream citizens by prohibiting *riba* (usury) (Qur'an, 2:275). Moreover, Islam also prohibits several other characteristics of a capitalistic economy that do not promote egalitarianism. First, capitalistic economies promote extravagance as a means to persuade the less fortunate to spend more and eventually, take out loans and pay high levels of interest. In Islam, *israf* (extravagance) is prohibited. Second, capitalistic economies support the idea of hoarding and using the rules of supply and demand for price determination (i.e., maximizing profits). This act can be detrimental for the citizens of a society who are unable to afford inflated prices based upon the rules of supply and demand. In an effort to help the needy avoid being exploited, Islam prohibits *bukhl* (hoarding). Finally, in capitalistic economies it is normal for industries to be monopolized. In Islam, *ihtikar* (monopolies) are prohibited so products and prices cannot be controlled. Thus, there is a stark difference between what capitalism promotes and what Islam prescribes. The next section will highlight the negative impact of capitalism on Afghanistan's politics.

Afghanistan's Politics
Capitalism not only impacts the society and economy, but also the internal and external politics of a nation. In the case of Afghanistan, capitalism has promoted unethical behaviors that have had somber ramifications on the society. When a society is dealing with a "survival" of the fittest mentality, it becomes imperative for "the fittest" to obtain high positions in government and then to assist and promote their own social group resulting in "tribalocracy," nepotism, and at times, being "above the law." In a recent debacle in Afghanistan, close to $900 million of the Kabul Bank was embezzled by 19 individuals and companies. Of these 19 individuals, several of them are related to the President and first Vice President of the country (Fox News, 2012). The example above clearly illustrates the consequences of capitalism in politics (i.e., widespread corruption). According to CBS News (2012), "The Kabul Bank scandal is a saga about money-grabbing, weak banking oversight, lax prosecution, nepotism, political contributions, and fraud."

Moreover, it should be mentioned that capitalism in politics creates a loss of merit. That is, those who deserve high-level positions based upon their experience and education are merely overlooked because of the sheer authority and power that the wealthy have. For example, there are currently several Ministers in Afghanistan's Cabinet who lack the experience, skills, and education to fulfill the tasks that are expected for their vital positions. There are also several warlords who are a part of Afghanistan's Cabinet. Moreover, several of these Afghan Ministers do not possess the educational requisites and justify their lack of qualifications with their military experiences (i.e., guerrilla warfare). This rationalization is eccentric and does not resonate with the masses. Unfortunately, capitalism has given the rich and the powerful privileged "rights" to buy votes, break laws, use coercion, and exploit the needy.

In Afghanistan, bribery has become the norm in all aspects of life. Corrupt practices and widespread existence of bribery in developing nations are likely to lead to greater inequalities and disparities between the rich and the poor. Despite a democratic government, greater inequality is being evidenced in Afghanistan today from the growing number of people who are living in poverty (Mujtaba, 2007). A research study by Mujtaba and Kaifi (2010) surveyed Afghans and analyzed their perceptions regarding business ethics. For the study, it was expected that the reported Personal Business Ethics Scores (PBES) for the Afghan and American respondents would not be significantly different. "However, this hypothesis was not supported because the study found a statistically significant difference in the business ethics scores of Afghan and American respondents" (p. 55). The results indicated that Afghan respondents reported significantly greater levels of approval for the unethical behaviors and decisions described in the eleven ethical dilemmas presented in the survey. Capitalism has promoted unethical behaviors among Afghans.

High levels of poverty, corruption, and inequality can leave a country and its people dependent on their neighbors and/or the international community. Graham and Chattopadhyay (2009) explain, "We also find evidence of adaptation to high levels of crime and corruption in Afghanistan; unlike most other places where we have studied happiness, being a victim of crime or corruption does not result in a decline in reported well-being, suggesting that individuals have come to expect such events as the norm" and the authors further state, "While adaptation may be a good thing – or perhaps even a survival strategy – from an individual well-being or happiness perspective, it may be bad for welfare in the aggregate, as it results in a collective tolerance for bad equilibrium, such as high levels of crime and corruption" (p. 127). The continuation of bribery and corrupt practices in Afghanistan will further harm, injure, and greatly impair the speedy development of infrastructure and economic progress. In addition, bribery and corruption will make Afghans more vulnerable to, as well as to remain dependent on, their neighbors and the international community in the coming decades.

Over the years, billions of dollars have been spent on building and rebuilding Afghanistan. Albeit this assistance is commendable, it should be mentioned that the countries that have helped Afghanistan have had many of their own conspicuous or inconspicuous expectations. As Adam Smith (1776) said so eloquently, "It is not from the benevolence of the butcher, the brewer, or the baker that we expect our dinner, but from their regard to their own interest." A case in point is how the Russians built roads and bridges in Afghanistan in the 1960s. Years later, the Russians used those same bridges and roads to invade Afghanistan and kill over one million innocent Afghans. From a political perspective, Afghanistan has always been regarded as a strategic buffer zone between empires.

Furthermore, it needs to be mentioned that Afghanistan has looked elsewhere for help throughout most of its history. For example, India has donated old planes, the Russians built the famous *Polytechnic* University and *Macreyon* apartment complexes in Kabul, the French helped create and establish the *Istiqlal* high school, the Germans helped create and establish the *Amani* high school, the Arabs donated millions of dollars to the Afghans during the Russian-Afghan war, the American army helped replace the Taliban regime, and the list goes on and on. As a result of this long-term foreign assistance and dependence, Afghanistan has regressed and has been struggling to provide food and electricity for its people while neighboring countries are developing nuclear arms (Kaifi, 2008, p. 17). In economics, the "dependency" theory concludes that poverty in developing nations is the result of their dependence on high-income nations, which is precisely the case in Afghanistan. Ultimately, "Dependency theory thus claimed to explain both continued underdevelopment globally and persistence in inequality and class structure within peripheral economies" (Perraton, 2007, p. 32).

In a research study by Kaifi, Mujtaba, and Xie (2009), the authors were able to conclude that different levels of education yielded significant viewpoints about whether foreigners (the international community) should or should not help Afghans. Participants with only a bachelor's degree agreed that foreigners should help; those with a master's degree mostly disagreed to the question and would prefer foreigners not to help; doctoral degree respondents all held the viewpoint that foreigners should not help in the development process. The more educated respondents perhaps believe that Afghans are capable of helping themselves without the unwanted influence of foreign governments which often comes with preconditions and hidden agendas" (p. 41).

The leadership of the country neglected the short-term and long-term implications of seeking assistance from the international community. As Kaifi (2008) explains, "The post 1929 laissez-faire mentality toward education has haunted the Afghan people for decades and has resulted in a life-long dependency on foreigners who have always had their own hidden agendas of strategically occupying the region" (p. 17). Thus, a capitalistic society demands a transformational leader that uses "referent power."

A prime example of a visionary and transformational Afghan leader is King Amanullah. Transformational leaders are able to transform the way people think and act. A more popular global example of a transformational leader is Mahatma Gandhi who transformed the way his society strived for independence by using peaceful protests and non-violence tactics. Referent power is when followers respect and admire their leader resulting in goal-accomplishment. If a leader portrays ethical behaviors, then the people will respect that leader, transform, and demonstrate ethical behaviors.

During his reign, King Amanullah took steps to "reform the legal structure, creating an independent judiciary, a system of courts, and a secular penal code"

(Ewans, 2002, p.93). Furthermore, he promoted monogamy and enforced a minimum age for marriage. He also took steps toward a modern economy with tax reforms to help develop the country. His economic reforms included reassessing, reorganizing, and restructuring the current economy and stressed the importance of filtering out the corruption and nepotism that became the status quo after his reign. "Judgments of a leader's ethical posture may play a particularly strong role in influencing follower satisfaction with the leader" (Vecchio, et al, 2008, p.79). He was able to provide peace and stability in Afghanistan while forming strategic allies around the world, which helped the country progress in numerous ways. In 1920, the Afghans and the Soviets signed a Treaty of Friendship which was Afghanistan's first international agreement since gaining full independence in 1919. According to Northouse (2004), "The transformational approach also requires that leaders become social architects" (p. 183). King Amanullah, one of Afghanistan's transformational leaders, influenced the people of Afghanistan by empowering them to be transformational leaders. In a research study by Kaifi and Mujtaba (2010), the authors were able to conclude that Afghan-American respondents scored in the high range for having a transformational leadership orientation (p. 48). Future leaders of Afghanistan should use this information to help transform the society into a merit-based and just society by not only promoting, but also exercising, democratic and universally acceptable ethical principles.

Summary

Capitalism has promoted *bay-iman* (no faith), *bay-nang* (no honor), and *bay-namoos* (no pride) behaviors in Afghanistan. Furthermore, Afghanistan is dependent on the global community, is a developing nation, and the people are divided (i.e., the "rich" and the "poor"). According to Agence France-Presse (2012), "Half a million Afghans displaced by war have been left homeless and struggling to survive because of government and international neglect." In its current situation, Afghanistan is unable to sustain capitalistic behaviors that mainly benefit the wealthy and suppress the poor. In order for capitalism to be successful, there needs to be law and order. Moreover, there need to be rules and regulations which are followed by all (i.e., starting with the leadership and government of the country). There should also be severe consequences for those who violate laws. Thus, capitalism is not feasible in Afghanistan at this current epoch. As mentioned above, almost all people in Afghanistan are Muslim and only principles aligned with their faith and culture will best resonate with the Afghan people. Accordingly, it is time for implementing Islamization, which is a process of nation-building by using Islamic principles to help the society flourish and thrive (Younos, 2008, p. 135).

Unfortunately, corrupt practices are likely to be around until Afghans become somewhat independent. In the meantime, education and capacity-building will be critical in helping Afghans become self-sufficient. Self-sufficiency in generating income through small business entrepreneurship will be critical in the elimination of corruption and reduction of bribery in Afghanistan. Public officials should thus "brainstorm" on the creation of effective ways to control and discipline the behaviors of their people. Harris (2002) explains, "the importance of developing processes which meet the requirements of procedural justice and equality of treatment but also of the flexibility to allow for sensitive personal interactions which take account of individual need" (p. 56). Ethical behavior should be expected, modeled, and enforced by using spiritual and religious teachings, particularly because the ritual of day-to-day prayers are part of the Afghan culture. In order for corruption and bribery to end in Afghanistan, the leaders of the country must model and emphasize the moral teachings of their faith which condemn corruption and unethical practices.

CHAPTER 5
China: Medical Corruption and Culture

Han Ping, The School of Management, Xi'an Jiaotong University, P. R. China
Ramón J. Venero and Yunshan Lian, Nova Southeastern University

China is a growing country with a mixed economic system where both capitalism and socialism concepts are being concurrently practiced. This chapter first provides discussion on China's medical industry challenges and its influence on trust related to doctors and patients. The second part of the chapter discusses foreign direct investment (FDI) in China and the culture of the country.

Practical implications and suggestions are presented for academicians and policy-makers.

China: Medical Corruption and Trust[2]
The medical corruption of China has already aroused great concern from society. This section analyzes the medical corruption expression, influence of China's medical corruption to trust relationship between doctors and patients, as well as the "downside" of reduced doctor-patient trust. Then, this part analyzes the fundamental cause of medical corruption. It results from the macro-economic system outside the medical system and current complicated social factors. It is directly related to the problems of morality inside the medical system and the supervisory institution. Medical corruption can also be attributed to people's psychological state, value orientation, and cultural background. Based on the analysis, the chapter brings forward some counter-measures to prevent medical corruption.

The People's Republic of China is a socialist country with its own characteristics. It is one of the developing countries. China lies in the east of Asia. It has an area of over 9,600,000 square kilometers. It consists of 34 provinces, autonomous regions, and municipalities directly under the Central Government. The People's Republic of China is one of the largest countries in the world. Now it has a population of more than 1.3 billion, making up a quarter of the world population

China is a socialist state with the Chinese Communist Party as the ruling party. Chinese politics has a strong influence on every aspect of the daily Chinese life. That is why Chinese business and politics can hardly be separated. From 1949

---

[2] Authored by Han Ping, The School of Management, Xi'an Jiaotong University, P. R. China

to 1979, China took on a Central Planning Economy. China has been conducting reforms and opening policy since 1978. After 30 years of reforming, China has transitioning to be a "socialist market economy". It is essentially a process of capitalism. Chinese economic structure is now a diversified one. It includes state-owned economy and non-state owned economy such as private owned enterprise, foreign investment enterprise and joint venture. Besides economic reforms, Chinese government also carried out a series of social system reforms, including politics, law, education, health insurance, healthcare, and taxation reforms. As a country with more than two thousand years history, Chinese culture plays an important role on the process of China's reforming.

Cultural Orientation
China is a country with many ancient customs, thanks to a huge history and culture. Although the famous Chinese philosopher, Confucius, died more than 2500 years ago, he is still influential today despite the impact of industrialism and Western culture in many aspects of Chinese societies (Bond and Wang, 1983). It can be argued that the standpoints derived from these philosophies are different from other countries. Because of the influence of traditional Chinese culture, "*guanxi*" (Chen, Chen, & Xin, 2004), "*face*," or "*renqing*" variables (Liu, Friedman & Chi, 2005) play important role in the Chinese context. Scholars have verified it.

Since Hofstede's (1980) original study on the cross-cultural field, numerous researchers have focused on studying individualism and collectivism. By using Hofstede's cultural framework, many scholars, including Chinese and foreign educators have launched studies of culture in China. Chinese culture, which develops from Confucian culture, presents the characteristics of collectivism and large power distance. Family and Guanxi are the nuclear and base of social network. Fei Xiaotong (1985) notes that there exists a Pattern of Difference Sequence in Chinese social network. Chinese scholars have researched interpersonal trust in Chinese background and found that Chinese are divided into two types--people on one's own side and outsiders--on the basis of guanxi. People intend to trust one of us otherwise distrust outsider. Fu and Yukl (2000) reasoned that U.S. and Chinese respondents would differ on the perceived effectiveness of "influence" strategies because of differences in cultural values of power distance, uncertainty avoidance, and short-term versus long-term orientation. They found that Americans rated rational persuasion and exchange as more effective than Chinese did. For Chinese, coalition tactics, upward appeals, and gifts were viewed as more effective influence tactics. Morris and colleagues (1998) compared the conflict-resolution approaches in the United States, China, India, and the Philippines using MBA students in each country. Chinese participants reported a greater tendency to use the avoiding style than the participants in the other three countries, whereas the U.S. participants reported a greater tendency to use the competing style relative to the others.

According to the reforming and opening policy, Chinese culture has changed a lot. Maoist ideology, traditional Chinese cultural values and Western life styles are found to exist side by side in China. Besides, reforming is not only bringing the advancement and changes for society, but also produced a negative by-product, corruption. On one hand, since the system is incomplete on the process of reforming, rent-seeking and corruption are regular phenomenon. On the other hand, since "guanxi", "face" and "renqing" is the core of Chinese culture, it gives a reasonable excuse and encourage corruption. Moreover, since China is collectivism and a centralized state, absolute centralization means absolute corruption. Corruption has been a "hot" issue faced by Chinese. Corruption does not only lead to the economic loss but also affect Chinese people's daily life.

Recently, the pressure of medical expenses has become more and more heavy, and as time goes on it is expected to get worse. Many ordinary Chinese people, especially the poor, are not affordable to pay for high level of medical expenses. According to the survey, higher medical treatment expenses and frequent medical dispute has become a big problem. What causes the problem in China? That is medical corruption.

China's Medical Corruption
There are different kinds of participants in the health care system, such as medical organizations, pharmaceutical manufactures, pharmaceutical agencies, government, insurance companies, and patients. Medical corruption may occur in different participants and in a variety of styles. In general, medical corruption in China has the following modality.

Pharmaceutical commission
Pharmaceutical manufacture and pharmaceutical agency will pay the commission to hospitals and doctors that use their medicine. The commission ratio is usually between 10-20%. For example, if a doctor writes out a prescription of 100 RMB medicines s/he can get 10-20 RMB commissions from it. One patient received 830 RMB prescriptions for an ordinary cold, even including a medicine for protecting embryo. Usually, the ordinary cold only needs fewer medicines, not more than 100 RMB.

Medical treatment red packet
Patients will send money, material objects, gift cards, and other economic benefit to doctors when they receive medical services. This practice has become an "unspoken rule," especially when the patient receives surgery treatment.

Excessive medical treatment
Some unethical doctors ask patients to receive excessive medical treatment in order to obtain extra money. For example, a six-year old girl was asked to conduct 104 tests and examinations for making a surgical operation of appendicitis, even including an AIDS checking.

Resell patients to collect and deduct a percentage

Some doctors may collect and deduct a percentage by passing and recommending patients to seeing other hospitals and doctors. The purpose of providing referral is not for patients' getting better treatment but for doctor's individual benefit. In general, the referee can receive 5%-6% of the patient's total medical treatment fee.

To influence and guide patients by using expert power

Some experts publish papers to enhance individual power, and then use this power to induce patients to receive a specified medicine, hospital, or doctor for personal benefit.

Influence of China's Medical Corruption on Doctors and Patients

The nature of medical corruption is depriving a large and feeble group, that is, patients, of good healthcare. The serious medical corruption in China has deeply hurt the trust relationship between doctors and patients.

Medical corruption has changed the perception of traditional doctor-patient relationship in China. In traditional Chinese culture, people usually regarded doctor as a kind and smart "god." People held high esteem to doctors and had high degree of trust to them. But a survey on doctor-patient relationship in 2007 showed that more than 70% of patients do not trust doctors. The effective sample is 13502. The interviewee is asked if he or she trusted the doctor when seeking medical advice. There were 3340 people answering that they trust doctor completely. Yet there were 7504 people answering that they hold only a half degree of trust to doctor. Moreover, 2658 people answered that they do not trust doctors at all, but they had to see a doctor since they were ill.

More and more patients take defensive measures when they go to see doctors. Some patients bring voice recording devices and video cameras when they go to see doctor in order to have evidence. While being examined, if doctor says the illness is serious, then the patient may think that this carries a foreshadow of the doctor's subsequent excessive medical treatment. If doctor says that the patient does not have a serious disease, then this doctor will be considered to have lower medical skill. If doctor writes a prescription of expensive medicine, then s/he will be regarded to get high profits from this prescription. But if doctor uses cheap medicine, s/he will also be queried.

There thus have been more and more professional hospital violator phenomenon in medical disputes, which has led to a serious negative impact on the hospital order and the safety of doctors. The Management Society of the hospitals of China has surveyed 326 hospitals. The data showed that 98.4% of hospitals have had medical disputes, and among those medical disputes, around 73.5% patients and their family members took extreme behavior, such assisting in the "mourning halls" and burning paper money in the hospital; and even 43.86% of those medical disputes worsened to become situations damaging to the hospital, even physically. Along with the frequent occurrence of medical damages and the rising awareness of safe-guarding the rights of patients, the system has created professional "medical dispute profiteers" in China.

The reduced trust between doctor and patient has adversely affected patients' benefits. Meanwhile, the lack of trust also has become the obstacle of development of hospitals and China's medical science.

Recommendations and Countermeasures

From the above analysis, we can see that medical corruption has reduced the trust of doctor and patient to a large degree in China. It is harmful for patients and hospitals. Why is there medical corruption in China? And how should one solve the problem? There are perhaps many reasons for the real or perceived corruption in China; and the following are some possible reasons.

Firstly, system and structure factors are the root cause of medical corruption. China has a management system that views hospital, doctor, and drug as a trinity. Most of the hospitals are state-owned. They cannot get enough financial support from the government. Hospitals get used to selling medicines to exist. And also, the Chinese medical security system is not complete. Government support is limited; and social funds cannot be smoothly included into the Chinese medical security system. There exist big problems in the distribution system of medicines and medical instruments. The legal system is not complete. All of the foregoing facts provide the "right" conditions for medical corruption.

Secondly, the social environment and the influence of the traditional culture is the external incentive of medical corruption. In the traditional Chinese culture, people pay attention to "*guanxi*" while "looking down" at public morality. "Courtesy demands reciprocity" has become common moral norm rather than a simple interest exchange criterion. Corruption is often inspired; and to be understanding or sympathetic by people is part of China's traditional interpersonal cultural atmosphere. This is the important social cultural foundation that leads to medical corruption spreading.

Thirdly, medical staff's individual interest is the direct reason of medical corruption. Doctoring is a profession with the key characteristics of high risk and low income in China. Some medical staff members who seek high personal earnings may fall off their moral standards and consequently practice corrupt behavior. Moreover, , there is a small probability to discover and punish medical corruption in China. The lack of sanctions fosters the medical corruption because of the puny "costs" of corruption.

Policy recommendations and countermeasures for solving China's medical corruption. Fighting against corruption is an extremely urgent task at present in China. Managing the medical corruption needs comprehensive administrative measures.

Firstly, the following must be accomplished: accelerate reforming medical system and reforming medical insurance system, perfecting the regulation, strengthening supervision and restriction mechanism, carrying out the model of separating pharmaceutical medical service; integrating anti-corruption agencies, completing relevant laws, increasing the transparency and strengthening objective social supervision. In addition, the government should increase financial input to medical and health services.

Secondly, standardize the medical market. In particular, make the medicine's sell and circulate in order; establish a scientific system of drug price; public the price of medical services; execute the system of purchasing by invitation to bid strictly; and rationalize the system of medicine sale.

Thirdly, pay attention to medical staff. Strengthen ethical education to medical staffs in order to respect patient's right. Improve the salary level of medical employees in order that medical staffs could have a reasonable compensation matched with their output. Strengthening the doctor-patient communication is another recommendation that could be helpful in removing negative perceptions and enhancing trust levels.

The Role of Culture in FDI in China[3]

This section examines the role that culture plays in Foreign Direct Investment (FDI) in the People's Republic of China (PRC). Using examples of inward FDI from mostly Western Multinational Corporations (MNCs), the implication of Chinese culture, Transaction Cost Theory, and modes of entry are discussed. The authors suggest that the increase in and the rate of direct FDI in the PRC (prior to the current worldwide economic crisis) raise important issues with respect to employment and talent management issues and organizations would be wise to consider the mode of entry and management practices if they are to be successful in China.

Firms often face difficult choices regarding the location of Foreign Direct Investments (FDI). Motivations to invest in foreign countries include nations with favorable economic, institutional, and regulatory conditions. In addition, foreign firms may be attracted to certain host country cultural characteristics (Bhadwaj, Dietz & Beamish, 2007). Cultural values underlie business practices. Culture has been defined as "a way of life, a conventional order, physically acquired and rooted in subliminal consciousness. The rule of culture extends from the family, village or circle of social acquaintances to the tribe or nation" (Mazakazu, 1996). Overall, the literature suggests that culture affects the firm's international business operations from selection of host country, to mode of entry, to its relations with government officials, to its operations in-country including the management of its workforce.

Theoretical Framework

Geert Hofstede is among the most eminent scholars in cross-cultural research. His 5D model is still the currency by which many MNFs analyze entry risks, modes and level of investment in host countries. His model of national cultural differences

---

[3] Coauthored by Ramón J. Venero and Yunshan Lian, Nova Southeastern University. A complete academic version of material is published by the authors in the *International Journal of Asian Business and Information Management*, 2013.

predicated on the following constructs: power distance, individualism, masculinity, uncertainty avoidance, and long-term orientation.

Transaction Cost (TC) Theory, while intuitive today, posits that firms will organize and direct their business in those markets where it is cheapest to perform. All costs are considered in the make-it or buy-it decision. When a market is competitively full, transaction cost theory assumes that the market will regulate transactions thorough price mechanisms. The process of internationalization involves the exploitation of a firm's completive advantages by acquiring complementary assets (thereby reducing transaction costs) in foreign target markets (Cheng, 2006). Under TC, firms view FDI primarily as a means to appropriate rents in oversea markets from the exploitation of their particular capabilities and economic resources through coordinating activities across national boundaries (Filatochev, Strange, Piesse, & Lien, 2007). Managing cultural distance can result in greater costs of information collection, transfer, and internalization, which is why some firms prefer an entry mode with a lower resource commitment.

Culture and Local Environmental Effects
Despite the cultural differences among nations, MNCs are sometimes herd-like in their behaviors and enter foreign countries with deliberate speed and consistency primarily motivated by the need among firms not to give their competitors any unchallenged advantage in a foreign country (Bhadwaj, et al., 2007). Notwithstanding this phenomenon, Bhardwaj, Dietz and Beamish demonstrated empirically a positive relationship between host country culture on the location choices of foreign firms. Host country cultural factors affected inward FDI after controlling for economic, human capital, institutional, and regulatory antecedents of FDI. Specifically, those countries with high level of trust combined with a low level of uncertainty avoidance (e.g. Ireland and China) appear to have the best cultures for FDI targets.

Using Hofstede's theoretical framework, DeJong, Smeets, and Smits (2006) use his cultural dimensions as surrogates for *openness* defined as the unrestricted integration of national markets in the global economy. These researchers concluded that Hofstede's Individualism has a positive effect on openness and Uncertainty Avoidance and Power Distance to have a negative effect. DeJong *et al.*, suggest that poor (i.e. less developed) countries sometimes need authoritarian leadership to realize changes.

China and India account for 40 percent of the world population and more than 18 percent of the global economy, based on purchasing power parity (Bhasin, 2007). China, with one-fifth of the world's population has achieved an average GDP growth rate of 12 percent from 1984 to 2004 and in recent years while other countries in the region have suffered economic slowdowns, China has managed to achieve a 7 to 8 percent rate of growth (Teng & Foster, 2006). This growth has been complemented and facilitated by FDI. This FDI has two primary sources, overseas ethnic Chinese investing in the "mother country" and Western MNCs in search of cheaper means of production.

The first and most important lesson for entry into China is that you have to be inside of China and cannot operate a business from a distance. Business in China cannot be conducted at a distance as the notion of *Guanxi* or personal contacts and relationships play an essential role in the way business is conducted in China (Dong & Glaister, 2007). Within the Anglo context, *Guanxi* might be operationalized as "it's not what you know, but who you know that matters" (Anonymous, 2007). Developing *Guanxi* is a pains staking and time consuming process which includes lots of personal contact, gift exchanges (particularly gifts wrapped in for what the Chinese consider the auspicious colors of red and gold) and never cause the Chinese to *lose face* (Anonymous, 2007). In addition, understanding the notion of *Guo Qing* (phonetically gwor ching- loosely translated the way things are done in China), a flexible approach to business, especially patience in navigating the very complex Chinese regulatory environment are critical to success (Teng & Foster, 2006).

Another important cultural construct is the notion of *tou bu* (toh bu meaning "flying smart"). In China this refers to an enterprise that that can gain earlier access than its competitor to its chosen market segment is likely to be able to build a competitive example over its rivals (Teng & Foster, 2006). This behavior is highly prized by the entrepreneurial Chinese business person. One example is the success of Audi in Chinese market: Audi was voted as "most preferred brand 2005" in China (Auto Pictorial), again Audi AG announced that its sales in China blew past those in the U.S. at a 26 percent clip (Autopia). Audi is not necessarily the best selling high-end car in global market but it is a dominant brand in China. This is just because of Auto's flying smart strategy. As the first FDI in Chinese high-end car industry, Audi easily and firmly took leading position since the joint venture agreement with its Chinese partner FAW in 1988.

On the other hand, Golf is the best-selling car in Europe (Carscoop), but as a hatch-back car, it was totally rejected by Chinese consumers at the very beginning due to the cultural factor. The car is pronounced as "Jiao Che" in Chinese language, and the meaning of that word is " sedan chair," which was a symbol of "high-profile" in "old" China. Thus, the image of the three-box-sedan is more likely to be a symbol of "high-profile" than a hatch-back car. And the explanation of such cultural phenomenon is "Mian Zi" – "the face." Thus, it is very important for a local marketing specialist to transfer important cultural information to the expatriate manager in charge of the FDI.

Another case is that of the insurance giant American International Group (AIG) which used *Guanxi* or personal contacts and relationships to re-enter the PRC insurance market, although restricted to foreign investment. AIG set up business in Shanghai in 1919 but went dormant during the period 1949 to 1978. To reopen its insurance business, it invested in several large-scale, real estate development projects. Through the good offices of its Chairman Hank Greenberg, AIG assisted in facilitating China's most favored nation status with the US, helped with its entry in the WTO, and even set up a foundation to buy a set of pagoda windows looted during the Boxer Rebellion. Mr. Greenberg and AIG are considered a "good friend" of China. So, by the time that China was admitted to the WTO in December of

2001, AIG had already established itself in wholly-owned subsidiaries in four major cities while the new entrants were only permitted in JV modes capped at 50 percent ownership (Teng & Foster, 2006).

Summary
The consensus of views from the literature is that Culture, and more specifically, the interaction of different cultures, add to the complexity of doing business across borders. Once companies have gained a foothold in China, the next step is to recruit, train and retain good staff. The current shortage of skilled workers in China means that wages have raised faster than the country's GDP which translates in employers having to use other incentives to achieve staffing goals. Rewards like on-site housing, sports facilities, health care benefits and extra vacation allowance can help to develop company loyalty, an important cultural construct and significant factor in staff recruitment and retention. While workers are important, developing homegrown Chinese executives and managerial talent is also a pressing concern. This fact may force MNCs to divert funds towards training and development activities to facilitate local college graduates from local to global thinkers.

Doing business in China's mixed economic system involves many challenges, yet the possibility of many rewards. Among these challenges are cultural misunderstandings, diversity among the workforce, especially as people from the countryside migrate to the cities seeking employment, and the vast size of the country. Communication problems stemming from cultural distance between host and home country firms raise integration costs. Integration capabilities, therefore, are usually built through post-acquisition experiences.

CHAPTER 6
Cuba: Remedies for Re-Building[4]

Pedro F. Pellet, Nova Southeastern University, FL, USA
Mario E. Delgado, Rural Development Specialist/USDA
María I. Méndez, Inter-American University, Puerto Rico

The intense isolation and deprivation Cuba has been "weathering" during the last five decades could unwittingly serve to provide a positive scheme for its reconstruction. Although its infrastructure has been drastically damaged and its human capital weakened, its deprivations, if we may, should provide a population in a state of being receptive to, and appreciative of, even drastic changes. These changes and transitions, however, should not be too hard to trigger since Cuba will be starting from almost "ground zero" in terms of socio-economic development.

Introduction
Before presenting our analysis and suggestions, and in order to understand the origins of the Cuban tragedy, it will be appropriate to make reference to a speech pronounced on July 26th, 1968 by Fidel Castro, in his official commemoration of the 15th anniversary of the attack to the Moncada Barracks that marked the beginning of his struggle against Fulgencio Batista's regime. This important ideological proposition represents the initiation of a whole era of irrational economic behavior that made Cuba highly dependent on Soviet aid and compromised any possibilities of escaping socio-economic alienation. The conclusion of this speech, presented as a tribute to Ernesto Guevara's numerous writings on socioeconomic incentives, represents the definite endorsement to an idealistic and, ultimately, historically proven catastrophic economic policy, based on a distorted version of the theory of the Fair Price, popularized by some of the Fathers of the Church like Clement of Alexandria, John Chrysostom, Basil, Ambrose, Jerome, Augustine, and others, during the first centuries of Christianity; and also presented in the Old Testament of the Bible by prophets such as Amos and Isaiah. Castro said at that time:

---

[4] For a complete reading on this topic, see the authors' article coauthored with Bahaudin G. Mujtaba, Nova Southeastern University, and published in the *RU International Journal, 2013,* Ramkhamhaeng University, in Bangkok, Thailand.

We should not use money or wealth to create political awareness. We must use political awareness to create wealth. To offer a man more to do more than his duty is to buy his conscience with money. To give a man participation in more collective wealth because he does his duty and produces more and creates more for society is to turn political awareness into wealth…The road is not easy. The task is difficult, and many will criticize us. They will call us petty bourgeois, idealists; they will say we are dreamers; they will say we are bound to fail. And yet, facts will speak for us, realities will speak for us, and our people will speak and act for us because we know our people have the capacity to comprehend these roads and follow these roads…What a magnificently just homage, what a magnificently just homage to the one who best symbolizes these ideals, the strongest defender of man's conscience as an instrument of development in the Revolution, …the eternally beloved comrade Ernesto Guevara!

The main themes of this utopian speech can be summarized by the struggle or dichotomy between ideology and necessity, as well as revolutionary ethics and economic rationality. The specific economic spheres of influence were: 1) moral versus material incentives; 2)- role of money and markets; 3) budgetary versus self-financed enterprises. These three spheres of influence were deeply linked and, ultimately, rested on the vision of the "Homo Comunista" and the Millennium.

Assuming the actual state of affairs as the result of years of accumulation of the socio-economic consequences of these utopian postures, we believe that at this historical moment, redemption is possible and the future of the Cuban people can be improved substantially if some or all of our forthcoming recommendations are implemented.

Policy Recommendations
The Post-Revolutionary Cuba should:

1). Appreciate and quickly internalize new and even radical national politico-economic processes and systems (such as deep and widespread popular participation and institutionalized competition) demanded by the shift to a more open society and economy. This latent adaptability and willingness to embrace constructive changes are essential to survive and thrive in our new age of rapidly expanding developments in technology, growth in competition, and globalization of businesses and national economies.

2). Become capable of introducing new technologies and processes without having to subsidize and/or politically struggle against a vast array of vested interests. There are relatively few processes to date, although this has been changing. Broad based and rapidly increasing rates of technological development are the international commercial equalizers for developing nations under emerging economic development schemes. A direction Cuba must undertake and hold if it is not to shift inadvertently from a category of economic leftover to one of a subservient or subordinate economy once more.

3). Enjoy employment gains even under the ever-expanding regime of modern labor saving technologies. Underemployment and unemployment could not be much worse than they are today. Gains are a sure bet from almost any developmental approach and will give instant credibility and support to development programs.

4). Absorb the lessons from the growing decay being observed in highly industrialized societies and avoid their pitfalls at the same time. Cuba must include in its strategic designs policies to help maintain through time and changes, the integrity of the family and community; the strength of moral values and ethical principles and an overall societal discipline aimed at supporting a cohesive and coherent national direction. Balanced economic development with a holistic human development orientation would provide the staying power for the long term.

5). Support emerging economic development and growth trends only if they prove to be complementary to predetermined cultural values and priorities with constructive moral underpinnings. Socioeconomic directions should not be left to random or self-serving individuals and institutions. The markets may, under special conditions, lead the national economy to an optimal allocation of resources, but not necessarily to an equitable, balanced, or even effective utilization of its human and natural assets. To avoid this bias, Cuba should reinforce rationally planned and managed processes only. Structural controls are a "must" so as not to waste scarce resources or have to justify and rationalize costly incongruent and dichotomous economic policies.

6). Cuba at the start of its transition should follow a form of mixed economy format in prioritizing the allocation of its resources and in supporting pre-selected industries. It should maintain this design until it delineates and gives clear direction and staying strength to its international industrial competitive strategy. Cuba must follow a similar approach to the Japanese developmental model. This model allows the national government to identify and "sponsor" national and regional industries in which the national economic resources can exact an international strategic competitive advantage. This approach does not imply giving monopolistic powers to any one company or even protective measures to the industries selected. What it entails is for the government to invest in association with and/or provide seed money to competing companies in the pre-selected industries. Open market forces are allowed to determine the survivors as any capitalist structure does. Government is not to be a majority or controlling force, but a partner responsible for providing strategic guidance, oversight and support to the surviving firms within the selected industries.

7). Tourism is too cyclical and too servile of an economic endeavor. It is an industry too unstable to be dependent upon or used to spearhead long-term economic development and sustained social pride. The health and socioeconomic costs in terms of, for example, sexually transmitted diseases, use of illegal drugs, organized criminal activities, etc. could be very high, indeed. However, due to its large labor/employment content, it could be used to provide part of the transitional and/or temporary employment required in the initial developmental and start-up structural changes. Later as the economy settles in its new framework, the tourist industry could be used as a safety valve for the modern more frequent output demand changes or outright death of entire industries. The rise in economic and market volatility is to be expected in the highly competitive and technological creative global market place that Cuba will be entering. Health tourism could be, however, an extremely interesting alternative to conventional tourism, given the experiences of countries like Argentina, Brazil, Colombia, Costa Rica, and Thailand.

8). Concerted national support should be provided to industries with high and expanding technological content no matter how complex they may appear at the onset. Continued advances in software and other computer aids have made initially intricate technological developments eventually user-friendly. So much so that in the near future not much sophistication or even formal education will be needed to make productive use of these advances.

9). Foreign investments should be welcomed with "open arms," but should only be encouraged and supported in the nationally prioritized strategic industries. If foreign investments are allowed to flow unperturbed and undirected, foreign direct investment will skew economic development towards a short range and narrow focus. They would reinforce current competitive advantage and resource combinations complementary to their institutional goals and organizational network's advantage and not necessarily invest in support of the national long-term economic strategies. Private capital, and especially foreign capital, by necessity, focuses more on short-term profits, synergy with other segments of "their" global network and market and political controls, than on capturing and developing national, unrealized, economic potential. Moreover, the intensifying international competition in quantity and quality of both products and companies and the exponentially increasing rate of innovation in technological advances, are shrinking the life cycle of products significantly. This condition is in turn making short-term gains and market control even more relevant than in the past, providing, therefore, an even greater incentive for global corporations to maximize short-term total gains at any cost.

10). The lead role required from the public sector in the development and support of key strategic industries, in addition to its traditional function of providing social services and infrastructure, will require a strong and equitable mechanism for assessing and collecting taxes. There will be, more than ever, the need to have access to sufficient funds to help the private sector finance both basic and applied research in the selected national strategic industries and in re-training the more frequently displaced labor. The public sector must also maintain a sophisticated national infrastructure of extensive telecommunications, roads, rail, air and marine transportation links. It should also endorse and sponsor a modern educational system responsive to more current and forecasted societal needs than to traditional preferences. Society should not be made to pay, encourage or tolerate the consumption of obsolete products and services, including education.

11). The development of modern financial services institutions, in the form of banking, securities, social security/retirement, and insurance, must also be given top priority. Not only to provide incentives to save and invest, but also to leave at home the expected higher returns to capital. As governments worldwide strive to maintain the prices of their domestic products and services so that they will be competitive in the international arena, there will be continuous efforts to control inflationary expansion of their respective money supply. This reductionist monetary policy will in turn exert an upward push in interest rates. Also the accelerating growth of competition and rate of technological change, with the accompanying increase in the mortality rate of new and established companies alike, will magnify the risk of doing business and thereby generate a naturally higher cost of capital. All of these forces will maintain interest rates at a naturally higher plateau than in the past. Well-developed financial services would not add excessively to costs and would channel inflows of foreign financial capital productively. Well-developed international financial market will help maintain monetary stability and diminish the need to apply extreme fiscal measures for control. Further, the growing sophistication and variety of financial vehicles, their increasing free flow across national boundaries and the expanding on-line capabilities of electronic means of communications will soon relegate the role of Central Banks to barely an accounting function.

12). Minimize the implementation of programs to balance the distribution of national economic resources through such up-front resource redistribution as land reforms, public cooperatives, etc. Instead, accomplish the same objectives through effective and efficient tax policies aimed to motivate the private sector to expand the economic opportunities by re-investing constantly. Private ownership of the factors of production combined with market allocation of resources under an active competitive environment, but always within national economic development strategies/parameters, will provide the best long-term approach to equitable, balanced and sustained socioeconomic development.

13). The Cuban population by now must be conditioned at least to tolerate centralized and authoritarian directions. This capacity will be much needed during the initial period of transition requiring the forging of the new socioeconomic plans and strategies. After so many years of psychological dependency on external controls, it will be a major mistake to require, all of the sudden, for its population to operate under a representative democratic political structure without a period of decompression and liberalization. Democracies in order to survive, do require populations dotted with patience, discipline, tolerance and understanding. These characteristics are not developed overnight: we have as example the repeated failures of Latin American nations that have tried overnight to shift from dictatorships to democracy. We now have the old Soviet Union as a current tragic play of major proportions. The transition to full democracy as well as to market capitalism must be gradual and well-timed. If this evolution is not carefully managed, the processes toward socio-economic development will be diverted and the final products distorted.

14). Social solidarity and responsibility were never developed in Cuba, and particularly during the second half of the twentieth century. What has prevailed, as a major cohesive force for the Cuban society is a desire for the exertion of power by the socialist ruling elite and their supporters? This drive has been glorified and cloaked under distracting and pseudo-idealistic populist moves and ideologies. The so called permanent revolution and its mandated sacrifices is nothing more than a superficial justification for ineptness, irresponsibility and ego plays by all involved. Rather than a truly internalized conviction in constructive principles, Cuba's revolution was based on and continues being nurtured by class hate and mistrust. Its controlling techniques have established the grounds for its own stagnation and destruction. Socioeconomic classes of one form or another will always exist under any regime or social structure. Attempts to evolve by accentuating and playing up class mistrust, will only serve to accentuate this natural rift and its worst features. Lasting social change must of course be supervised and mentored, but if it is to be productive, it must be planted and constantly irrigated with overall attitudes and expressions of understanding, tolerance and trust, especially by the national leaders. An economic system without foundations built on human trust is both inefficient and unattractive to investments.

15). Government imposed austerity measures over the purchase of imported consumer goods and services with hard currency, must be fully implemented. Foreign exchange utilization must be curtailed, with its uses for nationally determined investment purposes, given top priority. Its consumption must be centrally managed until the national economy achieves the desired self-sustaining growth and direction. Nevertheless, within these usage limitations, exchange rates must be left to fluctuate in the open market. "Hidden deficits" must not be allowed to build up unnoticed under the guise of parity, pride or outright protectionism. The economy must be guided but not protected. Once pre-selected public and private institutional and functional milestones have been reached, the participating players must be left to fend for themselves even more fully than during the transitional structuring period.

16). The existing overabundant supply of Cuban pesos need not be reduced any more than its natural devaluation has done in real terms; yet what is needed is for the supply of goods and services to increase. The surplus of pesos supported by the liberalized markets will translate the pent-up consumer demand into a matching peso-absorbing output of goods and services and relatively fast. The government should, in turn, and as previously suggested, actively embark in instituting policies and investments that would improve productivity and competition. Artificial (forced) reduction of the existing supply of pesos would only serve to delay economic progress and give unfair advantage to established interests.

17). Cuba must give immediate priority to the development of its communications and transportation infrastructures. It is a must to actualize its competitive advantages without undue delays. It would also serve to utilize productively some of its current large pool of under and unemployed labor. Innovation, speed, convenience, quality and price are the hallmark of the successful products and services of the future. These features are heavily affected by the conditions of the transportation and communication sectors of the domestic economy and its international networks.

18). The entrepreneurial spirit and know-how, so much needed to develop and sustain any dynamic economy, is readily available in the Cuban population now in exile. They have adapted well to and adopted the capitalist risk-taking and competitive mind set. A lot of the required start-up capital is also available in this quarter. Cuban officials must negotiate with exiled industrialists. They should be given first opportunity in the selected strategic industries and provided the established governmental support, but again without outright protectionism. Open competition must be the rule.

19). The Cuban society, through its elected government and institutions, must manage the selection and application of its socioeconomic policy structure just like a business would. Setting goals, objectives, and indicators, outlining programs and projects, implementing information systems and control and "feedback" mechanisms which would maintain a never-resting analytical eye on the ever-changing global environment, are imperatives The global arena is too volatile and too powerful to leave its impact to chance, even for strong and well-established players, and much more so for much weakened beginners. Again, the chosen programs and implementation processes must be managed under an organizational framework that minimized interference with competitive forces and individual business initiatives.

Summary
Cuba must take advantage of the new technological direction of the global economy, and not base its development policies on old industries or natural resources. The new development has to be based on intellectual and informational skills within the modern dimension, not on expansions or weak revisions of historical trends, no matter how successful they may have been in the past. Cuba is "starting fresh" and is intellectually capable of exploiting the new and constantly expanding technological frontiers as good as or better than any other competing teams in the global league.

Cuba's market should be the entire world; hence its scope and long-term strategies must not be bound by self-imposed limitations or by the ever present manipulation of private vested interests with short term objectives. The economy must be open, but also bounded by national vision and direction. Its very limited resources, especially at the outset, must not be wasted in endeavors with a limited future or become subordinate to the interests of foreign economies. Thanks to the economic equalizing power of the emerging technologies, "size" is not the issue any more, but rather intellectual capacity, creativity and courage are. And Cuba and the Cubans have lots to spare, and with a track record to support it.

Finally, growth just for growth's sake, or to cater to a manipulated endless demand for constantly "new and improved" goods and services, must be avoided. Socio-economic development must be seen as a tool and not as an end in itself. It is nothing more than a mechanism to help develop a more fulfilling and balanced human existence. This effective, if not also enlightened, approach will prevent the Cuban people from falling victims to greed and becoming "slaves" to a never-ending and unsettling speeding spiral of technological change and progressive social instability. Liberty and democracy, just like capitalism, must be bounded by moral values as well as a balanced behavior if they are not going to implode while exacting an unbearable price on both the natural environment and in human suffering.

Chapter 7

Ghana and Capitalism: Corruption in Public and Private Sectors

Osman Masahudu, Colorado State University – Global Campus

Ghana is located on the west coast of Africa. It is a country with flourishing democracy; and which appears to be an envy of the continent. Ghana is often referred to as an "island of peace" in a most troubling region of the continent. Investors around the world may soon have greater interest in Ghana because of the recent discovery of oil coupled with its "teething" democracy. Ghana has ten states and 110 counties. A former British colony, it was the first country in the Sub-Sahara Africa to gain independence, in 1957; Ghana practices parliamentary democracy. In the past decade or so, a series of events have enfolded to confirm Ghana's place as a "beacon of hope" for democracy in Africa (Gyimah-Boadi, 2009).

Introduction

Ghana is about the size of the state of Oregon with about 22 million people. The country covers an area of 238,500 square kilometers. In planning President Obama's visit to Africa in July 2009, the White House passed over Kenya, where Mr. Obama's late father was born, in favor of Ghana. This emphasizes the significance of the rule of law and order, human rights and freedom to the Western world. A year after Kenya exploded in political violence; it remains a tense and unsettled place. Ghana, by contrast, is seen as an outpost of democracy and civil society in a volatile region (NY Times, 2012). Most observers believe that the concept of democracy and human rights are the products of Western history; and that democracy may not be known in Africa (Haynes, 1991). Ghana and other African countries have disconfirmed this assertion.

Kwame Nkrumah, the country's first President, a visionary but autocratic post-independence leader, was an icon of anti-imperialism, setting out a Pan-African ideology that revolutionized the continent and beyond (NY Time, 2012). The Ghanaian people are hospitable. It is evident to see a Ghanaian treat a stranger like a family member. English is the official language; however, there are about 45 other spoken languages and ethnic groups in the country. The population relies heavily on foreign assistance and remittances from Ghanaians abroad, especially from the Western world. GDP is about 14 billion USD (WB, 2012). However, agriculture employs 60 % of the workforce and accounts for 37 % of GDP. Export products are gold, cocoa, timber, bauxite manganese, and electricity (WB, 2012).

In an effort to address an unspoken corruption in the country, the Government of Ghana, in 1998, established an anti-corruption institution called the Serious Fraud Office, to investigate corrupt practices involving both private and public institutions. The Government also announced plans to re-structure the roles of other institutions established to address internal corruption issues. In 2006, the Government of Ghana passed a comprehensive bill, which was very similar and popular in the United States and within the corporate world. The Whistle Blower provision was passed in Ghana, just as in the United States, to encourage citizens to volunteer information on corrupt practices to appropriate authority for investigation.

Cultural Orientation in Ghana

The root of corruption in modern society can be traced to the degree of power distance. Hofstede (2012) defines power distance as the extent to which the less powerful members of institutions and organizations within a country expect and accept that power is distributed unequally. It is evident that corruption emanates from how high or low a particular society scores on the power distance dimension. For example, western and southern European countries such as Belgium, Greece and Turkey that score high in power distance are notably corrupt societies. Therefore, corruption in Ghana can be traced to the country's score in power distance dimension.

Ghana scores higher in the power distance dimension. A higher score indicates the people accept hierarchical order and inequality. A society where superiors have privileges and are often inaccessible; a society with these characteristics is more likely to exhibit corrupt practices both in the private and public sectors. Unlike in western societies such as the United States; that exhibits low score in power distance. The United States low score in power distance underscores the premise of "liberty and justice for all." The American society promotes equal rights in all aspects of the American society and government. Hierarchy in the American society is established for convenience and superiors are always accessible unlike in the Ghanaian society. Subordinates are consulted in the American society and information is shared frequently unlike in the Ghanaian society.

Power distance and individualism closely relate to corruption and favoritism in the Ghanaian society. The Ghanaian society is a collectivistic society because of its lower score in the individualism dimension. The society has a close long-term commitment to member groups such as family, extended family, or extended relationships. People in power both in the private and public sectors will do every within their power to ensure families and extended families are being taken care of in terms of their basic needs regardless. Individuals in the Ghanaian society believe that taking care of their extended families is their sole responsibility; unlike in the American society where the expectation is that individuals look after themselves. This tendency promotes corruption and favoritism because family members may not be qualified to hold certain positions they are offered. For example, if there is a job opening in the public sector that requires job applicants to be screened for certain qualifications; a family member is more likely to be hired for the position and may not have the required qualification. Screening may be more relaxed for a family member at the expense of a non-family member who is more qualified. This breeds corruption and favoritism.

Uncertainty avoidance is closely related to capitalism in the Ghanaian society. Hofstede (2012) defines uncertainty avoidance as the extent to which members of a culture feel threatened by ambiguous or unknown situations and have created beliefs and institutions that try to avoid those uncertainties. Societies that avoid uncertainties are less capitalistic; because they expect the government to create jobs and build the economy or take care of individual needs. A high uncertainty avoidance society like Ghana avoids or restricts innovation; and security is an important element in individual motivation. Unlike a low uncertainty avoidance society like the United States; the American society is what one would describe as uncertainty accepting (Hofstede, 2012). There is huge incentive for new ideas and innovative ways of creating products and services whether they relate to technology or business practices. Americans tend to be more tolerant of ideas or opinions from anyone and allow the freedom of expression. At the same time, Americans do not require a lot of rules and are less emotionally expressive than higher-scoring cultures, such as Ghana. Gerring & Thacker (2004) maintain that a corrupt society is characterized by lack of transparency especially in the public sector, in adequate economic development and high illiteracy rate.

Cases of Corrupt Practices

Corruption in the Ghanaian society, especially in the public sector, has been widely publicized since independence. Even though, there has been significant initiatives in the last decade designed to fight this menace; a lot needs to be done to change the paradigm among politicians and public servants. Ghana has earned some credit in the last decade for significant improvement in their corruption perception. For example, in the 2006 corruption perception index, Ghana ranked higher than India, Italy, Mexico, China, and Egypt. When it comes to corruption in Sub-Sahara African, Ghana again, is a beacon of hope.

American investors are careful when they do business in Ghana. It is not uncommon for a public servant in Ghana to openly ask for bribe or to see government officials using their offices to enrich themselves. Public servants in Ghana, and especially members of Parliament, are known for their modest salaries. However, it is common for public servants and members of parliament to own mansions both in the country and abroad. A few years ago, a group of drug dealers were "busted" in the country's international airport carrying millions of dollars of drugs en-route to Europe. Initial testing of the drugs proved to be cocaine and other prohibited substances. The group was held in custody and was arraigned before the court as part of the due process. On the court date when the judge asked to see a sample of the drugs, the sample that was brought before the judge mysteriously turned out to be a substance used for soft drinks or soda (Adusei, 2012). The judge had to dismiss the case for lack of evidence or tampered evidence. That result apparently was an instance of corruption among government officials and others.

Every Ghanaian believes that their public officials are supposed to formulate policies that will lead to ending corruption. They also believe that public officials are supposed to lead the nation and to end poverty, which breeds crime and violence in the Ghanaian society. However, Ghanaians believe that their public officials have failed them in many ways. Public officials control all the nation's resources such as the oil, gas, gold, timber, diamond and what have you. They care more about themselves, and their immediate and extended families, as portrayed in their collectivistic tendency.

Elected officials in Ghana since independence have protected their own interest and thwarted the effort of the state to develop. They have failed to take measures that will stamp out corruption in the ministries or public departments because doing so will expose their own corrupt illegal behaviors. Public servants prefer that Ghanaians live in ignorance so that they can continue to disseminate their own opportunistic behaviors. The less talk of law enforcement in Ghana, the "better." The law enforcement sector is the most corrupt institution in Ghana because the personnel believe when they do not amass wealth while in office, no one will take care of them when they retire or leave public service (Adusei, 2012). A British construction company, between 1994 and 1999, bribed the Ghanaian minster of health in the amount of $6 million to secure a contract to build bridges in the rural areas of the country. Several British companies admitted in court documents how they have paid large sums of money in bribes to Ghanaian officials to gain unfair business advantage.

Corruption threatens freedom, liberty, rule of law, and economic growth and development around the world. Public servants in Ghana believe that the nation's wealth or resources are their "inheritance" and, for that matter, they will do everything to protect it for their selfish means. According to Bate (2012), corruption is not a single event, but a continuum, perpetrated day in and day out against citizens by crooked politicians and civil servants who enjoy positions of power. They can be heads of state who demand a payoff of millions of dollars on major government contracts. Or they can be lowly civil servants in small towns who have the power to grant building permits or allow access for children to schools or reserve hospital beds, and who use such powers to extort cash payments from poor and innocent people around the world.

Unlike in the United States, with its widely prosecuted provisions against bribery in the Foreign Corrupt Practices Act of 1977, codified into 15 U.S.C section 78dd-1. The two key provisions in the Act are the one that addresses accounting transparency requirements under the Securities and Exchange Act of 1934; and the second provision addresses bribery of foreign officials. These are serious corruption and "white-collar" crime prevention law that is widely known by senior executives of multinational corporations. The anti-bribery or corruption provision of the law states that:

Issuers, domestic concerns, and any person from making use of interstate commerce corruptly, in furtherance of an offer or payment of anything of value to a foreign official, foreign political party, or candidate for political office, for the purpose of influencing any act of that foreign official in violation of the duty of that official, or to secure any improper advantage in order to obtain or retain business.

In 2012, the U.S Department of Justice charged senior executives of BizJet, a U.S corporation that provides maintenance for civil aircraft around the world for bribing Mexican and Panamanian officials to gain unfair advantage for business contracts. BizJet had settled the charges with the DOJ for an amount of $11.8 million (Diaz, 2012). DOJ invokes a provision under the foreign corrupt practices Act in charging BizJet executives. Many U.S companies such as Hewlett Packard, Siemens, BAE Systems, Wal-Mart, to mention a few, were involved in one way or other in bribing foreign officials to gain unfair business advantage. Most of them settled the charges against them and others were prosecuted.

Whereas there is significantly disproportionate number of prosecuting corruption cases in Ghana; there exists no evidence of disproportionate prosecution of corrupt public servants in the United States. For example, in Ghana, according to Professor Amakye Boateng, a political science lecturer at the Kwame Nkrumah University of Science and Technology, the issue with Ghanaian democracy is that there is always "witch-hunting" between the leading political parties and the opposition. When party A is in office, most or all of the corruption cases prosecuted involve members of party B. He adds that it is very rare to see the ruling party prosecuting its members on corruption charges. Professor Boateng concludes that this needs to change to ensure even prosecution of corruption cases in the country. This result will strengthen investor confidence and more importantly improve the country's transparency and accountability to the people.

Implications and Suggestions
Most foreign media organizations agree that the press freedom in Ghana has not been fully utilized to serve the people. Chapter 12 of the country's Constitution guarantees freedom of the press and independence of the media; while chapter 2 outlaws censorship. The Ghanaian media is considered one of the most free in Sub-Sahara Africa. Regardless of the relative freedom, writers and journalists in Ghana are poorly paid and work under deplorable conditions. Because Ghanaian journalists and writers are poorly paid and work under deplorable conditions, they are prone to bribery and other unprofessional conduct. Some journalists and writers lack basic training. It is evident that the quality of radio and television broadcast is sub-standard. Most newspapers and radio stations work along "party lines," which makes it difficult to offer "constructive criticism" to either the ruling party or the opposition.

Serving the interest of the country and the people should be the utmost responsibility of journalists and writers in Ghana. Lack of adequate compensation and training has hindered the work of journalists to thoroughly investigate and expose corrupt practices. Journalists in Ghana are more likely to take bribes and close investigations into corrupt practices instead of boldly standing up to officials and individuals suspected of corrupt behaviors. The Government of Ghana and the Serious Fraud Office should team up to provide adequate training and advocate for good pay and benefits for journalists across the country. Providing good pay and benefits as well as adequate training may help journalists do their job more diligently.

Article 286 (1) of the Constitution of Ghana requires "a person who holds public office to submit to the Auditor General a written declaration of all property and assets owned by or liabilities owed by him directly or indirectly." Such public office holders include the President, Vice President, and the Speaker of Parliament; the Deputy Speakers of Parliament; Ministers and Deputy Ministers of State; Chief Justice; Justices of the Superior Courts; Ambassadors or High Commissioners and Secretary to the Cabinet. Other public office holders are Chairmen, Managing Directors, General Managers and Heads of Departments of Public Corporations or Companies, District and Municipal Chief Executives in the state has a controlling interest and the Auditor General. This Article needs a review to ensure those mentioned in the Article fully comply with the provisions of the Article. It is evident that the individuals cited in the provision are more often accused of corrupt practices.

In addition to declaring assets while in office, the Article may be amended to include existing declaration of assets. This means public officials leaving office must be required to re-declare their assets as they leave public office. This may help combat corruption and bribery among public sector managers. Education in ethics and transparency should be promoted among public sector managers. Annual ethics training should be part of the public sector managers' job requirements.

Summary

The Government of Ghana should implement programs to combat illiteracy and poverty. Lack of awareness and too much dependency on family members for livelihood are some of the "drivers" of corruption in the Ghanaian society. Elected officials are too pressured to provide for their family and extended families. So much pressure on public officials to provide for their extended families may lead to corrupt behaviors.

Sustainable education and job training for the youth may help relieve some of the pressure off public sector managers so they can focus on what they have been elected to do. It is important also for the Ghanaian Government to review salaries of ministers and department heads to ensure they are appropriately compensated.

Chapter 8
Haiti: Corruption and Reconstruction

Ruth Torres, HR Strategic Consulting
Jackson David, Olympas Corner Enterprises

Haiti is a small, beautiful Caribbean island of just 360km bordering the Dominican Republic and occupying 1/3rd of the island of Hispaniola, which is right in the middle of "hurricane alley." In 1697, Spain ceded to the French the western third of the island, which later became Haiti. The French colony, based on forestry and sugar-related industries, became one of the wealthiest in the Caribbean, but only through the heavy importation of African slaves and considerable environmental degradation.

In the late 18th century, Haiti's nearly half million slaves revolted under the leadership of Toussaint L'Ouverture. After a prolonged struggle, Haiti became the first black republic to declare independence in 1804. Yet Haiti became the poorest country in the Western Hemisphere, predominantly due to the stripping of natural resources during colonization, the forced payment of $90 million to France for the recognition of Haitian independence in 1825 (which amount took the island until 1947 to pay off) and the economic repercussions of the continuous civil unrest financed by various political opponents.

Introduction

Haiti has been plagued by political violence for most of its history. During the three-decade reign of François "Papa Doc" Duvalier and his son Baby Doc, the Duvalier clan terrorized Haiti — 30,000 opponents were abducted, kidnapped, and killed by their Gestapo-like secret police, the Tonton Macoutes — and Baby Doc alone, according to recent Haitian judicial investigations, allegedly stole some $300 million, including, in one case, funds appropriated for a major railroad that was never built. Their dynasty is a key reason why Haiti is still the Western hemisphere's poorest and most dysfunctional country today (Padgett, 2011).

The U.S. embargo and blocking of foreign aid and loans from 2000 – 2004 further contributed to the island's financial, political, and civil instability. Under U.S. pressure, aid was cut and international institutions were pressured to do likewise (their reasoning is extensively reviewed in Paul Farmer's Uses of Haiti, and in some current press commentary, notably by Jeffrey Sachs (Financial Times) and Tracy Kidder (New York Times))(Chomsky, 2004).

President Jean-Bertrand Aristide (the island's [first] democratically elected president) left the island in February 2004 in a highly controversial removal. President Aristide and his supporters allege that Aristide was forcibly removed to live in exile in Africa. Some U.S. officials claim Aristide was not forcibly removed but obtained the assistance of safe passage, as he requested (Rossier, 2005). An interim government took office to organize new elections under the auspices of the United Nations. Democratically elected President Rene Preval and Parliament were selected in May of 2006. The Republic government consists of an Executive Branch, bicameral Legislative Branch, and Judicial Branch. The Chief of State, President Michel Martelly, was democratically elected in May 2011 for a five year term; and is not eligible to serve a consecutive term. The President then appointed the Head of Government, Prime Minister, Laurent Lamothe, in May 2012, whose appointment was ratified by the National Assembly.

The bicameral National Assembly, or Assemblee Nationale, consists of the Senate (30 seats; members elected by popular vote to serve six-year terms; one-third elected every two years) and the Chamber of Deputies (99 seats; members elected by popular vote to serve four-year terms); note - in reestablishing the Senate in 2006, the candidate in each department receiving the most votes in the 2006 election serves six years, the candidate with the second most votes serves four years, and the candidate with the third most votes serves two years (CIA, 2012). However, Haiti has yet to obtain the full nine members of a permanent electoral council and create an electoral calendar. Haiti is already months overdue in filling empty Senate seats, one-third of which remain vacant, as well as all of its city and town councils. Additionally, just weeks after the superior judiciary council was formed, two of its nine members have already resigned, further handcuffing reform (Schneider, 2012).

Poverty, corruption, and poor access to education for much of the population are among Haiti's most serious disadvantages. The 2010 earthquake destroyed much of the capital city and made a severe impact on Haiti's economy. With 80% of the population living under the poverty line and 54% in abject poverty, the earthquake inflicted $7.8 billion in damage and caused the country's GDP to contract 5.4% in 2010. Following the earthquake, Haiti received $4.59 billion in international pledges for reconstruction, which has proceeded slowly. Two-fifths of all Haitians depend on the agricultural sector, mainly small-scale subsistence farming (consisting of coffee, mangoes, sugarcane, rice, corn, sorghum; wood); and thus remain vulnerable to damage from frequent natural disasters, exacerbated by the country's widespread deforestation. Other industries include: textiles, sugar refining, flour milling, cement, light assembly based on imported parts (CIA, 2012).

U.S. economic engagement via the HOPE Act passed in December 2006, has boosted apparel exports and investment by providing duty-free access to the US until 2020 under the Haiti Economic Lift Program Act (HELP); the apparel sector accounts for about 90% of Haitian exports and nearly one-tenth of GDP. Remittances are the primary source of foreign exchange, equaling nearly 20% of

GDP, and more than twice the earnings from exports. Haiti suffers from a lack of investment, partly because of limited infrastructure and a lack of security. In 2005, Haiti paid its arrears to the World Bank and received debt forgiveness for over $1 billion through the Highly-Indebted Poor Country initiative in mid-2009. The remainder of its outstanding external debt was cancelled by donor countries following the 2010 earthquake but has since risen to over $600 million. The government relies on formal international economic assistance for fiscal sustainability, with over half of its annual budget coming from outside sources. The Martelly administration in 2011 launched a campaign aimed at drawing foreign investment into Haiti as a means for sustainable development (CIA, 2012).

A massive magnitude 7.0 earthquake struck Haiti in January, 2010 with an epicenter about 25 km (15 mi) west of the capital, Port-au-Prince. Over 300,000 people were killed and some 1 million left homeless. The earthquake was assessed as the worst in this region over the last 200 years (CIA, 2012). Today, more than 400,000 of those residents still live in the tents and brace themselves regularly for tropical storms and hurricanes. Haiti also experienced a cholera outbreak in October, 2010 which killed more than 7,000 people and sickened more than 500,000, according to Nigel Fisher, the United Nations' humanitarian coordinator in Haiti. The risk of another cholera outbreak increases with the arrival of storms.

Cultural Orientation
The family is the most important relationship, function, and responsibility in Haitian culture. The actions of the individual impact the family's reputation. The extended family of elders is highly respected, participate in decision-making, and expect to be cared for in their old age.

Haiti is currently home to 9.8 million people, with over 20% of the total population living in or around the capital, Port-au-Prince. About 95% of the population is black and speaks French or Creole. Regarding religion, 80% of the population is Roman Catholic and also with approximately 50% of the total population practicing some form of Vodou. The spiritual perspective of Haitians has a significant impact on their views of health care and illnesses with many believing in spiritual causes of illness and/or foregoing Western medical treatment to pursue indigenous and ceremonial remedies (Cook Ross Inc., 2010).

Domestic elites and foreign interests have funded an unregulated, wide-spread arming of various groups within Haiti. The resulting and continuous social unrest and human rights abuses have been a historical normalcy in Haiti; marginalizing the value of life. Gangs, police, irregular soldiers, and even UN peacekeepers bring fear (Griffin, 2005).

No formal education structure exists throughout Haiti with almost 50% of the population being illiterate. However, of those that do have access to primary education, their learning comparatively rivals and sometimes exceeds that of the US. Absent language barriers, Haitian children have skills in math and science. Culturally, a select set of professions is desired and promoted: doctor, engineer, or accountant. Unfortunately, due to language barriers and/or lack of support services, many educated and experienced Haitian professionals arrive in the U.S. and other countries and end up accepting manual labor positions to survive. Many Haitians in the US work in intensive manual labor positions as well as a variety of service oriented industries, most notably in hospitality, tourism, and medical support positions.

Corruption
Corruption in Haiti is prevalent not only due to the abuse of power, lack of transparency, and lack of accountability in government; but is fueled by the lack of legitimate, fair, income sources for the average citizen. There are number of textile manufacturers currently producing for export in Haiti, which include those representing major worldwide retailers such as: Wal-Mart, JCPenney, Kmart, Sears, Gildan, Choose Haiti, Blanket America, Dockers, Dickies, Eddie Bauer, DKNY, Calvin Klein, American Eagle, Gap, and Old Navy (Business in Haiti, 2010).

An attractive business venture when minimum wage is kept at 31 cents an hour and workday earning about 125 Gourdes or $3.13 in U.S. currency (Business in Haiti, 2009). Plus, there are no U.S. tariffs; and there are also ongoing efforts to prevent unionization, with only 1 factory out of 23 unionized in Port-Au-Prince. Even after working 12-13 hours shifts, the wages are generally below what could be considered a "living wage." The AFL-CIO Solidarity Center released a study looking at the cost of living for factory workers in the SONAPI export processing zone near Port-au-Princes airport. The study found that for a single woman with two children, average monthly living expenses totaled $750. Assuming a 48-hour work week, that breaks down to about $29 a day (Center for Economic and Policy Research, 2011).

There was an attempt to raise the minimum wage two years ago to 61 cents an hour; however allegedly Hanes and Levi Strauss were able to gain U.S. government backing to prevent the increase. A U.S. based Haitian provides an insightful perspective, stating in Fowom Ouvriye (Fowom Ouvriye, 2008):

> But why should workers here in the US, why should progressive people here in the US, care about the minimum wage in Haiti and the struggles of Haitian workers to gain a just compensation for their labor? It is precisely because capitalist free market globalization is using extreme starvation wage economies such as Haiti to force US workers to negotiate their salaries and benefits downward to compete in this global economy. Capitalists are using the freedom of capital in free trade markets to shackle workers to lower and lower wages, forcing us to compete with the lowest paid workers. This is our plight as workers. Greedy bosses close down factories in the US and relocate them to so-called Third World dominated economies where we, as workers, have to endure starvation wages because of massive unemployment, political repression and USAID, World Bank and IMF policies. And because we can't earn a living in our native countries, we are forced to emigrate,

most often illegally, draining our native countries of their productive labor force. And when we end up as undocumented immigrants here in the US, we are again used as pawns to divide the working class and to drive wages and benefits downward, while these same capitalists and their paid politicians point to us as scapegoats and pass legislation to further persecute and discriminate against us. And again, as they set immigrant workers against native workers, these same capitalists are laughing all the way to the bank, their bank.

That is why as workers, we can't afford to be divided, because precisely as workers we belong to the same class and are all fundamentally engaged in the same struggle against capitalism world-wide. Only through our united struggle and solidarity can we overcome those who seek through their insatiable greed for more profits to exploit us ever more, to feed their corporate earnings and stock value. Only through our united struggle and solidarity can we attain better compensation for our labor.

Corruption leads to violence, as people attempt to simply survive, at all costs, when there appears to be no other options. Brutality, force, burn and destroy, theories of the end goal always justifying the means, have been ingrained into the Haitian population from the slave revolt days through modern times. Living in perverse corruption is the everyday reality in Haiti, especially in highly populated Port-Au-Prince. Specific examples of the everyday corruption experienced in Haiti are deep and wide, affecting the ability to obtain identification, operate a legitimate business, receive medical attention, and preventing kidnapping; all the foregoing result in high crime and ongoing civil unrest.

Need government documents or services? Rakètè (brokers) are needed to obtain birth certificates, photo IDs, passports, visas, and various government documents and services. Obtaining identification from government offices are discouraged by usage of long waits of a month or more. This extended delay funnels services to brokers who require fees high enough to profit themselves and pay off officials to obtain the identification from within a few hours to a few days. Depending on the level of desire or urgency to leave Haiti, individuals pay brokers for the identification, an appointment, and an average of $5,000 for a passport and/or visa.

Want to open a business in Haiti? If there is an existing competitor, be ready to bribe officials, who will facilitate a "bidding war" with competitors and allow only the highest bidder to prevail. This approach has resulted in proposed business ventures becoming a literal "life or death" battle. Social unrest is a common threat to businesses as mobs loot, burn, and destroy, and often without prejudice or discrimination. Extortion is also common in the form of payment to government officials, gangs, and whomever else claims territorial power in order to protect one's business, and without any guarantee or warranty of safety and security.

A highly criticized example of corruption was the eradication of a lucrative specialty pig market, the Creole Pig, which existed in Haiti until a new provider wanted the market. The pigs were very popular and served as a type of savings account for the Haitian peasant: sold or slaughtered to pay for marriages, medical emergencies, schooling, seeds for crops, or voodoo ceremonies. The official story is there was an alleged risk of African swine fever so USAID and the Haitian government ordered all pigs destroyed and replaced with unsuitable, inferior pigs. The "locals" see the move as a corrupt means to strip them of yet another resource to enable a new foreign provider to secure the market and prevent competition. For many, the pig trade was the only business they had, and they relied heavily upon it. Therefore, the systematic eradication of this key asset dramatically affected their ability to fund their children's education, as there is very limited free education available. Although an effort to repopulate the Creole Pig is underway, the original local people affected have little hope of benefitting.

Labadee is another long standing issue with Haitian locals. Labadee is a resort leased long-term by Royal Caribbean International. Although advertisements often describe it as an island in its own right, it is actually a part of Hispaniola. Labadee is separated from the surrounding area with fencing. Most tourists do not realize they are in Haiti. Haitian locals are only allowed very limited access to this area; however, U.S. Haitians as well as all Americans have open access. For "locals," it is just another example of exploitation of their resources.

Within a few days of the 2010 earthquake, international relief organizations hurried to build tent cities to provide shelter to displaced Haitians. Many used this opportunity and other relief efforts to profit in excess of the good intent. Those with homes, which were not structurally damaged and not displaced, waited at the site to secure a tent, which they have now "rented and subleased" to those who were actually displaced.

On medical care, "free care" was never free because even the most basic services had hidden costs. The General Hospital in Port-A-Prince was supposed to be free. However, it was surrounded by small for-profit private pharmacies and labs that counted on referrals and income from the sale of everything from surgical gloves, sold by the pair, to the most basic medicines and lab tests. The hospitals suffer from lack of funding and the imposition of a fee-for-service model in a country where the majority of people, and certainly those most at risk for illness and injury, didn't have money (NPR, 2011).

Haitians who leave the island for the U.S. or other countries often send much of their income to assist their families in Haiti; often, this is the only source of income for the family remaining in Haiti. Kidnapping is the most "popular" way of getting money from Diaspora (Haitians living in the U.S.) families. Ransom demands can range from $20,000 to several million dollars, based on the kidnappers' research of the family's ability to pay. Unfortunately, after receiving the ransom, they often still kill the kidnapping victim. Further disturbing is the fact that many kidnappings are orchestrated by family members, friends, or neighbors. There have even been instances where the supposed victim fakes his or her own kidnapping to obtain funding from U.S. family members. Paying the ransom is the only route families believe they have due to the lack of ability and trust in the local law enforcement.

The lack of capabilities of the Haitian police force is well known. The corruption within law enforcement compounds the problem. Police rarely arrive in time to prevent a crime or capture the assailant. In the rare instances where they do make an arrest, even in cases of murder, the suspect is usually released within a few weeks or even days and no further action is taken as long as the authorities are compensated accordingly. Citizens unite at times to attempt to stop robberies, gangs, and attempted murder. However, knowing that the suspect will not be punished, citizens sometimes kill the suspects to prevent retaliation upon release. This violence causes an escalation of civil unrest and instability.

The UN stabilization mission of 8,000, called Minustah, was formed in 2004 to keep a polarized Haiti from violent implosion, and then shared in the tragic loss of life during the country's catastrophic 2010 earthquake. (United Nations, 2012) Yet it has been blamed for a cholera epidemic that has caused more than 7,000 deaths and sickened 500,000; and some of its troops also are accused of sexual abuses. Its massive presence after eight years has irritated a proud nation. Nevertheless, Haiti's limited police force – in numbers and capacity – cannot protect its citizens without UN backing. Until Haiti builds a stronger, more capable, law-enforcement structure – and one hopefully is in the making – the resulting vacuum would almost inevitably lead to "spoilers" seeking to secure their goals through gun barrels rather than ballot boxes (Schneider, 2012).

Recommendations
Paul Farmer has been a Haiti advocate for almost 30 years; he is the UN's Deputy Special Envoy for Haiti, Chair of Global Health and Social Medicine at Harvard, and Founding Director of Partners in Health. His books, "The Uses of Haiti" and "Haiti after the earthquake" provide an in-depth analysis of Haiti's history and current status. He would grade the relief effort this way: "I would say for humanitarian relief, right after the quake, I'd give a pretty decent grade, like a B," he tells The Daily Beast. But, he adds, "For reconstruction, I would say we're lucky if we're at C- / D+." Farmer is emphatic that a large part of the solution is much more investment in Haiti's public sector. He's still worried about the cholera epidemic, which he says has not been contained, and cites that as a reason that public-sector utilities like water systems need to be strengthened. "For public health and public education, trying to bypass the public sector is a big mistake," he says. (Verger, 2011). What's needed, he says, is to (Maskalyk, 2011):
1. Put promised money into projects that create lasting jobs for Haitians,
2. build safe and efficient communities,
3. improve public health care and education, and
4. encourage transparent governance.

Noam Chomsky, an American Professor at MIT and author of over 100 books, is an outspoken activist in Haiti; and offers several suggestions within several publications and books such as Getting Haiti Right This Time include (Chomsky, Chomsky on Haiti, 2010):

1. France and U.S. payments of enormous reparations to Haiti (a demand of the ousted President Jean Bertrand Aristide, which has been flatly rejected).
2. Free, open, and accessible media throughout Haiti, limiting the propaganda of the existing media outlets in Haiti.
3. Allow and support of Haitian agriculture, not just low-wage textiles, by limiting the shipments of highly subsidized US commodities. (There has been a huge influx of imports into Haiti, which drove down the price of goods they were producing. For example, Haiti used to grow much of its own rice. Haiti's farmers cannot compete with the imported commodities, so imports havealmost completely wiped out local production, which caused an increase in food prices).
4. Funneling international aid - "the aid ought to be going to Haitian popular organizations. Not to contractors, not to NGOs-to Haitian popular organizations, and they're the ones that should be deciding what to do with it."

Lisa Ballantine is executive director of Filter Pure, which focuses on providing sustainable water sources in Haiti and the Dominican Republic. She concludes that the well-intentioned humanitarian aid was not fully utilized and inadequate in supporting the long-term needs. She states, "It's therefore essential that those wanting to assist consider whether the proposed plan will really meet the needs of the local population, and especially whether it is suitable (and affordable) for the long haul" (Ballantine, 2012). For example, aid should be supporting sustainable clean water sources instead of sending thousands of bottles of water.

United Nations, Assistant Secretary-General for Human Rights, Ivan Imonovic, finished a four-day visit to the Caribbean nation on September 15, 2012. His advice is focused on curbing corruption. He is calling for a Haitian National Police with an independent Inspector General and strong rule of law, which includes police reform, a more independent, reliable, and efficient justice system and ongoing penal code reform. The planned hiring of 5,000 police officers in the next four years has great potential for the country's safety, but only if selections are made based on valid and ethical merits and if the police force receives adequate training. Preventing corruption and human rights violators within the ranks is key to curb corruption, which would in turn, attract investment and create new decent jobs (United Nations, 2012).

Mark Schneider is the senior vice president of the International Crisis Group and former head of the Peace Corps during the Clinton administration. He also states, "Any exit strategy for the UN presence in Haiti has to be built on the country doubling the size of its police, ending impunity in its courts, and forging the rule of law as a foundation for economic growth and political stability" (Schneider, 2012). Schneider's additional recommendations include:

1. UN Security Council should gradually exchange its military-dominated mission to a larger, more robust, and competent police ideally be led by Brazil and the same Latin American countries that comprise a majority of the UN stabilization mission, Minustah.
2. Minustah to respond to the ongoing cholera threat with vaccinations in remote areas and a major commitment to water and sanitation infrastructure.
3. Better vetting, orienting, and training of future peacekeeping contingents. And they must work to ensure that those who violate the norms are held fully accountable.
4. Convince former Chilean Foreign Minister Mariano Fernández to continue his crucial support of the new Haitian government on critical decisions.
5. Full efforts on creating a national accord to preclude self-destructive impulses, which exceed the fragile coalition of parliamentarians that President Martelly just announced. A new mandate must also give the SRSG the internal political clout to direct the work of the entire UN country team to focus on Haiti's areas of greatest vulnerability, in support of the country's development priorities.

Based on the history and current situation, tactically, the following are suggested:

1. Implement a new minimum wage in line with fair living wage recommendations.
2. Reduce corruption and enable the establishment of a sustainable and independent Haiti the societal issues must be addressed; otherwise reconstruction efforts will result in futility. Peaceful democracy and simply "agreeing to disagree" are literally foreign concepts. Addressing this issue requires education and the broadening of perspectives throughout the population.
3. Build a team which leverages and unifies those who can look forward in creating a sustainable, democratic government, and economic stability in Haiti. Although both Aristide and Baby Doc have returned to Haiti; for now they do not appear to be openly participating in or undermining reconstruction efforts. This is a situation that needs to be continuously monitored as each of these men has the ability to throw the country back into complete chaos.
4. Build a system of accountability with "checks and balances" over local police forces. There is no national military in Haiti since Aristide disbanded the highly corrupt Army. With so many areas, communities, cities, etc. – many of them do not have jurisdictional law enforcement –

only the National Police force which could further explain the level of corruption as they each have political agendas.

5. Recruit police officers and key staff to support Haiti's economic and political stabilization from within the current estimated population of 2 million Haitian and Haitian descendants within the United States, predominantly in Florida and New York. Several hundred thousand more reside in Montreal, Canada, Mexico, Puerto Rico, Jamaica, France, Dominican Republic, French Guyana, and parts of Africa. These individuals should be able to utilize their education, skills, experience, solid reputations, and cultural understanding to make effective impact in their home country in many of the initiatives identified by Haiti subject matter experts.

6. When arming the police force or other law enforcement, utilize industry best practices. For example, weapons and ammunition must be assigned to individuals and tracked for usage to support holding officers accountable and avoid abuse of power.

7. Implement a gun "buying and reporting" program so that people can anonymously turn in or report the location of weapons, especially assault rifles, to receive reward money. Those weapons should then be secured for the expanded police force.

8. There are some workforce development initiatives underway in Haiti. This program is critical to enabling Haiti's economic sustainability and promotion of self-sufficiency. There is a need for developing long-term, independent, sustainable, economic vehicles which do not exploit Haitians.

Summary

The infrastructure needs to be "right" to attract ethical businesses like Knights Apparel, whose CEO, Joseph Bozich, operates a factory in the Dominica Republic paying nearly three and a half times the prevailing minimum wage, based on a study done by a workers' rights group that calculated the living costs for a family of four in the Dominican Republic (Greenhouse, 2010).

There are multiple governments, international organizations, NGO's, and privately funded initiatives participating in the reconstruction, although at what earning wage is not yet established. A few of the initiatives include:

1. USAID has developed a four pillar plan to support Haiti's development: Infrastructure and Energy, Food and Economic security, Health and other basic needs, Democracy and Rule of law. These initiatives include workforce training in construction and health.

2. The Clinton Bush Haiti Fund announced 1.5M in December 2011 for Workforce Development.

3. ReBuild Globally is using recycling initiatives and artistry to create jobs in Haiti making shoes and other items. They recently received a two year grant from the UN's Minustah.

4. RTI International is recruiting candidates for a large, three-year value chain and enterprise development project in Haiti.
5. Extollo International is in the process of establishing a contractor and construction training center and trade school in Haiti.
6. The Inter-American Development Bank is planning on building 39 schools throughout Haiti; and several U.S. governemnt entities, such as Miami Dade County, are facilitating economic development opportunities in Haiti.

Schools, hospitals, and other services must be concentrated throughout the country in order to reduce the numbers of those involved with the constant migration of citizens. Port-Au-Prince is over-populated due to the promise and hope of services sought after by those migrating from rural areas of the country. The high population contributes to the high crime in the area.

Within the plans for infrastructure building, transportation and workforce development, we sincerely hope planners are making considerations for the thousands of citizens who are disabled and plan with accessibility and inclusion in mind. Prior to the earthquake, those with any type of disability were social outcasts with most viewing these individuals as being cursed or receiving judgment. The significant increase of those with impairments, or perhaps the fact they are still alive, when so many have died, has reduced the stigma. However, the lack of accessibility and employment options is a real issue.

Protecting the environment using "Green" technology and policies is also an important initiative during building infrastructure and factories in Haiti. Otherwise, the environmental impact will immediate on the Caribbean and U.S.

Religion is a main component of Haitian culture. Utilizing the established religious systems to assist in developing and communicating the national accord and citizen activism is likely a key mechanism. A "grass roots" approach utilizing religious systems, which addresses, encourages, and issues a challenge to the main social issues, would be undoubtedly impactful. However, the people's hope in Aristide due to his priesthood was shattered and made thus became cynical. Therefore, caution should be used to avoid promoting an individual religious figure.

Chapter 9

India: Capitalism and the Path to Prosperity

Mohammed R. Ahmed, Webster University

Capitalism is the process of achieving personal, social, political, technological, and economic growth, with fewer constraints and boundaries, in order to provide opportunities for everyone in the society to participate in that growth. There are several explanations of capitalism presented by researchers, economists, and philosophers, and still there is no one single definition that clearly explains capitalism in a simple fashion.

Capitalism is understood in Eastern societies as a belief or process for the exploitation of markets and sowing the seeds of corruption. It is a system for choosing "winners and losers," and a system for eliminating small businesses. The reason for the lack of a clear understanding about capitalism is because the process of achieving growth involves multiple variables and outcomes. It is sometimes difficult to define or explain capitalism to the people of eastern countries because for decades it was labeled as a process to get rich at the expense of the poor. The growth in monetary value, or "getting rich," is one of the outcomes of capitalism, and if we focus on only one of the outcomes of capitalism, it becomes an unattractive alternative in South Asian countries for managing growth.

Introduction

Growth is essential to everyone in a society regardless of their political and social differences. To achieve growth in developed, underdeveloped, and emerging countries, their leaders have to select capitalism, socialism, or a communist approach for managing growth. The political changes around the world have forced most of the communist countries to move towards socialism, and to look for opportunities in the capitalistic markets. A rational explanation of capitalism is that it is a designer process for achieving growth. Growth in the context of capitalism refers to personal, economic, social, political, and technological growth. In order to maintain fair social growth we need to have few constraints and boundaries, and it is fair to define the new capitalism as a process of achieving personal, social, political, technological, and economic growth with few constraints and boundaries, to provide opportunities for everyone in the society to participate in the growth (Ahmed, 2010).

History of Economic Systems

Capitalism is not a new process of achieving growth in South Asian countries, and in particular India. The history of India shows that the seeds of capitalism were planted in the Indian sub-continent starting in the thirteen century. The history of India shows that the rulers of the Mughal Dynasty were actively involved in implementing a process to foster growth that may be labeled as early capitalism of the east. The Mughal Empire started in the fifteenth century and ended in the eighteenth century, and during this period India became the experimental ground for capitalism. Although all the Mughal rulers were interested in capitalism, only one of the rulers, Akbar (1542 – 1605) was successful in creating the environment for capitalism to succeed under his rule (Ahmed, 2012). This raises the question about why India is facing capitalism challenges, and looking to the West to learn about capitalism. The answer lies again in the history of India, after the Mughal Empire.

The British East India Company that was involved in developing trade and commerce with Asia entered India in the sixteenth century, and received concessions from the Mughal Empire for trade and commerce. As the Mughal Empire and other princely states started losing political power, the British East India Company started filling the void by transforming from trade and commerce to a parliamentary authority in the region, and ultimately establishing a British rule in India. As India became an occupied territory, or a British colony, the roots of capitalism were replaced by British rule. A controlled socialism designed by the British became the process for business and trade in India. After India's independence from British rule in 1947, the Indian leaders who were involved in rebuilding India were interested in making the country self-reliant, and they decided that the socialist approach was the best approach for the country at that time. Sixty five years after independence, India is facing challenges as it has entered the global economy as an emerging country. The purpose of this section is to explain the following:

1. How can South Asian public and private sector leaders effectively manage their economy?
2. Should South Asians move onto a path of full capitalism, or will a mixed economy be more effective?
3. What kinds of paths could lead to a better world in South Asia?
4. What kinds of roles can management educators play to encourage progress along these paths to a better world?

India, with its natural resources and knowledge base, has struggled for decades to achieve economic prosperity. Public and private sector leaders must understand that the choice of the process for achieving growth is the key to effective management of the economy, and effective management starts with recognizing that the changing environment demands the discovery of new tools and approaches for managing the economy. The traditional tools used by the Western countries to manage the economy in the past may not be best suited for emerging countries, for example, monetary and fiscal policies are good examples of economic tools used for managing the economy. Western countries, like the Unites States of America, which learned a lot from the great depression of 1929, realize that managing the economy involves monetary policy, fiscal policy, and managing the financial health of the financial institutions (Ahmed, 2009). If we look at the economic policy of the United States during 2008 to 2011, the Federal Reserve has maintained the discount rate at zero to loosen credit and maintain the circulation of funds in our economy. The federal government had bailed out failing financial institutions to maintain confidence and the availability of credit to businesses. The government has also injected billions into the economy by investing in our infrastructure, however economic recovery was slow and unemployment remained above 8%. This proves that the tools of the past are no longer effective in the present economic environment. South Asian countries like India must understand that capitalism is a process for achieving growth, but the tools used in this process change as the environment changes. Leaders who think that they can solve economic problems based on theories and past economic experiences may be proven wrong in the current global economic environment. The problem with that way of thinking is that the environment is changing, and the old theories and approaches are not enough to stimulate the new economy. To stimulate economic growth, we need to include behavioral and economic aspects, understand the role of digital technology in the economy, and recognize that our economic system has changed from a macro-cell to a micro-cell economic system.

Collective Focus

In a digital economy the focus of the economic policy should be on millions, not on just a few. Millions of people make the nation prosperous, and not the few so-called "essential" industries (Ahmed, 2010). The global and South Asian economy is a micro-cell economy. In a micro-cell economy, the growth of the economy depends on the growth in micro economic cells. The growth of a micro-cell depends on education, intellectual capital, monetary capital, digital technology, and communication. A "trickle-up" approach is needed to stimulate a micro-cell economy rather than a "trickle-down" approach (Ahmed and Pellet, 2010).

The history of economic policy shows that it takes decades for countries to move from one economic system to another. Based on the alternatives available for emerging countries like India, the optimal path is to move towards capitalism. India, as the largest democratic country, will be able to become an economic power in the world if she chooses capitalism as the ultimate choice for long-term growth. In the pursuit of capitalism, India will face challenges because India's economy is a four-sector economy. India is participating in agriculture, manufacturing, service, and knowledge based economies at the same time. It has an abundance of land, skilled labor, unskilled labor, and knowledge workers. The challenges for both public and private sector leaders are the allocation of resources to individual sectors, and raising capital to support the growth of each sector. It is a challenge for leaders and economists because India is experiencing a new economic growth pattern. The past economic growth models, such as the two sector (Lewis, 1950) or three sector economic models, do not provide any direction in understanding the possible resource allocations for economic growth. That is why there is the need for developing a four-sector model to understand the challenges India will face by choosing a mixed economy or the full path to capitalism. The decision to move onto the path of full capitalism or to a mixed economy will vary from country to country in South Asia based on their economic, political, and social environments.

The idea of capitalism motivates people in both the right and wrong directions. It sometimes creates conflicts between the cultures, religions, values, and beliefs of a society, and the economic processes for growth. This may be due to the understanding that capitalism is the product of a western culture. The history of India, on the other hand, shows that the Mughal Empire introduced capitalism to India, and the people were happy and prosperous during the Mughal Empire. If the so-called growth achieving process of "Capitalism" was part of the eastern culture in the past, it cannot be a product of western culture, or harmful to India's culture of today.

In this digital age, customers from around the world have the ability to change the market share of a company with the click of mouse, and product life cycles are becoming shorter every year. There is a high demand for innovation and price-based competition all around the world, and the Internet is breaking the barriers of trade and commerce (Ahmed, 2011). South Asian countries like India have the ability to participate in this growth opportunity, and to bank on the global opportunities that the country has to face from the challenges of capitalism that in turn will bring prosperity. This will be able to create a better world for India and South Asia.

Educators have the opportunity to review the history of early capitalism in India, understand the consequences of the current capitalism models in the west, and develop a new model of capitalism for South Asian countries. India and China's economies are comprised of four sectors, and there has been little research done on what capitalism challenges the countries will face if they move towards the full path of capitalism. Management educators must play the role of researcher and information disseminator. To encourage progress along these paths to a better world, management educators must encourage both the public and private sector leaders to recognize that we are part of a new economy, and we cannot generate economic growth by the traditional jump-starts of the past. The economy is more complex, and it is not a manmade machine. Leaders may think that they can solve their economic growth problems based on theories and past economic experiences, but the problem with that thinking is that the environment is changing, and the old theories and approaches are not enough to stimulate the new economy or generate growth. The average citizen in South Asia or India is not interested in economic theories, a debate between the two schools of economic thought, or a choice between "soft socialism," and a "hard capitalism." They are interested in finding well-paying jobs that provide an income to support their families, a house to live in, and credit to buy goods or services so that they can enjoy life and "pay as they go." India has entered into a new (digital) economy, and the leaders cannot use the tools that were used in agricultural and industrial economies to manage growth and be part of worldwide capitalistic market. Also, the "trickle-down" economic growth policy of the West will not solve current economic problems.

Summary
To stimulate economic growth, leaders need to include behavioral economics, understand the role of digital technology in the Indian economy, and recognize that Indian economic system has changed to a micro-cell economic system. To assist leaders in promoting capitalism in South Asia, including India, this chapter presents a definition of "new capitalism."

The "new capitalism" is the process of achieving personal, social, political, technological, and economic growth, with few constraints and boundaries, in order to provide opportunities for everyone in the society to participate in that growth. The new definition of capitalism or "new capitalism," and the fact that capitalism has a birthmark in India, will help both the public and private sector leaders in promoting capitalism to the people of South Asia, and the people will understand the benefits of capitalism. In addition, the definition of "new capitalism," a four-sector economic growth model, has been developed to provide guidance for public and private sector leaders to understand the challenges they will face in moving towards the path to full capitalism.

Chapter 10

Jamaica and Capitalism in the Caribbean

Donovan A. McFarlane
Keller Graduate School of Management, DeVry University

The Caribbean region has long suffered a great economic setback in terms of the prospects and expectations regarding capitalism, wealth, and progress. Often we consider the Caribbean region among the most impoverished and underdeveloped areas of the world, especially when we examine the gross domestic products (GDPs), per capita incomes, and standards of living of the various countries relative to their growing populations and increasing problems and challenges, as well as their present and future opportunities. Especially critical in this analysis is consideration regarding the factor of social development, an area in which many nations in the region are lagging far behind when compared to the progressive and growing nations of Asia and the highly developed and industrialized nations of the world.

When it comes to issues of health, education, and social justice, nations in the Caribbean are increasingly falling below standards, especially as resources constraint and a lack of focus on human development create situations in which the people of these nations, especially young people, find themselves facing a bleak future where survival is very uncertain. The nation of Haiti (discussed earlier in this book) has been a prime example of the potential future awaiting its neighbors in the Caribbean; and many of these nations are not doing enough to avoid such a future.

Introduction

The lack of effective leadership in many of these Caribbean nations is a current weakness and must be addressed before these nations can begin to strategically map their future paths to survival. Jamaica, having celebrated its 50th year of independence in the year 2012, has assessed its progress since 1962 and the majority perspective is that the country has not made enough efforts and preparation for the current and future needs in securing the well-being of its people. This perspective is not unique to Jamaica, as nations such as Trinidad and Tobago, Cuba, among others are faced with the same realization after having evaluated their current levels of growth and development, especially in light of world global economic crisis and circumstances which worsened beginning in the latter part of

2007. The global recession of late 2007-2008 has created concerns for many Caribbean and developing nations as their lucrative trades and dependence on wealthy foreign nations in North America and Europe, such as the United States, Canada, and Great Britain have dwindled, leaving them searching for new economic opportunities and ways of recreating the losses they have experienced in terms of money and supply of important basic as well as luxury products, employment and development opportunities.

Jamaica is now at a critical crossroad where its government must immediately recognize the need to develop strong and effective strategies to lead the country into a successful future by first evaluating its available opportunities in terms of its resources, its strengths in terms of the skills of its workforce and abilities of its current educational and health systems, its weaknesses in terms of underdeveloped and failing infrastructures; and its threats in terms of the competitive and natural-physical challenges, which can worsen its current situation or stymie the future of the Jamaican people and nation.

The Island Country of Jamaica
Jamaica is well-known for its beauty and desirability as a popular tourism destination, as well as for its unique culture and its various rituals and cultural art forms, including its globally loved and admired reggae music popularized by Bob Marley and other artists. It is also known for a harsher and unrefined "art form," called "dancehall music" with variously devised characters that have influenced the people and the world's perception of Jamaican culture through their lyrics that sometimes truly do not reflect what the country is really about, or the true values and endeavor communicated and expressed in the nation's Pledge of Allegiance: "Before God and all Mankind..." Nevertheless, such "art form" despite being highly stereotypical and even undesirable from a social-functional perspective, has come to be recognized as part of the culture. The Jamaican culture has a rich and interesting history influenced by the Spanish, French, and English and the age of adventure, colonialism, and British imperialism.

Jamaica is located in the Caribbean Sea close to Cuba and Haiti. Jamaica is slightly smaller than the state of Connecticut. The nation enjoys a tropical climate and boasts excellent rivers, waterfalls, and beaches. Jamaica is mostly mountains, with narrow, discontinuous coastal plains and has extensive woodlands, especially in the more rural parishes. The word Jamaica comes from the language of the island's first indigenous people called the Arawaks or Tainos who named it "Xaymaca" which means "Land of Wood and Water" or the "Land of Springs." With a current population of 2.8 million, Jamaica is one of the largest among the island nations of the Greater Antilles, and also one of the largest among island countries of the Caribbean. The capital of Jamaica is Kingston, its most important port with a population of almost 1,000,000 people. The country is divided into three counties: Cornwall, Middlesex, and Surrey, and fourteen parishes (Table 10.1 below). Jamaica has a democratic government, which is best described as a "Constitutional Monarchy" since Queen Elizabeth II of England is regarded as the

Head of State and is represented in the Jamaican government by a Governor General.

County	Parish
Cornwall	Hanover
	St. Elizabeth
	St. James
	Trelawny
	Westmoreland
Middlesex	Clarendon
	Manchester
	St. Ann
	St. Catherine
	St. Mary
Surrey	Kingston
	Portland
	St. Andrew
	St. Thomas

Table 10.1 - *Jamaica's Counties and Parishes*
(Lookfah Marketing, 2012, p. 1)

The country gained independence from Britain in 1962 and continues on the path to greater independence as it strives to strengthen its economy. By virtue of ethnicity, Jamaica is in majority, African-descent with approximately 91% of the population classified as Black, 6.3% as Mixed, and 2.7% as others including Caucasians, Mongoloids, and Islanders. The major language spoken in Jamaica is English, which it inherited from Britain as its "colonial mother." However, the native Jamaican speaks a dialect known as Patois, which is a combination of several languages, predominantly English, Spanish, and French, as well as several African languages which were derived from the many slaves brought from Africa. As of July 2012, Jamaica had a population of 2,889,187 (The World Factbook, 2012). This population consists of approximately 29.5% of people between 0 and 14 years old (male 433,686 and female 419,296), 62.8% of people between 15 and 64 years old (male 896,832/ female 917,543), and 7.7% of people 65 years and over (male 99,259/ female 122,571). The median age of the Jamaican population is 24 years old (The World Factbook, 2012). This means that Jamaica has a strong youthful population which it needs to provide opportunities for. Thus, in focusing on the future, its current leadership needs to understand how the current make-up of the population requires developing certain sectors of the economy for progress. This means that health and education are extremely important and that investment in its young people become a priority of government planning and advisory committees. Jamaica needs to create job opportunities for its young people and position the nation for a strong future where talented and brilliant young Jamaicans can earn a living rather than migrate to foreign countries, thereby creating "brain-drain." Jamaica's current birthrate is 19 (per 1000 of the population) while its death rate is 6.6 (per 1000 of the population). With its death rate much lower than its birth rate, Jamaica's population will continue to increase thereby changing the composition and needs of this small country. One of the major problems in development is the location of its population centers. Jamaica has a large percentage of its population living in the capital city of Kingston and this creates social problems including crimes and violence, health issues, overcrowding, traffic congestion, and other challenges. Many of the urban cities, such as Mandeville in the Parish of Manchester, Montego Bay in the Parish of St. James, and Ocho Rios in St. Ann. These are the most highly developed and wealthiest cities that attract both trade and tourism, and thus many Jamaicans, especially young people, flock from rural to urban areas to seek opportunities where they sometimes are disappointed by what they find. Jamaica needs to create more opportunities in non-urban areas; essentially urbanizing other cities and use government funds to build and develop viable community centers and projects.

Jamaica's Natural and Land Resources
Jamaica's major natural resources are bauxite, gypsum, and limestone. These three resources have brought significant economic activities and trade for the nation, but have been inefficiently exploited and ineffectively used to gain competitive advantage in the regional economy of the Caribbean and in international trade. Jamaica is able to rely on its natural physical beauty to attract a strong tourism industry to its tropical climate with beautiful beaches and a natural environment with great vegetation. The culture and the people are unique and have been two of the major factors that have fueled a lucrative tourism and entertainment industry. Unfortunately, these industries are now being eroded by extremely high crime rates that deter both foreigners and natives from participation. The loss to Jamaica from a decreasing tourism patronage is great in terms of the monetary-financial costs and the decline in economic activities, especially as vital cottage and linkage industries are affected that benefit from the influx of tourists from all around the world. Furthermore, the global economic crisis which began around late 2007 has also decreased the number of tourists traveling for vacations and spending money in

Jamaica. Thus, the country needs to plan effectively to adjust itself when travel and tourism are affected by global economic, political and natural-physical changes.

No other resource should be regarded as more valuable than a nation's people, and Jamaicans overall have never felt that they are the most valued by the government or administrations that have come and gone over the last 50 years, including the current Cabinet of Prime Minister Portia Simpson-Miller. The challenge of declining pride in the nation stems from this perspective as the government has lost touch with its people; and the people no longer possess the deep passion which the governments of Michael Manley and Edward Seaga were able to sustain during the previous decades. While Jamaica has a fairly high level of literacy (around 88%), there is greater need to develop the skills and abilities of the Jamaican people, especially in areas such as healthcare, leadership, innovation and entrepreneurship, as well as in sustainability and change management. Jamaicans currently need greater knowledge and understanding of their changing national environments and emerging challenges, as well as understanding of the global world in which various factors shape their success and the prosperity and future of their nation.

Jamaica after Fifty Years of Independence
Recently, in August 2012, Jamaica celebrated its 50th year of independence from British colonial governance. During this festive occasion, one of the country's former prime minister and opposition leader, the Honorable Edward Seaga, commented on the insufficiency of economic and social progress that has been made, particularly with regards to the development of economy, wealth of the nation, the standard of living of the people and their overall prosperity and well-being. Edward Seaga has been instrumental in Jamaica's 50 years of independence for 45 years, and thus, his observations and opinions are of particular importance when it comes to assessing and thinking about Jamaica's current economic well-being and potential. According to Martin (2012), Edward Seaga is the last surviving member of the Independence Constitution Committee and is the longest-serving Member of Parliament for 45 years, leader of one of the two major political parties for 30 years, opposition leader for a cumulative 23 years, and prime minister for eight years and creator of more than 20 national institutions. Thus, when Edward Seaga expresses the view that Jamaica has not progressed much in 50 years, it is not without forethought or understanding; and this view is held by many given the nation's current economic standing: declined currency value, high crime rate, high unemployment rate, high rate of poverty and other developmental issues.

Jamaica is currently experiencing a struggle in determining what direction the nation must take to set itself on the right path to economic development and prosperity. In fact, Martin (2012) and others believe that Jamaica is currently at a crossroads and that the prospects of wealth and freedom in economic choices promised by further embracing capitalism and its wide arms are not enough to motivate the level of actions and economic comfort that Jamaica needs to grow and become prosperous. While Jamaica has developed a plan to change its current economic position in the form of Vision 2030, the nation is believed to lack both the funding and other resources that are critically needed to jump-start a real capitalism that will grow wealth like the United States, but will not be vulnerable to its current woes. Under its quest to change its current course from increased poverty and dependency on foreign goods, services, and assistance, Jamaica has made Vision 2030 a priority. Vision 2030 is a national strategic economic plan that sets out four basic national goals for Jamaica: 1) Jamaicans are empowered to achieve their fullest potential; 2) the Jamaican society is secure, cohesive and just; 3) Jamaica's economy is prosperous; and 4) Jamaica has a healthy natural environment (Martin, 2012). Whether these goals will be achieved depends highly on how Jamaica proceeds in addressing its current social and economic problems and challenges.

The Independence Development Plan
Jamaica's current economic misfortunes and lack of progress have been blamed on the abandonment of what is called its "Independence Development Plan," which was drafted immediately before and after its independence in 1962. With this plan, some Jamaican scholars and politicians believe that Jamaica would have been in a better and more prosperous position today. The Independence Development Plan should have been constantly used to fuel Jamaica's economic growth through increased employment and greater equity in all the major economic sectors such as agriculture, manufacturing, bauxite, tourism, construction, and services, while pushing for increasing economic diversification and for increasing development, and reducing discontent (Martin, 2012). Furthermore, this plan was supposed to be a major push for increasing exports, improving utilities and infrastructure, and decreasing the fertility rate and population growth as well as maintaining control of development goals.

Further aspects of the Independence Development Plan included expanding education and training for increased productivity and developing, increasing and promoting culture, arts, sports, and community development for social transformation. These developments were to be supplemented by natural science and social science through several organizations established to launch and support the development plan. These organizations would have included a productivity center, a standards organization, a national volunteer service, a national airline, particularly in support of tourism, and community villages (Martin, 2012). Unfortunately, after such great ambitions were cast aside, Jamaica today remains hard-pressed on all sides for renewal in terms of economy, productivity, and growth. The country is currently hampered by a variety of social and economic problems that are not conducive to significant and smooth economic progress. The problems and challenges range from labor force coordination problems, declines in export and primary industries, such as agricultural production in bananas, yams, and other ground provisions, as well as the need for effective and strong leadership to bring the country onto a positive path.

Problems and Challenges to Capitalism

Jamaica is currently in a strategically weakened and uncertain position as far as capacity for progress and economic growth is concerned. The problems and challenges that the nation currently faces lead to many questions about its preparation for capitalism and its quest toward this direction so far. Jamaica can be characterized as a "developing capitalist" economy that lacks the resources, appropriate labor and technological skills, as well as effective leadership and governance that are necessary to bring the salient factors for growth toward a truly free enterprise and well-off economy. Over the decades, the country has lost so much of its import power due to decline in primary industries such as agriculture and mining as it experiences a hasty and premature transition into the dominant global service-sector economy model. This is caused by the changing nature of national interests and the fact that much of its young population is rapidly urbanizing. Furthermore, there seems to be a failure to recognize the importance of fostering domestic subsistence before the country can really have the foundation for worthwhile economic progress toward a capitalism as prosperous as those of developed nations and other developing economies across the globe that are getting the growth and prosperity formula correct.

With regards to the obstacles and challenges to economic growth and greater free-enterprise orientation and prosperity, two major factors currently stymie the nation's prospects. The first factor is the social problems, especially the nation's current high levels of crimes, including murder. Jamaica has in recent times received extremely bad press, even being referred to as "the murder capital of the world." Furthermore, drugs and other crimes seem to have become mainstays of Jamaican society as we have seen in the case of Jamaican "drug lord" Christopher "Dudus" Coke and his former network of illegal activities across the island and extending even into other territories. Additionally, over the years Jamaica has experienced a rapid, unprecedented decline in literacy and morality. The deteriorating values are an indication of worsening economic conditions and lack of pride in the nation. Jamaicans are cultured into being proud of their nation and heritage and are taught to express these in conforming and acceptable values and ambition for self and society. However, the various happenings in Jamaica over the past two decades are socially, ethically, and morally alarming: from the fascination with "questionable" and explicit oral and physical pseudo-cultural overtures stemming from uncensored media presentations in the form of "dancehall music" to the lack of regard for human life, law, and society. There seems to be a connection between morality and progress and Jamaica is, sadly, currently a rapidly demoralizing society where there needs to be some form of cultural revival and resurgence before any economic or national development requiring the collective conscious efforts, labor and cooperation of the people can be a success.

The second problem that stymies Jamaica's prospect toward prosperous free enterprise development and growth is an economic one where the country's economic variables, including labor and resources, as well as industry concentration have dramatically changed over a short period of time. This creates a kind of premature capitalism as many smaller and developing nations have a tendency to emulate their wealthy and highly developed counterparts without having the key ingredients and preparation. This is also the direct result of globalization, changing and emerging market demand, and the need to keep up with current trends. However, growth and development need monitoring if nations such as Jamaica are to really experience the prosperity and the capitalism they seek for their future. Sheckleford (2006) seems to fully understand the economic obstacles to Jamaica's growth and development as the prerequisites for capitalism's venture. Sheckleford (2006) believes that "The Jamaican economy has suffered numerous challenges and setbacks in the increasingly competitive global environment" (p. 1). Jamaica is currently under-producing, over-importing, and under-exporting, and the nation is in serious financial debts with the World Bank. Furthermore, there seems to be little action on the part of the current government in terms of any significant plans for Jamaica's economic and social future. While examples of American and British capitalism provide Jamaica and many small nations with valuable lessons in pursuing development and they benefit from wealth and trade with these nations, they are also negatively impacted by the woes of these wealthy capitalist nations, and must also take the negative lessons in capitalism as part of the wisdom needed in deciding on an appropriate course for growth, development, and managing and leading change for national prosperity.

Environmental and Natural-Physical Challenges
Jamaica like several of its Caribbean nations currently faces several environmental and natural physical challenges. Located in the Caribbean Sea, Jamaica has always been vulnerable to hurricanes as the prime natural-physical, environmental uncontrollable problem, especially between July and November of each year. For example, Jamaica was devastated by Hurricane Gilbert in 1988, and since then, has been through several other hurricanes that have caused millions of dollars in damages to physical and social infrastructures. The nation, which has consistently been heavily indebted to the World Bank (formerly International Monetary Fund – IMF) faces increasing challenges when it must find financial and other resources in responding to natural disasters. Furthermore, the impact of hurricanes on the physical-natural environment has affected Jamaica's tourism industry over the past several decades. Tourism is a primary earner for Jamaica, along with agriculture; and the hurricanes and accompanying flooding and other effects sometimes destroy acres of vital export crops such as bananas, yams, sugarcane, oranges, among many others. When this happens, Jamaica has to increase its borrowing from the World Bank and depend more extensively on foreign imports. This drives up the cost of living for its people as well as the nation's total debt and deficit.

Jamaica currently has several revolving environmental and natural-physical problems and challenges: heavy rates of deforestation; its coastal waters are polluted by industrial waste, sewage, and oil spills; there is heavy and increasingly significant damage to its coral reefs; and heaving and increasing air pollution affects the capital city of Kingston from vehicle emissions and overcrowding (The World

Factbook, 2012). Other challenges that Jamaica faces with regards to its natural-physical environment include the nation's failure to renew or replenish resources such as soil and water, as well as to have a beneficial waste disposal and recycling systems and processes that are geared toward pollution reduction and conservation. One of the very disconcerting things to observe about Jamaica in its present state is the decline in agricultural activities and care for the land and native plants that are of significant uses for medicine and foods, as many young people abandon agriculture - farming, livestock rearing and fishing - to seek blue-collar activities, which are, in the country's current economic state, unrealistic and unavailable to majority of job seekers.

Health Issues and Challenges
Jamaica is currently facing the same health issues and crises that other nations are grappling with. These problems include inadequate healthcare and health education for its increasing population of youths and elderly, failure to recognize the role and impact of health on national progress and economic growth, and failure to reach certain basic needs of the country's population. Jamaica currently lacks enough physicians, doctors, nurse practitioners, nurses, and healthcare educators to meet the needs of the country. In 2009, it was estimated that the country had roughly 0.85 physicians per 1000 of the population (The World Factbook, 2012). Furthermore, the country lacks healthcare infrastructure in terms of hospitals and ambulances, and other medical facilities adequate enough to meet the people's healthcare needs. Jamaica is also wrestling with health problems such as HIV/AIDS which has a prevalence of about 1.7% and affects about 32,000 people with an estimated 1,200 deaths from HIV/AIDS in 2009. This is a large number for a small country of 2.8 million people. Other health issues such as heart problems, diabetes, cancer, other STDs and other diseases and illnesses are also inadequately addressed both medically and educationally because of poverty and lack of planning by both central and local governments. The majority of Jamaicans lack health insurance; and many rural cities lack health services facilities.

Apart from the regular health problems that plague nations, Jamaica has a higher level of cancer among its male population than many other countries; and this problem needs to be addressed, especially by focusing on male healthcare programs. This requires more education and more awareness through community engagement and development. Problems of hunger and malnutrition are still issues in Jamaica, especially among children and the elderly. Mental health issues prevail and are on the increase as many more homeless and abused and neglected people are left to survive on their own due to lack of care from community and governmental leaders, as well as the unavailability of capital to finance these efforts. National healthcare and health awareness will become important considerations in Jamaica's future growth and performance.

Security, Crimes, and Political Corruption

Jamaica is currently facing some serious security challenges, especially as its national crime statistics is on the constant rise and illicit trades become more prevalent. This includes drug-trafficking, especially of marijuana and some "hard drugs." The internationalization of the Jamaican drug problem was evident in the arrest and extradition of Jamaican drug lord Christopher Coke to the United States, who is now imprisoned for his extensive trafficking and crimes in the nation. Furthermore, political corruption stymies Jamaica's growth and during the events surrounding the manhunt for Christopher Coke, it became evident that his illicit activities also involved members of the Jamaican government including law enforcement officials. The Jamaican Constabulary Force (JCF) which is supposed to maintain law and order has also been a challenge in terms of effective leadership as over the past several years several members of the police force have also engaged in criminal activities ranging from murder to extortion. More importantly, the high crime rate currently plagues Jamaica, and is rapidly damaging its global image and reputation, as many foreigners now fear going to Jamaica on vacation because of the fear of being victims of crimes. This leads to decline earnings from the globally admired and well-known Jamaican tourism and entertainment industries. This also results in increased unemployment and decrease in Jamaica's gross domestic product (GDP), which depends highly on the health of these two industries.

Two severe crimes that are currently plaguing the small island nation are murder and sexual assault in the form of rape. The murders are especially gruesome, ranging from decapitation to gang-related shootings. The prevalence of illegally-owned guns is a major problem for Jamaica. These guns are believed to arrive in majority from Haiti and neighboring islands and Jamaica's ports are not secure enough to track and prevent the influx of drugs and guns. The government has failed to establish adequate and strong border security that would decrease these illicit trades, and when such security is marginally in place, it gives way to corruption, greed, and bribery. The Jamaican Ministry of National Security needs to work to resolve the current levels of crimes and reform its police force and control urban crimes that are accounting for much of its losses. National security is important for progress and there is a critical challenge to improve national security in Jamaica.

Unemployment and Poverty

Jamaica currently has a very high rate of unemployment and this is really difficult to address by any ordinary means. With its rate of unemployment standing at around 28% percent as of 2009, Jamaica needs to find opportunities for its people. This high rate of unemployment represents a complex of problems and challenges as it contributes to poor health, inadequate nutrition, increased vulnerability to crimes, increase in criminal activities, increases in illness and diseases, and the inability of a great number of people to socially advance themselves. Poverty has long plagued Jamaica; and the lack of planning by its government is a key factor contributing to the vicious cycle of poverty. Providing education has always been the key approach to addressing the poverty problem. However, it is far inadequate when thousands of students are graduating from secondary schools, vocational institutes and colleges and universities without any job opportunities awaiting them. Many Third World countries are trapped in poverty and Jamaica is no different, and the types of foreign assistance it receives are inadequate and come at a heavy cost to the country. For example, the major assistance has been in the form of loans from the World Bank. However, these loans act as a trap to keep the nation like many of its Third World sister-nations in heavy debts and with high deficits. The country has to strategically wrestle its way out of this vicious cycle by identifying and developing internal opportunities for growth and the survival of its people. This means looking toward its primary industries, such as agriculture, fishing, and mining, in order to create more jobs and basic necessities.

A major problem that creates poverty and hardship for Jamaicans is the failure to exercise good economic decisions with regard to currency value. The Jamaican dollar is constantly experiencing devaluation against the United States Dollar (USD), the British Pound, and the Canadian dollar as well as other currencies. This increases the costs of goods for Jamaicans, especially some of the vital basic food items that are imported from these nations. The devaluation of the currency provides insights into the declining power of the Jamaican economy and this should become a major concern as the government seeks to renew and institute economic and financial order.

American Examples of Capitalism at Work
Small developing nations like Jamaica and many in the Caribbean tend to emulate the United States when it comes to economic positioning and policies regarding capitalism and its adoption. However, the past few years of United States' economic decline and financial crisis should bring some weariness and thinking about the price that nations must pay for capitalism and its benefits. Thus far, since the "Great Recession" which began in or around 2007-08, there have been mostly negative or bad examples that only serve to increase the fears, myths, and reservations in moving rapidly toward capitalism. For example, recently, with three more bank failures resulting from the closure of two small banks in Florida and one in Missouri, bringing the number of U.S. bank failures in 2012 to 46 (Associated Press, 2012), many small nations have but to fear what capitalism might bring to them. In 2011, by around November, the United States experienced 80 bank failures, and when added to the current 46 failures for 2012, that is a total of 126 bank failures within less than a two-year period. According to the Associated Press (2012), "Bank closures peaked in 2010 in the wake of the financial crisis. In 2007, just three banks went under. That number jumped to 25 in 2008, after the meltdown, and ballooned to 140 in 2009" (p. 1). Furthermore, 157 U.S. banks were seized by regulators in 2010, and bank failures cost the deposit insurance fund an estimated $88 billion between 2008 and 2011 (Associated Press, 2012). Given these grim financial statistics and occurrences in the world's foremost capitalist economy, small and developing nations such as Jamaica and its neighbors in the Caribbean are

rather educated on the woes and weaknesses of capitalism, especially a capitalism that is becoming increasingly liberal in its standards and guarantees. Despite these facts, the challenge that capitalism faces in small nations like Jamaica, and especially Caribbean nations, is simply not one that rests solely on finance and economy, but also on culture and values as these are impacted by capitalist ideals and practices.

Summary
Jamaicans like many other developing nations' peoples are fascinated with the prospective wealth and benefits of capitalism; and this fascination has been a great driver of change in consumption and industry changes and development in the nation. At the same time, many traditionalists in the nation question the exact gains in following a model of capitalism, which the United States and many other nations use, given the negative impacts of such a model on social values and tradition. This is especially a concern for those who still feel that Jamaica's declining moral and social values stem from a decisively capitalist orientation which places materialism and individualism above values and community. Nevertheless, Jamaica has a long way to go to enjoy the great fruits of an ideal capitalism, and Sheckleford (2006) believes that four factors or problems and challenges make this dream a rather difficult one:

a) The Jamaican economy suffers from serious debt, high inflation, and uneven growth rates;

b) Current economic policies, such as exchange rate devaluation and debt-servicing, only exacerbate Jamaica's economic downslide;

c) To resolve this crisis, the government must implement measures aimed at sustainable growth, such as improving the quality of education and facilitating credit access for small borrowers; and

d) Ultimately, Jamaica may be forced to walk the Argentine road of debt renunciation in order to keep from going under (Sheckleford, 2006, p. 1).

Jamaica needs economic progress, but most importantly, it begins with effective leadership that can strategically plan and bring together the right factors and opportunities that the nation needs. The nation will become crippled in the next several years by the lack of growth and development and the inability to provide adequately for its people if the current leadership does not strategically plan for its immediate and distant future. The many problems and challenges need to be addressed effectively; and the nation needs to make "nation-building" a priority. This means endeavoring to make the next 50 years significantly superior in accomplishments compared to the last 50 years that ended in August 2012.

Chapter 11
Japanese Capitalism and its Challenges

Kazuhito Isomura, Graduate School of International Accounting
Chuo University, Japan

This chapter first points out several varieties of capitalism, and then explains the overview of the Japanese economy.

When the Soviet Union and other socialist regimes began to collapse at the end of the 1980s, the victory of capitalism was proclaimed. However, this does not mean that the entire world now is dominated by one type of capitalism. Several researchers argue that there are several varieties of capitalism (Boyer, 2004; Hall & Soskice, 2001; Michel, 1993); they suggest that capitalism takes different forms as a result of being combined with the socio-cultural factors of each country and region.

Introduction

Polanyi (1944, 1977) proposes three types of human interactions: reciprocity, redistribution, and market exchange; he suggests that market exchange is dominantly embedded in a capitalistic society. However, several differences occur to determine the extent the market exchange is embedded in a society. Michel (1993) discusses two models of capitalism: the neo-American model and the Rhine model. According to Michel (1993), what is regarded as commercial goods is culturally different. In the neo-American model, company, house, transportation, and media are regarded as commercial goods; therefore, they are easily exchanged in markets. In contrast, these services are basically considered to belong to communities in the Rhine model; therefore, these services are provided by public institutions. However, the company, house, transportation, media, education, and medical services are also actually considered as commercial goods and partly exchanged in markets. Michel (1993) suggests that Japan shares some characteristic of the Rhine model. Moreover, Dore (2000) presents a similar view of capitalism with the Anglo-Saxon, Japanese, and German models. The Anglo-Saxon model regards a company as goods, whereas the Japanese and German models consider a company as a community; therefore, they deal carefully with merger and acquisition. Moreover, Boyer (2004) and Hall and Soskice (2001) explain varieties of capitalism by how government, market, company, and society play coordinator roles and build relationships among them. The nature of each player is culturally different, and their relationships depend on social and economic backgrounds. Thus, the literature review shows that capitalism develops its own form by being combined with socio-cultural factors.

The Japanese Economy
The Japanese economy developed steadily after the Second World War through the 1980s, despite the fact that it encountered several significant difficulties, such as two oil crises and the drastic rising of the value of the yen. Consequently, Japan grew as the second largest economy in the world until the end of the 1980s. The success of the Japanese economy was often examined and argued (Abegglen, 1958; Abegglen & Stalk, 1985; Vogel, 1979). Abegglen (1958) points out several features of the Japanese style of management: lifetime employment, seniority-based wages, periodic hiring, in-company training, and enterprise union. The strength of Japanese companies was considered to be created by these features. The unemployment rate used to be 2–3 % for most of the post-war period until the end of the 1980s. Therefore, it is possible to say that the Japanese people enjoyed the prosperity of economic success.

However, in the 1990s, the Japanese economy was suffering a long recession caused by the burst of the "bubble economy." Nippon Keidanren (the Japan Federation of Economic Organization) reexamined its labor policies and divided its employees into two categories: regular and non-regular employees (Mujtaba & Isomura, 2012; Asahi Shimbun, 2009). Most representative companies built a new framework for employment in the 1990s to cope with the long recession (Kobayashi, 1996; Isomura & Huang, 2012). In fact, Nippon Keidanren proclaimed the elimination of lifetime employment. Moreover, the pay system has shifted from a seniority-based system to a performance-based system (Japan Institute for Labor Policy and Training, 2005). Thus, key representative features of the Japanese style of management were reconsidered in the 1990s.

In the early 2000s, the neo-American model was introduced in Japan. Comprehensive financial deregulation was implemented by the government, causing a shift from indirect to direct finance (Asahi Shimbun, 2009). In addition, Japanese accounting standards were revised to minimize the differences between the two countries. Moreover, Japan's employee-based corporate governance was in transition and had a large presence of outside directors as board members in the 1990s. Therefore, the influence of shareholders is rising and Japanese companies now are closely monitored by modern-day investors (Abe & Shimizutani, 2005). Consequently, Japan accepted the neo-American type of financial capitalism in the 2000s; the Japanese style of management came under the pressure of short-term economic performance. Then, in 2008, the global financial crisis hit the Japanese economy; and in 2011, a big earthquake and tsunami and the Fukushima nuclear disaster damaged the eastern part of Japan. Japanese capitalism is facing many difficulties, and searching for ways to address them.

Japan's Cultural Orientations
To understand Japan's cultural orientations, this section reviews several representative studies on Japanese culture (Hall, 1976; Hofstede, 1980, 1991; Nakane, 1970; Ouchi, 1978, 1980, 2004). This section is based mainly on at joint study by Mujtaba and Isomura (2012).

First, Hofstede (1980) provides four criteria to assess culture: power distance, individualism, masculinity, and uncertainty avoidance. Then, Hofstede (1991) adds one more criterion, long-term against short-term orientation. According to Hofstede (1980, 1991), power distance and individualism in Japan are in the medium range, whereas masculinity, uncertainty avoidance, and long-term orientation are in the high range. On the one hand, power distance, individualism, and masculinity are useful as criteria mainly related to styles of communication, authority, decision making, motivation, and leadership. On the other hand, I utilize uncertainty avoidance and long-term orientation to help understand how people and organizations build mutual relationships.

Second, Hall (1976) divides culture into two extreme types: high context and low context. In high context culture, people share their ways of thinking, feeling, and acting; therefore, they often use non-verbal communication. According to Hall (1976), Japan is regarded as a high context society. This research aids in explaining the reason that Japanese people tend to avoid uncertainty and are long-term oriented. Japanese build strong and stable relationships with others, which facilitates communication with each other.

Third, Nakane (1970) explains that the group consciousness of the Japanese depends on the immediate social context called "frame." Frame is circumstantial; it can be a locality, or a particular relationship that binds a set of individuals into a group. Frame means a location or field. Nakane (1970) points out that the dependence on frame produces a strong sense of belonging for the Japanese, a deeply emotional involvement of people, a strong sense of exclusiveness, and an emphasis on tangible interactions.

These studies indicate that Japanese culture is basically collectivism-oriented and that Japan is a high context society. Japanese build strong and stable relationships, and understand each other deeply by keeping long-term relationships.

Next, I explain how these long-term and people-oriented attitudes influence the nature of organization and produce their management practices. Nakane (1970) emphasizes that the vertical relationship is a central principle in Japan, and is used to create cohesion among group members. As tangible interactions and long, stable relationships are regarded as important in Japan, those who belong to an organization for a long time play a major role; as a result, a delicate and intricate ranking system develops. The system of ranking is based on relative age, year of entry into the company, or length of continued service, not necessarily always on ability. Therefore, it is a system of ranking by seniority.

In addition, Nakane (1970) points out that Japanese organizations produce a set of groups tied vertically to one organization so that many factions can be formed. This is because tangible interactions and immediate relationships are considered as a first priority in their organization. These factions are competitive and in conflict with each other. Those who belong to the same faction exchange information within the faction, with the result that informal organizations or networks are highly developed.

Ouchi (1978) explains that Japanese organizations have evolved in a society in which individual mobility is low and where the culture supports norms of collectivism. Ouchi regards Japanese culture as incorporating low rates of social mobility. In general, Japanese prefer staying in one company and enjoy long-term employment. Consequently, employees will be more familiar with the workings of the organizations and more likely to develop friendships among their co-workers. Moreover, employees become integrated into the culture of the organization, a positive contributor to long-term sustainability.

Furthermore, Ouchi (1980) regards Japanese organizations as clans. Clans basically control an organization by socializing members. Ouchi (2004) insists that organizational culture plays an important role in harmonizing individual and organizational goals in a large organization. Therefore, the Japanese approach appears to be effective for managing a large organization in Japan. According to these studies, Ouchi (1978) points out several characteristics of Japanese organizations: lifetime employment, consensus decision-making, collective responsibility, slow evaluation and promotion, implicit, informal control, non-specialized career paths, and holistic concern.

Challenging Issues of Japanese Capitalism
This section points out two challenging issues that Japanese capitalism is currently facing: increasing mobility of employment and corporate transparency.

Japanese culture has long-term and people-oriented attitudes; lifetime employment was generally prevalent among large companies, and the employment was stable. However, the Japanese economy suffered a long recession in the 1990s; the pressure to reduce labor costs caused an increase in non-regular employment and a high unemployment rate among young people. Regular employees are full-time worker who are hired, in principle, until the age of mandatory retirement. In contrast, the definition of non-regular employees is not clear; it include four types such as contract employee, part-time worker, temporary worker and dispatched worker. In general, non-regular employees are different from regular employees in that the period of employment is limited. The rate of non-regular employees is rising from 20.2% in 1990 to 35.1% in 2011. The rate rose by about 15% in two decades. More than one third of employees currently work as a non-regular staff. The unemployment rate used to be 2–3 % for most of the post-war period, whereas the recent rate has doubled; the highest rate was 5.4 % in 2002 (Minister of Health, Labor and Welfare, 2012). Moreover, as I showed in the introduction section, representative Japanese companies changed their employment policies and built a new framework of employment. They divided their employees into three main groups: the long-term competence accumulation group, the highly professional competence utilization group, and the flexible employment group. The first and second groups are regular employees; the third group is non-regular employees. The third group is utilized to reduce labor costs in a recession. In fact, a large number of non-regular employees were laid off during the Global Financial Crisis in 2008 and after the Great East Japan Earthquake in 2011. The Japanese government supported this trend by eliminating the regulations on temporary workers step by step from 1997 to 2004 (Asahi Shimbun, 2009).

Lifetime employment was accepted as management practice among large companies in the post-war period in Japan; therefore, companies played a real role in protecting social security on behalf of the government. However, on the one hand, severe global competition destroyed lifetime employment. On the other hand, the Japanese government depended on companies; hence, the government did not build a safety net for unemployed people. Consequently, many people became homeless in 2008, and the number of households receiving livelihood protection has drastically increased lately (Asahi Shimbun, 2009). The long recession since the burst of the bubble economy and severe global competition necessitate a revision of the roles of the government and companies.

Let us now address the shift to neo-American financial capitalism. To enhance the international presence of the Tokyo Stock Market, the Japanese government engaged in a comprehensive reform of the financial system, sometimes described as the Japanese version of the Big Bang, from 1996 to 2002 (Minister of Finance, 1997). The principles of this policy are free, fair, and global; the government enacted the Financial System Reform Act in 1998 (Minister of Finance, 1998). The boundary between banking and securities services was basically removed, and the activities of foreign financial institutions in Japan were deregulated. In addition, Japanese accounting standards were revised to be more compatible with International Financial Reporting Standards (IFRS) and US Generally Accepted Accounting Principles (GAAP) (Isoyama, 2002). Thus, number of main ideas of neo-American financial capitalism was introduced in Japan from the second half of the 1990s to the first half of the 2000s.

What happened as a result? The transparency of the stock market improved and the pressure of the market increased. The negative legacy of the Japanese style of management gradually clarified. Japanese are long-term and collectivism-oriented; hence, most Japanese companies built cross-shareholding relationships and the main financial banks played a crucial role in binding a business group. Consequently, company scandals in the past were often hidden. However, the fundraising of companies now depends more on the stock market and the transparency of the stock market improved; therefore, many company scandal surfaced. Yamaichi Securities Company went bankrupt in 1997 because of stock shuffling. The CEO of Seibu Railway Corporation was arrested for misstatement of financial statements in 2004. Similar scandals occurred at Olympus and Daio Paper Company in 2011. Thus, it is possible to say that neo-American financial capitalism brought about positive impacts on Japanese capitalism by bringing to light some negative aspects of the collectivism orientation. Corporate transparency has improved significantly, and companies try to enhance their compliance (Asahi Shimbun, 2009).

Summary

Japanese tend to have long-term and collectivism orientations; long and strong relationships are built not only among individuals and between an individual and an organization but also among organizations. As a result, management practices such as lifetime employment and seniority-based ranking systems and payment are formed in companies; and companies build business groups both vertically and horizontally. It is possible to say that the role of coordination among organizations and government is stronger than that of the market. Therefore, as presented by Albert (1993) and Dore (2000), Japanese capitalism is community oriented rather than market oriented. However, globalization encourages market orientation to compete severely, exposing Japanese capitalism to several changes. On the one hand, the strength of the Japanese style of management is considered to be produced by the long-term and collectivism orientation; however, these can also become weaknesses. On the other hand, market pressure of transparency brings to light negative sides of Japanese capitalism.

Thus, each type of capitalism is formed in its economic and socio-cultural environment; its advantages and disadvantages depend on changes in the environment. It is not easy to determine which model of capitalism is favorable, both because success depends on each environment and because the environment is always changing. Therefore, balancing economic and socio-cultural factors is important for each culture or country to build its own capitalism. In Japan, declining birthrate and aging population reduce domestic markets; the Japanese economy inevitably needs to expand its market globally, particularly in the Asia Pacific region. Japanese capitalism must adjust to globalization and build its own way continuously and flexibly.

Chapter 12

Nigeria: An Institutional Based View of Corruption[5]

Ikwukananne I. Udechukwu, Columbia Southern University

Corruption in Nigeria has been well documented. However, the basis for the corruption has not yet been fully studied. Some studies have approached corruption in Nigeria from a judiciary, executive, labor, law enforcement, and legislative perspective. This chapter attempts to use the institutional and architectural perspectives to glean into the nature and consequences of corruption in Nigeria. Despite its vast natural resources, the average Nigerian has not benefited from it due to the high level of greed and mismanagement allowed under market-based capitalism which is not very well regulated by the government. It is hoped that other developing economies with abundant natural resources, as is the case in Nigeria, using the matrix provided below, can study the nature of the formal and informal institutions that exist within their boundaries.

Introduction

Corruption remains an omnipresent and troubling issue for most Nigerians and for potential investors in Nigeria. It is often a subject of great concern and discussion amongst Nigerians and investors, regardless of the context and focus of such deliberations. It is apparent that no one is more interested in resolving the issues of corruption in Nigeria than Nigerians themselves, and in some cases, foreign investors who see the vast investment and economic potentials in the country. But a part of the corruption problem in Nigeria finds root not just in policy, behavior, culture, and processes, but also in the abundance of natural resources, specifically crude oil, for which the country is well endowed. Crude oil is both a symptom and a manifestation of the institutional and architectural misalignment, existing in the Nigerian context.

According to *USATODAY*, "Nigeria, an OPEC nation, is the fifth-largest crude oil exporter to the U.S. Nigeria has proven natural gas reserves of about 5.29 trillion cubic meters. It produces about 2.4 million barrels of crude oil a day.

---

[5] *Source*: Udechukwu, I. I., and Mujtaba, B. G., (March 2013). An Institutional and Architecture Based View of Corruption in Nigeria: An Analysis of a Developing Economy's Formal and Informal Structures. *Journal of Business Studies Quarterly*, 4(3), 230-239.

However, more than 50 years of oil and gas production has taken a heavy environmental toll" ("Nigeria: 2 Presumed Dead", 2012).

This link between corruption and crude oil has well been established, documented, and acknowledged by interested parties and observers; and consequently, has led to numerous acts of sabotage and labor unrest against Nigeria's crude oil production capacity. Corruption is an act of sabotage on formal rules, systems, and institutions. According to the *USATODAY*, among innumerable episodes of labor unrests related to crude oil, and hence corruption, a severe strike threatened to derail the Nigerian economy as the government tried to remove subsidies for domestic production of crude related products at the beginning of 2012. Unfortunately,

> Anger over losing one of the few benefits average Nigerians see from being an oil-rich country, as well as disgust over perceived government corruption, have led to demonstrations across this nation of 160 million people and violence that has killed many people. The Petroleum and Natural Gas Senior Staff Association of Nigeria, which represents about 20,000 workers, said it would be forced to "apply the bitter option" of closing down all oil and gas production if the government refused to reinstate the gasoline subsidies (Ibukun, 2012).

Furthermore, Gboyega, Soreide, Le, and Shukla (2011), also acknowledged this history, as they noted:

> Nigeria is recognized as a country with the most known reserves of petroleum and gas in Sub-Saharan Africa. Petroleum has long become the most important aspect of the national economy, accounting for more than half of GDP, about 85 percent of government revenues, and over 90 percent of exports. Since oil was discovered in Nigeria more than five decades ago, the country has had a turbulent and disappointing development record and remains significantly oil-dependent. The scramble for control of natural resource rents has contributed to weak oil sector governance and to political upheavals and conflicts. (p. 7).

While there is no shortage of articles describing corruption in Nigeria and its consequences on that nation, what is clear from these assertions is not whether corruption is an issue there or if the abundance of Nigeria's mismanaged crude oil reserves spurs corruption, among many other valid reasons for corruption in the country, rather, this discussion is about a new and better understanding of the framework of corruption from a Nigerian perspective. Gboyega, *et al.* noted, "Thus, although Nigeria is rich in petroleum resource as a result of its geological endowment, the fact that it remains highly dependent on petroleum reflects its failure to manage these resources to develop a broad-based economy" (p. 8). This excessive dependence on crude oil is a tacit and innate recognition by Nigerians, through a resource-based view of organizations, suggesting that the competitive advantage of an organization, partly depends on the value, rarity, and inimitability of available resources and competencies of that organization.

Illustrated in Table 12.1 is the Corruption Perception Index for Nigeria for the last decade, as documented by Transparency International. Whether or not the perception of corruption in Nigeria is improving, based on the data below, is debatable. However, Gboyega *et al.* (2011) suggested, "Over the last decade, Nigeria has shown some signs of improving governance, including the return to democratic rule since 1999" (p. 7). It is not clear if the signs of improving governance clearly demonstrate the nature of its institutions and the relationship between the architecture of that nation and the nature of its institutions.

Table 12.1- *Corruption Perception Index for Nigeria in the Last 10 years*

Year	Ranking Among Other Nations	Score	Number of Nations
2011	143	2.4	182
2010	134	2.4	178
2009	130	2.5	180
2008	121	2.7	180
2007	147	2.2	179
2006	142	2.2	163
2005	152	1.9	158
2004	144	1.5	145
2003	132	1.4	133
2002	101	1.2	102
2001	90	1.0	91

The data in Table 12.2, while it is a combination of data drawn from IMF research on actual, estimated, and projected economic indicators, suggests that with inflation rate greater than real GDP rate, the average Nigerian must come to terms with how to supplement the dwindling value of their personal income and fortunes, and the purchasing power of the Nigerian currency, the Naira. Thus, suggesting one of several reasons Nigerians engage in questionable practices and transactions, or acts of sabotage that invariably weaken formal institutions while strengthening informal institutions, with the intent of making up for this potential income shortfall, due to inflation, which harkens to the term, corruption. With inflation rates exceeding real GDP growth, corruption in Nigeria is expected to be a vicious cycle of an unending exploitation, leading to the weakening of existing formal institutions and the strengthening of informal institutions, based on the manipulation of existing architecture in Nigerian institutions, to include their organizational structures, processes, controls and incentives, and culture.

Table 12.2 - *Nigeria: Economic Indicators* (% of GDP)

	2005	2006	2007	2008	2009	2010	2011	2012
	Actual	Actual	Est	Proj	Proj	Proj	Proj	Proj
Real GDP growth (Percent)	6.5	6.0	6.3	9.0	8.3	7.0	7.0	8.1
Consumer price inflation, annual average (percent)	17.8	8.3	5.4	7.3	8.5	8.5	8.5	8.5
Current account balance	7.1	9.4	0.8	5.7	2.4	3.1	2.9	3.4

Sources: Nigerian authorities and IMF staff.

It does make sense to approach the Nigerian scenario rather carefully, particularly from an organization and management orientation. Though a nation, Nigeria is still fundamentally an organization of people with collective but disparate cultures and needs, whose primary goal is to take advantage of its internal resources and capabilities (crude oil). This harkens to the resource-based view of firms, which suggests that competencies and resources required for competitive advantage of firms, and in this case, a nation, have to be valuable, rare, and difficult to duplicate, as is the case with the high quality crude oil found in Nigeria. However, the allocation and distribution of these resources across Nigeria, has been uneven, since the discovery of crude oil in the late to early sixties, and has encouraged corruption at an architectural and institutional level, not because the resource is a curse, as most Nigerians and observers might view it, nor because Nigeria lacks the capacity or competency to engage in fair distribution of these resources.

The structural and institutional factors associated with Nigeria, as can be gleaned from an organizational architecture perspective and institutional-based view of organizations, may help provide a deeper understanding of what the Nigerian government must do, to help address the issue of corruption, this is if it is to enjoy the full benefits of its nascent democratic ideals. In fact, Peng (2011) suggested, "In harsh, unattractive environments, most firms either suffer or exit" (p. 10). In the Nigerian case, while corruption is attractive to its domestic beneficiaries by strengthening its informal institutions, corruption is simply unattractive to investors who would prefer a stronger formal institution. Nigeria already suffers from the ill-effects of corruption in many ways, as illustrated by examples provided elsewhere in this chapter.

Thus, this chapter discusses Nigerian corruption from an organizational architecture perspective, which entails the nature of its architecture, processes, culture, and incentive and controls; and through the institutional-based view of organizations, which entails formal and informal institutions.

The Architecture Perspective

Every organization is fundamentally built around a design or sets of design that serves to enhance its existence (short-term or long-term) and legitimacy in that particular environment. Whether or not that design is ordered or chaotic, or whether the design is a function of conscious or unconscious thought processes, or whether the design truly serves the purpose for which it is intended, has been a never ending source of discussions about the nature of collective entities and systems, to include firms and nations. In this case, the complex nature of any national architecture might be a source of some of the issues that nation might be facing. Organizational architecture allows us to think of organizational designs in terms of formal organizational structures, control systems and incentives, organizational culture, processes, and people (Hill, 2009 & Morgan, 1986).

According to Hill (2009), "By organizational structure, we mean three things: First, the formal division of the organization into subunits such as product divisions, national operations, and functions…; second, the location of decision-making responsibilities within that structure (e.g. centralized or decentralized); third, the establishment of integrating mechanisms to coordinate the activities of subunits including cross-functional teams and or pan-regional committees" (p. 381). Within the current Nigerian structure the relationship between the executive branch, the judiciary branch, and the legislative branch, fails to find unity of purpose in establishing an "integrating mechanisms to coordinate the activities of subunits including cross-functional teams" (Hill, 2009, p. 381). This provides unexpected opportunities and "loopholes" for informal entities to legitimize informal rules and agreements with the electorate in that particular environment. In the absence of effective structures borne from formal institutions, and uncoordinated with a national interested purpose, corruption then morphs from being perceived as a criminal behavior to becoming an acceptable cultural ideal and belief system. Controls and incentives to impede this phenomenon is usually ineffective because of differences in incentives accrued through formal institutions compared to incentives accrued through informal systems. Due to the strong informal institutional framework of the Nigerian polity with allegiances to religious, ethnic, and regional loyalties, informal institutions tend to be seen as being more profitable than structures that can be found in formal institutions. The difference in incentive is thus, wide enough to encourage acts of national sabotage we now refer to as corruption.

The system of controls for formal and informal institutions in Nigeria, differ in the nature and type of incentives extended by the principals (country) to its agents (officials). Hill (2009) defines controls as, "metrics used to measure the performance of subunits and make judgments about how well managers are running those subunits", while incentives "are the devices used to reward appropriate managerial behavior" (p. 382). Formalized entities of Nigeria, due to institutional constraints, incentivize its agents much less competitively than the agents of informal entities. Thus, the opportunity cost to maintain the required behavior or value congruence, in the national interest, becomes fairly expensive, while becoming a source of motivation to engage in activities that are ultimately defined as corruption, when one takes into account the data published in table 2, which clearly illustrates how inflation significantly prompts Nigerians to act against the interest of the state, thus weakening formal institutions.

The extrinsic nature of this motivation as a result of a national culture that encourages the public display of wealth is blatant and glaring. The longitudinal reinforcement of higher incentives due to informal rules, and the corresponding high opportunity cost due to formal rules, eventually signals to the electorate in that environment that corruption is not only a profitable behavior and venture, but an acceptable cultural ideal and belief system. This also does something interesting: It diminishes loyalty to formal entities, nationalism, and dignity in labor, while encouraging domestic sabotage of formal rules and policies of formal institutions, whose opportunity costs are that much greater and dire than those in informal systems. The net effect of this phenomenon, is higher transaction costs for both citizen and investor, who has to engage in one form of economic, social, and political activity or the other, with formal institutions in Nigeria. These concerns are reinforced in the processes as well.

Hill (2009) defines processes as "the manner in which decisions are made and work is performed within an organization" (p. 382). Incentives support the processes whether in an informal or formal system. Since informal systems are more likely to be better incentivized, one would expect a more responsive service in informal systems than formal systems. This is a segue to the conclusion reached by Williamson (2009), who argued that nations with strong informal systems tend to enjoy more economic development than nations with strong formal institutions.

Processes in formal systems, will then attempt to bring to equilibrium, the incentives accrued to agents of the informal system. Thus, inefficiencies are then designed into the processes of formal systems, in order to attract a part of the corruption funds being enjoyed by agents of informal systems. This act of sabotage then takes a life of its own, sometimes leading to collusion between agents of the formal system and agents of the informal system, leading to new processes designed to benefit both parties, at a cost to the collective national interests. The structure, control and incentives, and processes, eventually become integrated enough while embedding itself in convergence to/with the existing religious, ethnic, and regional polity of Nigeria.

Hill (2009) defines organizational culture as "the norms and value systems that are shared among the employees of an organization" (p. 382). In this sense, the culture of corruption is actually a culture based on value congruence. This implies members of either formal and informal systems whose values are not congruent with the nature of incentives and processes borne from the competitive relationship between informal and formal systems, are generally considered out-group members because a collective culture sometimes has more sway than the principles of a single individual under these conditions. This would also suggest that simply indicting members engaged in a culture of corrupt practices in Nigeria, may actually turn out to be exercises in futility, since the structure, incentives and controls, and processes, from which such members emerged, remain intact, while continuing to support the culture of corruption at all levels in the system, regardless of who is indicted, if an indictment exists, or not.

The Institution Perspective

Peng (2011) elaborated on the institution perspective by stating, "An institution-based view suggests that the success and failure of firms are enabled and constrained by institutions. By institutions, we mean structures that define the rules of the game" (p. 9). These institutions when they follow the "formal rules of the game", which includes "laws and regulations", are classified as formal institutions (Peng, 2011, p. 9). On the other hand, informal institutions, or "informal rules of the game, include culture, ethics, and norms" (Peng, 2011, p. 9).

The emergence and embedded nature of corruption in Nigeria appear to be an equilibrium between weakening or weakened formal institutions functioning in competition with strengthening and strengthened informal institutions. In this case, formal institutional structures, processes, controls and incentives, and culture, generate much higher and dire opportunity costs for members maintaining any level of value congruence in those formal institutions, than do members of informal institutions.

Busse (2010) discussed several mechanisms by which informal institutions influence the activities of formal institutions. They include replacement, undermining, support, and competition (Busse, 2010). "Informal institutions can replace (and be replaced by) formal institutions" (Busse, 2011, p. 318). The Nigerian experience here is one where it is more efficient to rely on informal institutions to speed up government services than rely on the processes, structure, culture, and controls and incentives of formal institutions. Thus, suggesting that informal institutions provide a template upon which to replace the normal functions in formal institutions. In the colloquialisms of Nigeria, informal institutions are recognized as "Oluwole". Busse (2010) supports this position by adding that, "Informal institutions can also serve as templates for formal institutions. Informal rules may generate precedents and prevalent practices that are then formalized for efficiency's sake" (p. 321).

Busse (2010) states that, "informal institutions can undermine and thus weaken formal rules. Informal practices and institutions are seen as promoting corruption, delaying the consolidation of democratic institutions, and eroding emergent formal rules. Yet undermining can also redress the violation of social norms introduced by formal rules" (p. 321 – 322). The idea behind undermining formal rules is the innate tendency for agents of informal institutions to seek justice and redress at any cost. By justice, we mean organizational justice, and more specifically, procedural justice where the traditional social norms for distributing resources are sabotaged through acts of corruption. These informal institutions undermine the structures, the processes, incentives and controls, and culture of formal institutions because they believe it is more just and perhaps, more efficient to do so than to allow rigid formal institutions that are perceived to serve the needs of the political elite, to decide who gets what and when. "Informal political institutions can also support or reinforce formal institutions. They do so both by "reifying" formal institutions—delineating the domains where formal institutions rule—and by providing information and enforcement that promote the functioning of formal institutions. Informal rules also can enforce formal regulations via informal sanctioning (truthful gossip), or reporting to formal authorities" (Busse, 2010, p. 324; Ellickson, 1991).

Finally, Busse (2010) suggests that "informal institutions have a second-order effect: they help to shape elite competition, which in turn affects both the timing and type of formal rule emergence, and the mechanisms by which informal institutions influence formal rules" (p. 326). In the Nigerian context, in some cases, the lucrative nature or services provided through informal institutions, drives formal institutions to provide value added benefits to its electorate, not with the intention to improve services rather with the goal of competition with the efficiencies accrued through the structures, incentives and controls, and processes of informal institutions.

Williamson (2009) went further to create a typology of nations based on the strength of their institutions—strong or weak or both. Williamson (2009) noted that, "Conceptually, the strength of an institution implies either well-developed (strong) constraints or lack of constraints (weak)" (p. 373). While Williamson's model was designed to focus on economic development in institutions, it could also serve to enhance our understanding of corruption since corruption is in fact, an institutional variable and a constraint to economic development. Thus, the extent of corruption existing in a nation, as a constraint, should also be a strong determinant of the strength and extent of a nation's economic development within the institutional and architectural framework of that nation. Williamson presented the model using four quadrants.

Table 12.3 - Strength of Formal and Informal Institutions

Strong formal (1)	Weak formal (2)
Strong Informal	Strong Informal
Strong formal (3)	Weak formal (4)
Weak informal	Weak informal

Source: Williamson, C. R. (2009). Informal institutions rule: institutional arrangements and economic performance. *Public Choice, 139*, 371 – 387.

Williamson (2009) argued that nations with strong informal institutions enjoyed higher levels of economic development, irrespective of the strengths of their formal institutions. Cited in that paper was Nigeria, which was located in the fourth quadrant, thus indicating weak formal and weak informal institutions. Williamson's analysis appears as a paradox to the prevailing circumstances in Nigeria, since Nigerians tend to believe they exist in a strong informal institutional setting, with a weak formal structure. The history of Nigeria is fraught with primary loyalties to these informal institutions in the form of ethnic, religious, and regional affiliations, which continue to undermine the need for a national identity. These affiliations also have the property of diminishing the value congruence between agents of formal institutions and their loyalty to formal institutions. Thus, suggesting that Nigeria maybe plagued with strong informal institutions and a weak formal institutional system, contrary to the conclusions reached by Williamson (2009).

Implications
Corruption must be viewed very systematically for analysis, training and development perspectives (Yasmeen, Begum and Mujtaba, 2011). Based on this analysis if we are to combine the factors noted in the architectural perspective and the institutional perspective, then the idea of addressing corruption using the tools available in Nigeria today, to include the use of formal institutions such as the Economics and Financial Crimes Commission (EFCC) to combat corruption, would likely fail, for precisely the reasons stated in this paper. If the goal of informal institutions is to "replace" or "undermine" the structure, processes, controls and incentives, and culture of formal institutions, attempts at impeding that effort could lead to more costly forms of national sabotage, beyond corruption, to include assassinations, death threats, arsons, etc. The relocation of the former EFCC Chairman, Nuhu Ribadu, to the United Kingdom, whose life was in constant danger, exemplifies this noted concern in this paper. His life remains in danger and under threat, even after so many years off from the job.

Table 12.4 - Architectural and Institution-based Corruption Solution Matrix

	Replacement	*Undermining*	*Support*	*Competition*
Structure	Privatize	Bonded Agents	Contractors	N/A
Processes	Privatize	Bonded Agents	Contractors	N/A
Control and Incentives	Privatize	Bonded Agents	Contractors	N/A
Culture	Privatize	Bonded Agents	Contractors	N/A

The matrix in Table 12.4 is not a solution but a way forward in studying corruption in developing nations and particularly in Nigeria. It is a combination of factors identified from the architectural perspective and the institutional perspective of organizations, with a realistic acknowledgement that barring other crude forms of eliminating corruption can include decrees from military juntas, that some form of corruption will likely remain part of the Nigerian platform for the foreseeable future, even with draconian decrees from a military junta. The matrix simply provides a transparent method of auditing formal institutions of the Nigerian system with the aim of classifying each institution and role, in terms of its architecture relative to the pressures it experiences from the services provided by informal institutions. This audit should be conducted by reputable, outside third party organizations that are independent of the Nigerian system.

For example, is the formal institution facing the potential for "replacement" or "undermining" from informal institutions? If the formal institution is facing "replacement", then an audit should encourage an outright privatization of that formal institution. If it is facing "undermining, then informal institutions should be encouraged to vigorously participate in providing the same services as the formal institution, with the caveat that they do so as bonded agents acting on behalf of formal institutions. And, if the formal institution is being "supported" by informal institutions, then those informal institutions should be encouraged to serve as contractors to the formal institutions.

Thus, equilibrium between formal and informal institutions should be accepted as a first step in that process. Secondly, the transparency and control, using modern information systems, would be helpful in this process. Third, reform of the architecture of formal institutions with the goal of creating more flexible structures, shorter processes, competitive incentives, and encouraging a collective vision of all agents, under a technology-based system of accountability, may be required. Fourth, some form of recognition and validation for informal institutions may be required to the extent that government services can be provided through informal institutions whose processes, structure, and incentives remain informal but whose accountability to the services they provide, can be validated through formal means. These informal institutions can act as contractors or bonded agents of formal institutions, and may be required to undergo annual audits and reconciliations to ensure that the codes of conduct for the formal system remain intact. This could potentially swell the Nigerian bureaucracy; however, it could provide a more transparent environment for foreign investors, as the Nigerian economy continues to grow.

Summary

The nature of corruption in developing nations remain little understood even though evidence of such corruption abound. The idea of indicting single or groups of individuals has done little to impede corruption in these nations, particularly in Nigeria. Yet, a deep failure to recognize the need to bring informal institutions from the shadows and the dark, has remained elusive because a systematic study has yet to be done so far to provide a critical analysis of the corruption phenomenon in developing nations.

The Nigerian corruption situation shows clearly that the architecture of formal and informal institutions has a huge role to play in reinforcing practices that ultimately sabotage the national interests of all Nigerians. It is hoped that these suggestions are given some considerations as the Nigerian government forges ahead in its democratic future, while paving the way for a fair and entrepreneurially regulated spirit of capitalism to eventually flourish.

Chapter 13
Pakistan: Capitalism Realities

Talat Afza and Naseem Habib
COMSATS Institute of Information Technology
Lahore, Pakistan

Capitalism is often seen as an economic system where individuals own the means of production and they are free to control the means of production in accord with their interests. Such a system confers the responsibility of providing peace and justice upon government. Government also imposes tolerable taxes but does not intervene in price mechanism of market which is adjusted in the best interests of society through coordination of the forces of supply and demand.

This chapter discusses capitalism in Pakistan as a case which has fallen prey to the moves of nationalization and new liberal economies in alternative periods. In more than sixty years the country could not devise an effective economic policy which best suits its circumstances.

Introduction

Pakistan is the clear example of a system which lacks proper control and which allows the small group of people comprised politicians, military higher-ups, civil bureaucrats, feudal and industrialists to control the fate and wealth of the country and make accessibility to political, human, and physical rights very cumbersome. Advocates of free market contend that free market will generate bourgeoisies who will pressurize government for more freedom, human rights and political participation; but in Pakistan's case the bourgeoisies has induced a system of bribes and misappropriation of state assets. Political power is vested in feudalists and industrialists who have purloined the state assets.

The objective of this chapter is to bring forth the reasons of the failure of neoliberal policies in the backdrop of Pakistan's socio-politico environment. Though Pakistan has tried socialism in 1970s, but out of six decades since its birth, five decades it has put in place private sector led growth model. The discussion of various factors has led us to believe that neoliberal economic policy can prove best economic policy when state has power to curb corrupt practices especially in redistribution of wealth and in the provision of equality of opportunity.

Pakistan – An Overview

The Islamic Republic of Pakistan is a sovereign country in South Asia and is the sixth most populous country in the world with a population more than 180 million. Located at the crossroads of the strategically important regions of South Asia, Central Asia, and Western Asia, Pakistan has a 1,046-kilometre (650 mi) coastline along the Arabian Sea and the Gulf of Oman in the south and is bordered by India to the east, Afghanistan to the west and north, Iran to the southwest and China in the far northeast. It is separated from Tajikistan by Afghanistan's narrow Wakhan Corridor in the north, and also shares a marine border with Oman.

Pakistan is a federal parliamentary republic consisting of four provinces and four federal territories. It is an ethnically and linguistically diverse country, with a similar variation in its geography and wildlife. It has a semi-industrialized economy which is the 27th largest in the world in terms of purchasing power and 47th largest in terms of nominal GDP.

Pakistan's post-independence history has been characterized by periods of military rule, political instability, and conflicts with neighboring India. The country continues to face challenging problems, including terrorism, poverty, illiteracy, and corruption.

Culture and society

Pakistani society is largely hierarchical, emphasizing local cultural etiquettes and traditional Islamic values that govern personal and political life. The basic family unit is the extended family, although there has been a growing trend towards nuclear families for socio-economic reasons. The middle class has increased to around 30 million and the upper- and upper-middle classes to around 17 million in recent decades; and power is shifting from rural landowners to the urbanized elites.

Political system

Pakistan since its independence has been spearheaded by fourteen elected governments and four military rulers; and every decade of democracy is preceded and followed by a decade of military regime. Years 1958-1969, 1977-1988, and 1999-2007 were the long periods when military ruled the country which had seen economic growth (though it was limited to a class of people and could not spread to lower echelons of society) while the periods of democracy were characterized by corruption, misgovernment, lack of political will, and political instability. Elected governments work under parliamentary system, while military rulers instill a semi presidential system in Pakistan and through amendments in the constitution in their reign they tried to strengthen their position by vesting more power to the position of president who acts as the head-of-state.

Economy

When it gained independence in 1947 from the UK, Pakistan's average economic growth rate since independence has been higher than the average growth rate of the world economy during the period. Average annual real GDP growth rates were

6.8% in the 1960s, 4.8% in the 1970s, and 6.5% in the 1980s. Average annual growth fell to 4.6% in the 1990s with significantly lower growth in the second half of that decade.

During the 1960s, Pakistan was seen as a model of economic development around the world, and there was much praise for its economic progression. Karachi was seen as an economic role model around the world, and there was much praise for the way its economy was progressing. Many countries sought to emulate Pakistan's economic planning strategy, and one of them, South Korea, copied the city's second "Five-Year Plan," and World Financial Center in Seoul is designed and modeled after Karachi. Later, economic mismanagement in general, and fiscally imprudent economic policies in particular, caused a large increase in the country's public debt, and consequently led to a slower growth in the 1970s and 1990s.The economy recovered during the 1980s via a policy of deregulation, as well as an increased inflow of foreign aid and remittances from expatriate workers.

During the mid-2000s, Pakistan experienced a period of tremendous growth, averaging 7% yearly GDP growth between 2003–07. Due to its large population of 186 million, it was included in 2005 by the Goldman Sachs Global Economics Group as one of the "Next Eleven (N-11)" – a group of countries with economies that "might have the kind of potential for global impact that the BRICs projections highlighted, essentially an ability to match the G7 in size."

By October 2007, Pakistan raised back its Foreign Reserves to a handsome $16.4 billion. Exceptional policies kept Pakistan's trade deficit controlled at $13 billion, exports boomed to $18 billion, revenue generation increased to become $13 billion and attracted foreign investment of $8.4 billion.

Since the beginning of 2008, Pakistan's economic outlook has taken stagnation. Security concerns stemming from the nation's role in the War on Terror have created great instability and led to a decline in FDI from a height of approximately $8 bn to $3.5bn for the fiscal year 2011-2012. Concurrently, the insurgency has forced massive capital flight from Pakistan to the Gulf. Combined with high global commodity prices, the dual impact has shocked Pakistan's economy, with gaping trade deficits, high inflation, and a crash in the value of the Rupee, which has fallen drastically.

Capitalism in Pakistan
At the time of its independence, Pakistan consists of East and West Pakistan which were separated by Indian territory.. East Pakistan consists of a large province of Bangal and West Pakistan comprises four provinces including Punjab, Balochistan, Sindh, and North West Frontier Province (Present day Khyber Pakhtonkha). Power struggle, linguistic and ethnic issues, regional disparities and physical separation between East and West Pakistan paved the way for the civil war in Pakistan and the separation of East Pakistan as an the independent state of Bangladesh in 1971. In the formative days of Pakistan's early life, it met so many other challenges that economic reforms and policy took a "back-seat." Pakistan has shown the average

growth rate of 3.1 % in the first 10 years from 1947 to 1958 despite insignificant foreign inflows and host of problems.

Having faced an unstable political atmosphere for a decade, the country was taken over by a military dictator Ayub Khan, in October 1958 and this dictatorship perpetuated for a decade. Pakistan saw an impressive growth rate in this decade showing 6% GDP growth rate per annum along with manufacturing sector expansion of 9% and agricultural growth rate of 4% with the introduction of Green Revolution Technology. Government's initiatives and support through Export Bonus Scheme in manufacturing export sector witnessed a rise in manufactured exports such that Pakistan's exports were higher than the collective exports of Thailand, Indonesia and Malaysia together. While Pakistan's growth was taken as an example by other newly born or developing countries, which emulated the five year development plan of Pakistan and emerged as miracle economies in international arena, but within Pakistan these plans were seen as "pro-rich" policies, which resulted in the concentration of economic assets in the hands of twenty two families and aggravated regional and class disparities.

The initiative taken by Ayub Khan's regime in 1960s in the realm of agriculture, named Green Revolution, made a significant difference in raising the overall level of yields and the productivity of land in Pakistan, but the main beneficiaries were the rural rich, who constituted less than 5 percent of rural population and owned mostly irrigated land. The important factor to mention here is that distribution of the land is highly skewed because large landholdings of irrigated land are operated by few landlords, while poor mainly subsist on rain fed areas. Green revolution technology accelerated growth by the application of seed-water-fertilizer package in the irrigated lands of large land holders with greater access to required resources.

Other public policy initiatives taken in the realm of agricultural sector to boost agricultural performance to provide a strong base to industry in this period included subsidies to make use of ground water reservoirs and availability of easy or subsidized credits for tractors and other mechanized equipment; but all met the same results in the presence of existing rural power structure which accentuated the income disparities further.

The economic policies pursued in Ayub's regime also worsened the levels of inter-regional disparity between East and West Pakistan. Whether these disparities were reality or misperceptions are debatable, but it resulted in the secession of East Pakistan in 1971. The breakup of Pakistan had traumatic effect on economic growth of the country as 50% of Pakistan's exports and 20% of its imports were from East Pakistan.

Zulfiqar Ali Bhutto's populist regime promised to establish a more egalitarian economic order in the country. The nationalization of key industries and financial institutions was considered the only panacea for reversing the economic concentration of the assets which pro-rich policies of Ayub Khan let accumulate in few hands. This nationalization program of Bhutto government only improved public sector employment but it failed improving efficiency and productivity of public corporations. This public sector employment growth is seen not more than a political patronage. The country slipped badly in perpetuating previous decade's economic growth performance. The only thing that was in alignment with the previous government's performance was the perpetuation of widening gap of income between rich and poor.

Pakistan's economy was least prepared to absorb exogenous shocks from internal and external market. The public corporations suffered financial losses because of mismanagement, lack of accountability, lack of enthusiasm and motivation and non-availability of capital and skills to modernize the corporations to improve efficiency and productivity (Siddiqui, 2011). The damage of crops especially cotton by flood in 1974-175 resulted in the decline of export revenue as cotton was the key export item. While internally it was hit by bad performance of public sector industries and institutes, and floods, externally it was battered by global recession. Due to global depression in early 1970's, global markets for exports shrank and rise in the import prices led to striking increase in import bills. The remittances of Pakistani workers abroad especially in Middle East after oil price boom served as a "safety valve" against all aforementioned exogenous shocks during Bhutto's government (Hussain, 2009)

In 1977, once again, the military came forward to rescue the country from economic crisis and ascendency of a military dictator again inhibited the democratic process for another decade. The reversal of the Bhutto policies by General Zia-ul-Haq brought an end to the uncertainty but political power was again centralized in the hands of a dictator. Zia-ul-Haq used religion to provide his rule legitimacy and it is perceived that present Islamic Fundamentalism was rooted in Zia's period (Hussain, 2009). Zia got huge military and economic aid from the U.S. for participating in the campaign of overthrowing Soviet Union in Afghanistan. Though the long-term costs for the country by participating in this war were colossal, Zia benefitted from this war as he got full backing of the U.S. and thus was able to prolong his authoritarian rule for a long eleven years. Fiscal deficits widened to 8 percent of GDP and to finance these deficits domestic borrowings were used which weakened the economic growth, both in the short- and long-run (Hussain, 2009)

Economic indicators showed a healthy trend, as GDP grew at almost 7%, with manufacturing industrial average growth at 9% per annum and agriculture at 4%, but the manufacturing sector was unable to generate new jobs. The insignificant employment growth, despite relatively high growth in manufacturing industry in the 1980s, partly represents an increase in capital rather than labor intensive industry during the period of accelerated expansion (UNIDO, 1990).

After the death of General Zia, democracy restored for another decade, i.e. 1988-1999, during which 4 elected and 4 interim governments ruled Pakistan. This decade is marked by political instability, uncertainty, misgovernment, corruption, and a lack of political will. Economic indicators fell sharply; GDP decelerated to 4 percent. Prime Minister Benazir Bhutto - elected in 1988 -launched neo-liberal reforms under the supervision of the IMF and World Bank with the main concern of lowering fiscal deficit to 4% of GDP. Both the Pakistan Muslim League and the

Pakistan Peoples Party (PPP), which took turns in office during this decade, pursued the same economic policies of liberalization, deregulation and privatization but dismissal of governments without letting them complete the term in office did not allow the positive trends to persist. It is speculated that poor governance would have been offset by continuity in policies. Large scale privatization was carried out in this period under the wave of denationalization to raise revenue. Privatization process was accused of being inconsistent and devoid of transparency. According to the Institute of Developing Economics Study (1994), the process allegedly suffered from favoritism as some bidders had privileged access to information and competing bids. The decision of Pakistani government to carry out nuclear test in 1998 to create a power balance in the sub-continent after the nuclear test by India the same year led to withdrawal of any aid by IMF and economic sanctions were imposed on Pakistan by the western world. Depletion of foreign reserves and huge capital flight from the country exacerbated the economic situation of Pakistan further. Exports were stagnant around USD 8 billion; worker's remittances and foreign investment flows dwindled by US$ 500 million and US $600 million respectively; and Pakistan had no access to private capital.

Amidst such economic crisis, General Pervaiz Musharraf took charge of government. Shaukat Aziz was appointed as finance minister in 1999 and then he became prime minister in 2004. Aziz's policy of deflating the economy to control inflation and domestic demands declined the growth rates to 2 % in 1999. The policy of privatization of state owned enterprises to tackle the balance of payment crisis was pursued like previous governments. During US invasion of Afghanistan after 9/11, Pakistan became a strategic ally of the U.S. in the war on terrorism and extremism, and consequently economic and military aid again flew in. The IMF approved new aid and previous debts were rescheduled. This foreign aid, like in the past, created a "bubble-boost' in the economy; and so in 2005 the economy again began to slow down as it proved to be ill prepared to cope with sharp rise in global food and petroleum prices. Trade deficits rose to US $15 billion in 2008 from US $10 billion in 2007, and inflation rose to 22% in 2008-2009.

In 2008, the Pakistan People's party once again came into power after the assassination of the party's leader in December 2007. The assassination of a popular political leader plunged the country into an extremely uncertain state. Government's failure to find viable economic strategy to address economic issues of Pakistan together with global financial crunch has deteriorated the living conditions and exacerbated the incidence of poverty.

Capitalism's Challenges in Pakistan
The previous section has given an overview of Pakistan's economic policy that it has pursued under different military and civilian rulers. This section is dedicated to the analysis of the economic policy decisions taken in the backdrop of various factors and their bearing on the economic performance of the country. Further, it will also discuss the reasons why growth could not penetrate the lower echelon of society and the socio-politico environment which was not favorable for market

economy as individual rights were seriously curtailed, corruption and bribery culture vitiated the notions of open competition, justice, equality and freedom, and the rule of law.

Pakistan was largely an agrarian nation at the time of independence in 1947 with manufacturing sector almost nonexistent. This situation was further exacerbated by two predominant factors, i.e. the absence of national bourgeoisie and the composition of the ruling class which was drawn largely from rich landholders, tribal chiefs, civil bureaucrats and military officers. The economic policy of a country reflects upon the social structures and political complexion of the country.

The liberal private sector led growth model was introduced in 1950s and gathered pace in 1960s. It was just once rolled back by Bhutto's government in 1970 but since its revival in 1980s general thrust of economic policy has remained unaltered. Pursuing the same policies, the growth rates in Pakistan are very different in different periods of time. Since 1980s, neo liberal reforms underpin the economic direction of Pakistan but income disparities widened and growth remained concentrated to upper echelons and could not penetrate to lower echelons of society.

The question arise do neoliberal policies have some inherent flaws or are there factors pertinent to Pakistan which relegated the positive effects of neo liberal policy and aggravated the economic situation of Pakistan? This question can best be answered by examining the socio-politico-economic environment in which the initiatives were taken.

After just one year of its inception, Pakistan lost its "father figure." Formative years were subject to political upheaval and power struggle among military, bureaucracy and feudal lords. Since its birth, Pakistan has had the problem of corruption, political patronage, favoritism, and military interventions, which time and again curbed the political rights of people and weakened the institutions of country and did not develop democracy, which is *sine qua non* for the neoliberal reforms.

Political Patronage: Among the biggest problems of Pakistan is the patronage politics, which seems to be deeply rooted in the structure of Pakistan. Instead of promoting meritocracy in public sector employment, the appointments made on political affiliations and favoritism led to inefficient performance of the public sector. Dr. Mehboob Ul Haq, in an interview with Professor Anatol Lieven of King's College, has given an apt description of this state-of-affairs (10/12/1988):

> And every time a new political government comes in they have to distribute huge amounts of state money and jobs as rewards to politicians who have supported them, and short term populist measures to try to convince the people that their election promises meant something, which leaves nothing for long-term development. As far as development is concerned, our system has all the worst features of oligarchy and democracy put together.

The political parties, after coming into power, instead of focusing on infrastructural and human development initiatives, become embroiled in distributing favors and protecting influential groups, which can espouse their inefficient political policies and help them complete their terms in office despite all their inefficiencies and incompetence.

Military Interventions: The Pakistan military is the best institution of the country because of merit-based induction and promotion coupled with superb professional training and conduct. The military considers itself the best guardian of the national interests and thus will overthrow the elected governments on the charges of corruption and inefficiency. Continuity, certainty, and transparency could never be embedded in the political and economic structure of Pakistan and the absence of these is the real anathema to market based economy. Moreover, like all political parties, military also controls some of the largest business conglomerates in the country (Baker, 2005). Like politicians and businessmen in the country, rich generals also have foreign bank accounts. It seems the country is cursed to have ruling elites – either civilian or military- who are thoroughly corrupted.

Human Development: Hussain (1988) notes that subservient population is a big reason that ruling elites can get away with their corrupt practices. The educational system, like all other systems in the country, has perpetuated class divisions and reinforced segmentation. English medium schools charge exorbitant fees which only upper- and upper-middle-class people can afford, while the children of the poor go to state-run schools that are deprived of basic facilities and qualified teachers; and thus the children of poor end up with apprenticeship in workshops from very early ages. The children of the rich - who are educated at private English medium schools to go to foreign universities - come back to Pakistan to run family businesses, or occupy political offices occupied from generations after generations, and thereby carry on the legacy of injustices and inequalities of the existing system. Others from the upper-middle-class who do not have large business conglomerates or political inheritance take hold of top professional jobs in the country and become embroiled in self-enrichment. Almost half of the population is illiterate, as the official literacy rate of Pakistan is 58% in 2012. Intensity of deprivation is reported 53.4%, while the percentage of those who are vulnerable to poverty is 11% and those living in severe poverty make 27.4 percent and living below poverty line make 22.6 percent of the population (UNDP, 2011). Human development index for 2011 is .504 according to UNDP 2011 report. Above 60 percent of population is living in rural areas of Pakistan where incidence of poverty and illiteracy is more heightened so populations with such characteristics cannot be expected to look much different from the description of Hussain (1988).The poverty allows the poor to sell their votes for few free bags of flour, and at other times on the promises by politicians of getting their children low paid jobs like lower division clerk in some public sector institute or enterprise.

Large Land Holding: The concentration of land in the hands of small proportion of the rural population appears to be the main cause for the exploitation and misery of the rural poor. Land reforms legislation passed in 1959, 1972, and in

1977 does not impinge upon the concentration of lands. In rural areas, the access to land is the expression of social status as well as economic and political power. The large concentration of landownership is being regarded as prime obstacles to sustained growth and economic development. Therefore, demand for radical land reforms is seen as crucial on the grounds of social justice as well as a pre-requisite for economic development. This was the reason that the "green revolution" could not remove the impoverishment of the small farmers because nature of technology favored the rural elites with large irrigated lands.

Hussain notes, "The new technology made it possible to accelerate agricultural growth substantially through an 'elite farmer strategy', which concentrated the new inputs on large farms. Now the crucial determinant in yield differences became not the labor input per acre in which small farms had been at advantage, but the application of the seed-water-fertilizer package over which the large farmers with their greater financial power had superior access. Thus, the technocrats felt that the Green Revolution had made it possible to accelerate agricultural growth without having to bring about any real change in the rural power structure (Hussain, 1988:178).

Though division of lands among family members has changed the shape of the feudalism still it has many years to go to disentangle the power of land holdings through subdivisions generations after generations. Furthermore, landlords diversified their assets in urban property, and businesses still exercise huge influence on Pakistan's politics.

Low Value-added Export Goods: Industrialists in Pakistan always focused on low value-added products making Pakistani export market highly vulnerable to fluctuations in the international market. Pakistani policy-makers proved to be hostage of powerful lobbying of industrialists for low value added products and simple consumer durables instead of high value added, labor intensive products and high tech capital goods. Pakistan could have expanded the textile industry by producing labor intensive garments but it forewent the lucrative opportunity as the industrialists earned profits from producing low value added yarn from home grown cotton procured at subsidized prices and exporting the yarn in international market at world prices.

Moreover major protected industries belong to political parties, so only they reap benefits of subsidies and other measures. For instance, sugar is the second largest agro based industry in Pakistan owned by politicians and more than 50% sugar is being produced in sugar mills owned by politicians, so sugar industry enjoys high protection.

Reduction in import tariffs has its own implications on Pakistan's economy. When import tariffs were reduced to 25% in 2004 from 125% in 1992 (World Bank, 2006) the domestic market suffered a huge loss as it was unable to compete with cheap imported products. This resulted in closure of various industries and huge job losses along with decrease in tax revenue for the government. Lesser trade restrictions at the time when there was a need to provide protection to domestic market and encourage new industries to take off proved lethal for the economy. Every developed country promoted their national industries through subsidies and tariffs and did not practice free trade when they were in developing phase (Chang, 2003).

Corruption: Corruption is widespread in Pakistan. To get the right things done, one has to "cut" private deals with enforcing agencies or with the agents of influential higher-ups. Corruption cases regarding the political parties and military are now an "open secret." All political leaders and military higher ups have foreign bank accounts and properties. They have made millions of dollars from direct appropriation of state assets or indirectly by avoiding paying what was owed to state and have moved all their money to foreign countries and because of this country has lost billions of dollars. Legal and judicial mechanisms are so painfully slow that people would bribe officials to get their work done to avoid obfuscations, unnecessary delays and complexities. Businessmen are favored by politicians by giving state loans which will be written off ultimately in return for different favors to politicians and political parties by these businessmen. Corrupt officials are protected by politicians to get part of the deals made by these officials. Tax evasion has become a norm because of the tacit arrangement between unscrupulous tax officials and tax evaders of business class. Regressive taxation has further accentuated the impoverishment of the salaried and lower income class. The incidence of indirect taxation falls proportionately on all classes, but it is practiced in Pakistan as the contribution of both productive sectors of Pakistan, i.e., agriculture and manufacturing, and thus is negligible in tax generation and accounts for only 4 percent of GDP.

Summary

The attempt to introduce neoliberal policies in Pakistan aggravated the economic performance of the country in the absence of land reforms and laxity in fiscal and monetary policies. Only those domestic industries were given protections which were owned by political parties, like the sugar and textile industries, and import tariffs were lowered in a time when industry was in dire need of protection from government, which harmed the local industry to great extent.

In the political economy of Pakistan, rent-seeking activities of a narrow minority of influential elites drawn from the landlords, political parties, the military civil servants, big businessmen, and the professional class proved to be the main stumbling block in securing access to public services by the poor and their acquisition of physical and human capital

Hussain (2009) aptly described the economic growth model of Pakistan as the "elitist" growth model. We can see variety of capitalism working in different western countries with different names. Every country has tried to reconcile capitalism's challenges and the state's role in different ways. But in Pakistan, unlike other progressing nations, the state's role in the provision of equality of opportunity is negligible. On the contrary, some administrators and legislators are looting the country along with strong ties with other powerful groups in the country.

The role of state in economic development of the country is pivotal in that the state acting as regulatory body tries to correct the failures of the market; and also its role is crucial in the redistribution of wealth being generated in the economy. The state also safeguards the interests of masses by protecting the property rights and guaranteeing easy access to justice. The corruption, political patronage, plutocracy in the guise of democracy, feudalism, and the concentration of wealth in few hands, all are contributing to the declining economy of the country. *Capitalism seems to open up further avenues of corruption for the elite and the ruling class of Pakistan.*

In the backdrop of current globalized world, only those developing countries are able to grow which have shielded their economies from global capitalism through market interventions and in some cases through central planning. We can see the example of China, which is able to show a positive growth trend amidst global financial crunch. Pakistan needs to improve its exports, which could not penetrate in foreign market because of nature of products which are agricultural based as well as producing low-tech products. Government needs to realize its role in administration of laws and regulations, the provision of infrastructure, and modernizing market frameworks in accordance with changing circumstances.

Chapter 14

Singapore's Capitalism

Noel Fernandez, Ramkhamhaeng University, Thailand

Singapore is an island country in Southeast Asia with a total land area measuring about 273 square kilometres. Singapore is located in a major sea route between India and China, and is made up of 63 islands. Singapore has a population of approximately 4.8 million made up by the three official ethnic groups of Chinese, Malay, and Indian origins. Due to its ethnic diversity, the country has four official languages: English, Chinese, Malay, and Tamil. Singapore got its independence on August 9, 1965. It is a unitary, multiparty, parliamentary republic with a Westminster system of unicameral parliamentary government.

Introduction

Singapore is governed on the basis of a strong state and prioritizing collective welfare over individual rights like freedom of speech. This form of governance has been criticised by many people and organisations, like Freedom House, which ranks Singapore as "partly free" (Freedom House, 2010). The President, who is ceremonial, is elected through a popular vote and has veto powers on limited key decisions like national reserves and the appointment of judges. Parliament is the legislative arm of the government (Singapore Academy of Law, 2007). The country is led by a Prime Minister.

The Singaporean economy majorly relies on exports and the refining of imported goods, especially in its manufacturing sector, and has one of the busiest ports in the world. It has a highly developed market-based economy characterised by free, innovative, competitive, and friendly business practices (Li, 2010; The EuroCham, 2010; World Economic Forum, 2009). It was one of the original Asian tigers along with Taiwan, Hong Kong and South Korea. Singapore is the only Asian country with a credit rating of AAA from the three major credit rating agencies and was ranked the second freest economy in the world in 2011 (Fraser Institute, 2011). The country's economy also depends on tourism, and to this end has legalised gambling, developed casino resorts and marketed itself as a medical tourism destination. Singapore has the second largest casino gambling market in the world, is ranked as the fourth world leading financial centre and is the leading oil trading centre in Asia (Singapore Economic Development Board, 2012). Due to its corruption-free environment, low taxes, skilled labour force and advanced infrastructure, it has been able to attract great amount of foreign direct investments. Singapore uses the Singaporean dollar as its currency. The currency is issued by the Monetary Authority of Singapore.

Cultural Orientation

Singapore is a very diverse, multi-ethnic society composed of 77% Chinese, 6% Indian, 15% Malay, and expatriates making 2%. Due to the diversity in the country, people in Singapore speak different languages, and their religions and culture are seldom delineated according to ancestry or skin colour (Knights and Willmott, 2007). Those who speak English are seen as leaning towards Western culture. Those who speak Chinese, who are the majority, embrace the Chinese culture and Confucianism. The large percentage of Chinese in Singapore makes Confucianism background dominant (OPPAPERS, 2012). Confucianism believes in the stability of the society based on relations between people. In Confucianism relationships are based on mutual and complementary obligations. Under this background there is a chain of command with centralized power where managers rely on their bosses and rules for guidance and instruction, and junior employees also expect to be told what to do. This makes Singapore a collectivistic society where people tend to belong to a clan, family or organisation. Communication in a collectivistic society like Singapore is direct, and conflicts are avoided at all costs, with politeness taking precedence over honesty (Xueying, 2009).

According to Hofstede's 5-D model, of power distance, individualism, masculinity, uncertainty avoidance and long term orientation, Singapore is a collective society where modesty and humility is important (Hofstede, 2012). Generally conflicts are avoided with harmony and sympathy for the underdog is encouraged. Support for the community and individual respect is important. Singapore has an uncertainty avoidance score of 8 with its people considering their nation a fine country and almost answer 'fine' for everything. The country's long term orientation is linked to the Confucius teaching of societal virtue where the society exhibits a future oriented approach over short term oriented approach (Black, 2003). Singapore exhibits societal virtues such as perseverance, thrift, being scant with resources, and sluggish results. As their Western counterparts look for the truth, Singaporeans lay emphasis on virtue with open options to problem-solving. When Westerners believe that if party A is right then party B must be wrong; the people of Singapore and Southeast Asia often believe that both A and B can be combined to give superior results.

Cases of Corrupt Practices

Most professional Singaporeans speak English, are hard-working, well-educated and loyal. These professionals adhere to rules and processes. The professionals tend to adhere to these rules because the consequences of deviation are dire. The Confucianism culture is so dominant that instructions are followed religiously and without question (Zuliani, 2011). The employees depend on receiving instruction which they follow because a deviation would mean humiliation and guaranteed failure. Everyone wants to "play it safe" in Singapore; no instructions often means no work. There is no passion in the Singaporean work place because people sit around and wait for instructions. Most institutions and organisations are against individuality and individual rights and freedoms (Soek-Fang, 2001). Singapore's single party dominance offers a model of authoritarian capitalism. Because of the economic success in Singapore, the effects of authoritarian capitalism have been ignored. In an authoritarian capitalism, commerce is politicized when the profitability of the economic participants depends on the relationship that they have with the ruling party (Paul, 2003). This relationship overrides the efficient use of resources.

An authoritarian capitalistic regime is characterised by a heavy government intervention in the economy (United States Country Review, 2010). The fact that people are accustomed to following instructions and are compliant with the courts has led to a situation of lawless order; and that is why the corruption levels in Singapore are low. Under authoritarian capitalism, politics is also criminalized with the opposition to the ruling party being accused of criminal defamation for criticizing the actions of the ruling party (World Bank, 2010). To some extent, the involvement of the government in the country's economic activities has helped Singapore become one of the least corrupt countries in the world. The country's ruling party, People's Action Party (PAP), leads through consent; this means that policies are implemented on consensus. This gave Singapore a second ranking worldwide for government efficiency in 2010 (IMD World Competitiveness Yearbook, 2010). While her Western counterparts have diluted their capitalistic ideologies to give their citizens equality and social welfare, Singapore has stuck with the conventional liberalism, where social inequalities are justified and social welfare is provided by non-governmental institutions (Gittins and Tiffen, 2009).

Summary
There is lack of freedom in an authoritarian capitalistic nation like Singapore (Dimitrov, 2009). Freedom should therefore be encouraged in Singapore to increase the current levels of efficiency, innovation, and competitiveness. As much as the country can be described as free, government involvement in and the politicization of commercial activities should be at a minimum (Berteaux, 2005). The awarding of government contracts should be on merit and not pegged on the organization's loyalty to the ruling party. Democracy and freedom of speech should also be encouraged, and intimidation and criminalization of opposition abolished.

The workplace culture of workers depending on instructions should be minimized and employees should be encouraged to find solutions without waiting for instructions from their seniors (Immanuel, 2003). Individualism should also be encouraged to some extent, so that people are not afraid to venture out individually. The consequences of not following the laid down procedure should also be made less dire so that people are not afraid to "think out of the box." People should be encouraged to be innovative and at the same time loyal and obedient to their superiors (Gary, 2004). This will ensure that culture is not compromised and at the same time innovation, efficiency, and competitiveness are improved.

Chapter 15

Thailand's Sufficiency Economy

Acheraporn Plangmarn

Rajamangala University of Technology, Lanna Lampang, Thailand

We live in the age of markets. While markets have been around for thousands of years, we are just beginning to understand their power for organizing society and creating value. In the last 200 years, markets have unleashed a tremendous amount of innovation and progress in the West. The industrial revolution, the rise of consumerism, and the dawn of the global marketplace have each in their own way made life better for millions of people. Many of us now know comforts, skills, and technologies that our ancestors could only dream of. Alongside these great strides forward, are a set of deeply troubling issues. Capitalism and markets have also notoriously increased the divide between the rich and the poor, both within and across nations. In the pursuit of innovation, we have become blind to some of the harmful consequences of our actions on others, such as environmental degradation, dominance of less privileged groups, and the inequitable distribution of opportunities. The seeds of these deeply troubling issues are beginning to germinate. Global warming, global financial crises, and global terrorism threaten to destabilize our world. It is more imperative than ever to carefully study and understand the power of markets and capitalism (Freeman, Martin and Parmar, 2007).

Capitalism in South East Asia

With the world's three largest economies (namely the USA, China, and Japan) situated within the Asia Pacific region, and with regional gross domestic product (GDP) representing a major proportion of global GDP, the global economic, social, and environmental landscape will be significantly influenced by the cultural values, societal practices and operational environment of the Asia Pacific region. By the end of the 19th century, Thailand had been fully integrated into the world economy. The Thai monarchy signed the Bowring Treaty with Britain in 1855 and, thereafter, 14 more international treaties with other countries (Ingram, 1971). The treaties allowed foreign capital to establish business in the country and engage in domestic and international trade. Thailand's early integration into the international economy pushed the national state at the forefront in the development of domestic capitalism.

Since attempts to build a manufacturing sector ran counter to the roles the countries played as sources of raw materials and markets of manufactured goods in the traditional international division of labor, domestic manufacturing only prospered under the cover of state policies that mediated between international capital and domestic elites. The new set of industrial development policies reflected the new regime's more open attitude toward foreign investments.

Thailand's Culture[6]

Thailand is part of the eastern cultural tradition; and thus the Thai society possesses certain Asian cultural components. Thailand is considerably different from Western societies in terms of fundamental values as well as work-related values. Some of Thais' dominant values tend to be caring for others and the quality of life. In particular, the Thai people are more collectivist and more accepting of power than people in the United States. Thailand also has a more "feminine" culture in that Thai people tend to prefer more nurturing behavior over assertive conduct and they make more of an effort to avoid situations of uncertainly. The social structure in Thai society respects its elders, superiors, and patrons. The social status, seniority, and personal connections govern the relationships in Thailand. There are more community influences in Thailand; and core values are considered to be collectivistic, fatalistic, and externally power controlled. Thais give priority to maintaining good relationships since loyalty and trust to seniors are important to them, rather than task achievement and material rewards. Naturally, there are reciprocal obligations in Thai culture, that is, the relationship between superiors and subordinates means that there tends to be obligations on both sides. The Thai subordinates expect to be treated with respect by their bosses. Thais also place a great deal of emphasis on living and working in a pleasurable atmosphere, while also fostering a strong spirit of community through pleasant and congenial social relations.

The authority aspect of Thai culture is reflected in its education system, which stresses memorization and the taking of copious notes in lectures. Another key concept in Thailand is taking another person's feelings into account. A very important norm is that the lower ranks must respect the superior. Another expression of this relationship is gift-giving and gift-receiving, which in Thai society are very important acts. When one gives a gift, or does something to benefit another, the recipient of this gift or favor, is obligated to do something of benefit in return.

In the collectivist culture of Thailand, it is the duty of everyone (employees, for example) to accumulate BUN in order to belong to the merit group. In return, the manager should recognize the good effort and work from the subordinates. Furthermore, for Thai people in a collectivist environment, it is important to satisfy the group, to give more rather than less; working with the BUN

---

[6] This section is coauthored with Bahaudin G. Mujtaba and Frank J. Cavico, Nova Southeastern University as well as Peter Williamson and Bob McClelland, Liverpool John Moores University.

(do good things) means you will receive good things in return, and that is how the team works with enthusiasm. In Thailand, which is a high power-distance culture, the emphasis is on the Patron-Client, superior-subordinate relationship, which entails a traditional, formal, hierarchical structure. The Thai culture can be considered more feminine than some western countries like the United States, with greater value placed on maintaining warm personal relationships with a Patron-client situation. The relationships in the Thai society require obedience and respect for one's managers. Of course, superiors are expected to reciprocate by taking care of their employees and treat them with respect.

Capitalism in Thailand

In the early 1970s, the Thai state had transformed itself into a full-blown capitalist state (Hewison, 1990). What demarcated this earlier period from 1972 and beyond was the shift in the direction of promotional toward export manufacturing activities and the development of more liberal incentives for domestic and foreign investors. A corollary to the drive to expand industrialization for both external and domestic markets was the push to bring in more foreign capital. During this period, the country's economy was more closely linked to the global economy. The proportion of exports and imports was equal to one-third of GDP, and this caused the Thai economy to be more vulnerable to changes in global situations. For example, in 1973, there was the oil price crisis, which caused stagflation. The government adopted a direct income transferring approach through job creation in rural areas, in order to alleviate poverty. Fiscal reserves were utilized for this purpose.

In 1982-1991, the country had gained more political stability, but was facing several domestic problems due to the second oil price crisis, excessive external (public) debt burden, trade and current account deficits, in addition to the world recession. The incidence of poverty was relatively high at about 20.6 percent of the total population in 1981. Factors attributed to rural poverty were lack of education, poor health and sanitary conditions, malnutrition, etc. Therefore, the development plans set multiple objectives emphasizing the restoration of economic growth and stability, and income distribution. To achieve these objectives, the government employed both fiscal and monetary measures, such as restricted public expenditure at 17-19 percent of GDP and set ceilings on external borrowing, currency devaluation, structural adjustment, coupled with promoting consumption of Thai goods, and export promotion.

During the 1990s, the country modernized, but also faced rapid socio-economic changes and fierce competition in the global economy. Each National Economic and Social Development Plan, from the First to the Seventh, had a similar concept regarding planning and social development that relied heavily on the public sector role – people were considered only as "manpower input" in the production process (Teokul, 1999).

Financial crisis and Sufficiency Economic

Until mid-1997, the dramatic growth of the Asian economies was widely regarded as a miracle, and Thailand was part of this miracle as well. Within a day, the Thai government was forced to abandon the peg of the baht to the dollar on July 2, 1997, as a result, the currency crisis spread rapidly throughout the region and beyond.

Now, more than ten years have passed since the financial crisis. In many ways, an air of normality has returned. But, despite the recovery, it is perhaps time to look back at the causes of the crisis, the lessons learned, and what can be done to prevent the crisis from happening again. As a result of the financial crisis, His Majesty the King Bhumibol Adulyadej advised Thai people to change their economic philosophy in order to cope with present economic adversity and withstand economic insecurity. His Majesty's words have become very well known as the philosophy through which the royal has remarked on many occasions over the past three decades. The philosophy provides guidance on appropriate conduct covering numerous aspects of life that will lead to a sustainable way of living, and also to be able to meet the challenges arising from globalization and other changes. This applies to conducts starting from the level of the families, communities, as well as the level of nation in development and administration so as to modernize in align met with forces of globalization. "Sufficiency" means moderation, reasonableness, and the need for self-immunity for sufficient protection from impact arising from internal and external changes (Bunyasrie, 2010).

The "Sufficiency Economy" concept then brought into public's interest and was taught and implemented nationwide. The government played a key role to support this concept by assigning local government agents to be the liaisons between the government and the locals. The goal of adopting Sufficiency Economy concept is to sustainably develop the economy based on a principle of self-reliance (Sathirathai & Piboolsravut, 2004). "Sufficiency," according to this concept, means to lead a reasonably comfortable life at all times, without any excesses, or overindulgence in luxury…the key is to know one's limitations and realize when enough is enough (Ninnart, 2010).

During the Tenth Plan, the Philosophy of Sufficiency Economy was applied extensively in Thailand's development, resulting in greater resilience in various aspects of Thai society, enabling Thailand to cope effectively with the impacts of the 2008 global economic crisis. This achievement was well reflected in the Green and Happiness Index (GHI) of 65-67 percent, with contribution from strong economic performance, high employment, strong communities and family ties. However, major obstacles remain, such as political unrest, environmental and ecological degradation, low quality of education, and severe drug problems. The evaluation of the Tenth Plan also indicated improved economic foundations for development and increasing quality of growth. Quality of life has improved with better access to various economic and social security measures and gains in poverty reduction. It is, however, essential to emphasize the development of human capital and human security, promotion of good governance and fair competition, and distribution of development benefits in order to reduce social inequality. During the

Eleventh Plan (2012-2016), Thailand will encounter more complicated domestic and external changes and fluctuations which present both opportunities and threats to national development. Thus, it is necessary to utilize the existing resilience of Thai society and economy, and to prepare both individuals and society as a whole to manage the impacts of such changes and pave the way toward well-balanced development under the Philosophy of Sufficiency Economy.

Implications

Development in the financial and capital markets through the sufficiency economy perspective primarily lies in the need to foster the country's immunization against external volatility. The country should promote higher levels of domestic saving, and lower levels of dependence on external capital. Equally important is the development of efficient and diversified capital markets with sufficient instrument in order to make balanced choices, while borrowers should have appropriate mechanisms to tap long-term domestic savings. At the same time, strong financial institutions should be able to manage external volatility to the level that it is not harmful to the organizations and the overall system. Strength of financial institutions can be instilled through promotion of good governance and ethics among financial executives (Bunyasrie, 2010).

Summary

Thailand's development has led to a society that is too receptive of external influences without enough screening and sufficient institutional preparation. While opening to trade and capital flows have benefited the country in its development and growth, negative effect of external volatility need careful assessment and management.

The fundamental approach to the sufficiency economy is the holistic adaptation of attitude, behavior, and way of life both at the micro and macro levels. It emphasizes being satisfied with what is considered enough, minimizing greed, being reasonable, and applying moderation. It enables people to better cope with external and internal shocks and live more sustainably. The philosophy is not against, but in support of, the market economy regime.

The concept of good governance embodied and implied by the philosophy could verify that it, in fact, complements the market economy philosophy. Thailand will be able to develop with a balanced strategy so as to modernize in line with the forces of globalization while shielding against inevitable shocks and excesses that arise as a result of it.

Chapter 16
Uganda and Entrepreneurship[7] Education

Terrell G. Manyak, Nova Southeastern University
Isaac Wasswa Katono, Uganda Christian University
Warren Byabashaija, Makerere University Business School

Uganda is a comparatively small East African country that is roughly the size of the United Kingdom or the state of Oregon. It has a population of 35 million with a median age of 15 years. For decades, Uganda's economy has suffered from devastating economic policies and political instability, leaving it one of the world's poorest countries. Some strides have been made in the last quarter century to improve life in Uganda. Under the controversial leadership of President Yoweri Museveni, the country's economy has grown at approximately 7 percent despite the world economic downturn. A number of factors account for this positive economic picture. The country has been politically stable for 25 years, mineral and oil deposits have been discovered, self-sufficiency is largely maintained in agriculture, and strong financial support continues from the international community.

The Ugandan[8] Culture
The cultural foundation of Uganda evolves out of a diverse range of ethnic groups that make up this East African country (Manyak and Mujtaba, 2013). While English is the official national language of Uganda, the east, central and southern regions are dominated by Bantu-speaking peoples, most notably the Buganda. In the north, the Lango and Acholi people speak Nilotic languages while the languages of the Iteso and Karamojong in the east are of the Nilo-Hamitic group. Uganda has a very young population with a median age of 15 years. Universal education is a legal requirement in Uganda, but only two-thirds of the population over 15 years of age is considered literate.

Ugandan culture contrasts markedly from the American culture. For instance, Ugandans feel more comfortable with a "Kiganda" approach that emphasizes ties to a collectivity, respect for social structure, good manners, and

---

[7] An earlier version of this material appeared in the *Review of Business Research*, 12(4), 16-31 by the same authors.
[8] This material on the Ugandan culture is coauthored with Bahaudin G. Mujtaba, Nova Southeastern University. See: Manyak and Mujtaba, 2013.

consensus building. Another example of cultural difference is in the role of women within Ugandan society. Ugandan women reflect the broader African culture in terms of facing more disadvantages than men because of entrenched patriarchal attitudes and practices. In Uganda, it is common to hear demeaning phrases like, "Are you a woman?" when a man fails to meet performance expectations.

While Ugandan and American cultures are unquestionably distinct, broader global forces may be bringing them closer together. From the Ugandan perspective, many Western practices have been adopted as a consequence of the country's British colonial past. More recently, Ugandan culture has evolved due to the widespread availability of information over cyberspace highways. Radio, television, cell phones, and, increasingly, Internet services are becoming available in even the most remote areas. Most important, Ugandans living in the economic center of Kampala exhibit individualist values that are associated with Western economies. Moreover, despite entrenchment of the patrimonial social structure, women are emerging as a force in the political and economic life of Uganda. Women contribute 50 percent of GDP and own 39 percent of registered businesses. They also represent 80 percent of the unpaid workforce.

The forces of globalization are also bringing about changes in the American work force. Many high-context cultural practices have been introduced as employers encourage their employees to work collectively in achieving organizational goals. The role of women in the workforce has also changed. Similar to Uganda, the number of working women is expected to increase by 9% between 2006 and 2016 to comprise 47% of the U.S. labor force. While the percentage of women in the labor force is increasing, women in both countries remain under-represented in management and have yet to achieve wage parity.

Entrepreneurship Education
These positive economic statistics hide a serious problem that inhibits the long-term economic health of the country. Uganda has virtually no indigenous entrepreneurial middle-class to build and sustain a capitalist society. Entrepreneurship is dominated by Indians working through companies in Kenya. Larger businesses are owned by South African and an assortment of European and Asian companies. The infamous Idi Amin attempted to change this situation by forcibly removing Indians from the country and giving their businesses to his cronies. These businesses quickly failed and, following Amin's fall, Indians were invited to return, but they never returned in their original numbers or economic dominance. The point is that Ugandans have never played a significant role in the capitalist life of the country and have never learned to be entrepreneurs. At best, they aspire to be shopkeepers who open small stores that are exactly like the stores in the next block, hardly rising to what one thinks of as capitalist style entrepreneurship.

The Uganda government is actively seeking to build an entrepreneurial culture through an ambitious education program. Beginning in 2000, the Uganda National Curriculum Development Center added entrepreneurship as a required subject in all secondary schools. The goal was to reduce youth unemployment by building the student's ability to be innovative, creative, flexible, and self-driven in building their own futures rather than relying on the government for employment. While the goal of the curriculum reform is admirable, it does raise interesting questions about the teachers of entrepreneurship. Does it make a difference in building entrepreneurial values in students if the teacher has never owned and operated a business? What part do institutional and cultural factors play in developing a desire to become an entrepreneur in Uganda?

These questions were examined through a country-wide survey of 244 teachers of entrepreneurship that focused on studying personal attributes, intent to be entrepreneurs, and the institutional and cultural factors that might intervene in bringing intent to fruition.

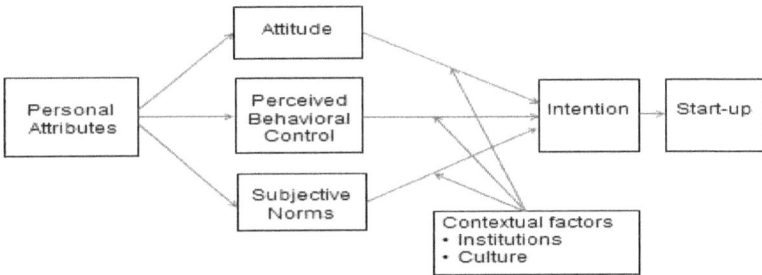

Figure 16.1 - Research Model

Personal Attributes
The research literature has long debated whether entrepreneurs are "born" or are "made." This same debate extends into identifying the attributes associated with successful entrepreneurs. Is the capacity to innovate a trait developed early in life or shaped in response to the social context of the individual? Do entrepreneurs have higher internal locus of control than non-entrepreneurs? Is there a specific skill set associated with being a successful entrepreneur? While these questions cannot be answered in this study, the attribute variables can be used to determine if Ugandan teachers of entrepreneurship that have entrepreneurial experience differ from those teachers with no experience. Thus a research questionnaire, based on the work of Canizares and Garcia (2010) and Linan (2008), was administered to the study population. The results clearly show statistically significant differences ($p < .05$) between the two groups. Teachers who had started businesses scored much higher than their fellow teachers with no experience in terms of creativity to solve problems and enthusiasm to start new projects. They also show an even greater

difference (p < .01) in expressing a desire to be an entrepreneur and in terms of their locus of control being much more internally oriented.

Intent to Become an Entrepreneur

The next stage of research utilized the Theory of Planned Behavior (Ajzen, 1987) which contends that intention to become an entrepreneur is the best predictor of an individual actually engaging in entrepreneurship in the future. Intention is measured by three variables:

- *Attitude* – holds a positive view toward entrepreneurship.
- *Perceived Behavior Control* – personal belief that a venture will be successful.
- *Subjective Norms* – support of family and friends in becoming an entrepreneur.

Using a 20-item questionnaire (Linan & Chen, 2007) and step-wise regression, the data analysis found that perceived behavioral control (p < .001) had the strongest value in explaining the lack of intent to start a business among teachers with no entrepreneurial experience. Attitudes toward starting a business had slightly less explanatory value (p < .005) while the Subjective Norms reflected in the support of family and friends had no value in predicting intention to start a business.

Institutional Factors

This phase of the research model utilizes the assertion that country institutional patterns, such as government regulations and access to funding, help to determine the entrepreneurial drive toward innovation. Indeed, the World Bank Doing Business Index (2011) ranks developing countries like Uganda very low in having systems and policies in place to assist entrepreneurs. To measure this variable, five items developed by Busenitz, Gomez, and Spencer (2000) were included in the questionnaire. The results show that institutions did negatively moderate the relationship between perceived behavioral control and the intention to start a business for those teachers who have not started businesses. While the Beta weights were positive, institutions had no statistically significant effect in moderating attitudes and subjective norms toward the intention to start a business.

Cultural Factors

Culture represents the shared values and beliefs that affect the emergence of entrepreneurs in a society. For example, studies show that entrepreneurs exhibit tendencies toward high power distance, low uncertainty avoidance, high individualism, and high masculinity (McGrath, MacMillan, Yang, and Tsai, 1992). These differ dramatically from African culture that emphasizes social order, respect for tradition, and family security. The tendency is to avoid unnecessary risks (Onuejeougwu, 1995) and restrain actions that might disrupt the traditional order (Munene, Schwartz, and Smith, 2000). To examine risk taking, the study utilized Yoo and Donthu's (2005) cultural orientation instrument. The results show that uncertainty avoidance moderates the relationship between perceived behavioral control (self-confidence) and intention to start a business, while no significant moderation was found in the case of attitudes and subjective norms.

Discussion

All teachers in Uganda are poorly paid. With the government's unwillingness to address the problem, sit-down strikes are common and teachers are left to fend for themselves in terms of their immediate and long-term financial security. The expected reaction, particularly for teachers of entrepreneurship, is to start a business on the side. The question then arises, why would a teacher trained in entrepreneurship hesitate to enter a business venture? Something must be holding them back.

Based on the research findings, one inhibiting factor is personality attributes. The results show that teachers who have started a business are more creative in solving problems and are more inner-directed in terms of local of control. They are more enthusiastic about starting new projects and are also better at networking and making professional contacts. Another inhibiting factor is how teachers of entrepreneurship perceive institutional and cultural problems in Uganda. Those teachers who have not started a business, with their low sense of perceived behavior control (self-efficacy) reinforced by outer-directed locus of control, have more difficulty handling challenges like the shortage of resources and other institutional problems that inevitably face business start-ups.

Summary

The study confirms that significant differences do exist between teachers of entrepreneurship who had set up a business and those who had not. Those teachers who had entrepreneurial experience show positive attributes of innovativeness, skills, and locus of control. These are the very attributes that are needed to overcome the institutional and cultural barriers that confront entrepreneurs in starting a new business. If certain teachers of entrepreneurship lack these attributes, how can they be expected to stimulate these desired attributes in students?

What good is it to teach entrepreneurship if many of the teachers who lack the necessary personal traits, self-efficacy, and inner-directed locus of control reinforce the cultural belief that any new entrepreneurial enterprise is most likely doomed to failure. Moreover, given the high institutional and cultural barriers that confront entrepreneurs in countries like Uganda, the government needs to find ways to reduce these barriers to make the teaching of entrepreneurship more effective.

Chapter 17

Venezuela: Corruption and the Bolivarian Revolution

Guillermo Gibens, Sp Jain School of Global Management
International Academic City, Dubai, United Arab Emirates

Venezuela's transformation from an agricultural producer to an oil producer has dramatically changed the social, political, and economic environment of the country from its inception as an independent nation to the current state of affairs with the late President Hugo Chavez. Corruption has been a malady that exploded especially after the 1950s with the advent of the well-built oil industry, democratic governments, and the growth of capitalism propelled by a strong middle class. The advent of Hugo Chavez in 1999 under the promise of wiping out corruption infused new hopes for a new kind of clean democracy among Venezuelans. Nevertheless, the late Hugo Chavez's administration had fallen into the same corruption patterns.

Introduction

On June 21, 1821, Venezuela cut its ties with the Spanish empire in South America and became an independent country. After 10 years of war, the colonial power of Spain surrendered to the Venezuelan forces under the command of Simón Bolivar, the Venezuelan Liberator.

From that moment onwards, politics and the economy would remain intertwined in the history of Venezuela. First, it would be the agricultural production of the late 19th century and early 20th century, then it would be the discovery of petroleum with the first oil well drilled in 1914 (Organization of Petroleum Exporting Countries, 2012), followed by efforts in the 1940s to democratize the nation's government.

Throughout these years, Venezuela transformed itself from an agricultural producer to an oil-rich country that would sustain a viable industrialization within the different economic sectors of society. But, the industrialization and the oil production, in addition to a society not very well adapted to the practice of a free-market capitalism, would create a fertile ground for the practice of paying additional amounts of money to gain access to a preferred status with governmental organizations. This would guarantee that your product or services would be given preferential treatment, or services that one requires from the government would be expedited.

This chapter is an attempt to explain how Venezuela was transformed from Spain's colonial producer to a modern capitalist nation with an infection of corruption and bribery that has permeated all segments of Venezuelan society. Even at the end of 2012, the Chavez government that back in 1999 came to power with the goal of fighting the "cancer" of corruption has succumbed to the addiction. Are there solutions in sight? An exploration of some tactics is offered in the conclusion of this article.

History of Capitalism in Venezuela

Darlene Rivas in her book *Missionary Capitalist: Nelson Rockefeller in Venezuela* (2002) described in detail Rockefeller's struggle to introduce capitalistic practices in Venezuela.

When Rockefeller visited Venezuela in 1937, he thought that if the country established new and up-to-date businesses and capitalist enterprises related to agriculture, there would be consequently more food production and better circulation of supplies (Rivas, 2003). For Rockefeller, capitalism would improve people's lives.

Although at that time the oil industry was already active, the agricultural production in Venezuela was not technologically advanced, and production was very communitarian and local.

By the 1940s and 1950s, Rockefeller and his investors would realize that capitalism like in the United States would be difficult to implement in a country like Venezuela, where local merchants (difficult to call them capitalists) preferred low-risk business, and where the rural population was used to traditional forms of farming, with little knowledge of marketing practices, or technical skills needed to improve production (Rivas, 2002).

Rockefeller's efforts ended up being side-tracked by some Venezuelan nationalists that looked at his enterprises in agriculture and food distribution as a way to get the United States involved in Venezuelan domestic issues. Rivas (2002) described Rockefeller's precarious situation in the following text:

> Within Venezuela, Rockefeller's initiatives became enmeshed in local political and economic debates. The Acción Democrática Party, which ruled Venezuela from 1945 to 1948, distrusted Venezuelan capitalists and embarked on state-led development. The A.D. government invested public funds in some of Rockefeller's projects but was criticized by economic nationalists and the business community who sought to restrict and regulate foreign investment that might compete with their own interests. The Federación de Cámaras de Comercio, Venezuela's principal business organization, strongly opposed the government's policies, arguing that a modern democratic state is not able nor must it dedicate itself to activities that are reserved to the individual (p. 107).

Another military coup in 1948 put General Marcos Perez Jimenez in charge of the Venezuelan government until 1958. During his tenure, Venezuelan capitalist economy grew to the point of being considered one of the highest in the world. Figures from the late economist Angus Maddison (as cited in NationMaster.com, n.d.) indicate that Venezuela's GDP in 1950 ranked the country as #4, just after New Zealand, Switzerland, and the United States.

After the overthrowing of Perez Jimenez in 1958, Venezuela began a democratic process that would result in presidential elections held every five years. For the rest of the 20th century, the country would see an economic development that would surpass original expectations. Nevertheless, the economic boom was not evenly distributed and masses of poor Venezuelans would move to the outskirts of Caracas (Venezuela's capital) and other large cities in search of better job opportunities, and abandoning the rural areas in detriment of the agricultural production.

From the 1950s onwards, the middle-class grew up, bringing a standard of living and purchasing power that were considered the envy of many other Latin American countries. Middle-class Venezuelans were able to buy many goods and services. But at the same time, the poor continued to pay the price of an economic boom that was being controlled and dominated by the economic elites in alliance with many officials in the Venezuelan government.

Galeano (1997) indicates that the discovery and production of oil in Venezuela attracted what he called "the vultures" (p.165) in reference to the U.S. oil companies that controlled the production and marketing of the oil products in the country. At the same time, the elite controlling the marketing forces in Venezuela were being grouped into major organizations which would play a significant role in how the production and imports of goods to Venezuela would be managed to get the maximum possible profit.

Galeano (1997) illustrates the city of Caracas' metropolitan life in the 1970s with the following words:

> The capital, Caracas, has grown 700 percent in thirty years: the old city of airy patios, central and silent cathedral is covered with skyscrapers as Lake Maracaibo covered with oil wells. Today it is a supersonic, deafening, air-conditioned nightmare, a center of oil culture that might pass as the capital of Texas. Caracas chews gum and loves synthetic products and canned foods; it never walks, and poisons the clear air of the valley with the fumes of its motorization; its fever to buy, consume, obtain, spend, use, get hold of everything leaves it no time to sleep. From surrounding hillside hovels made of garbage, half a million forgotten people observe the sybaritic scene. The gilded city's avenues glitter with hundreds of thousands of late-model cars, but in the consuming society not everyone consumes (p.166).

As Venezuelans became more adapted to consumerism, corruption and bribery to find specific services or to receive preferential treatment in the acquisition of products turned "into a normal way of life" as described by anecdotal references from Venezuelans "on the street."

Many stated that corruption began at the highest level and trickled down to lower segments of the society, turning into an industry where one needed to pay more to get something fast or of the quality one wanted. Getting services from governmental offices were considered the most prone to bribery.

The Power of Corruption
One of the best observers and writers on the issue of corruption in Venezuela is Gustavo Coronel. As former director of Petróleos de Venezuela (Oil of Venezuela), commonly known as PDVSA, between 1976 and 1979, he was able to take a close and personal look at the government politics in Venezuela that have taken the nation to the corruptive path which continues to be confronted in late 2012.

Coronel (2008) represented Venezuela at Transparency International, an organization devoted to confronting and fighting corruption around the world, between 1996 and 2000. He is well recognized as an expert in the field of the oil industry and politics in Venezuela and has written significantly on the subject.

In 2006, Coronel wrote that as far as 1813, when Venezuela was at war against Spain for independence, Simon Bolivar was already tackling the issue of corruption in the government institutions. In 1824, Bolivar defined corruption as "the violation of the public interest" (p.2). Bolivar also affirmed the application of the death penalty for "all public officers guilty of stealing 10 pesos or more, including those judges who disobey these decrees" (p.2).

In his writings, Coronel (2006) strongly criticized the management of the oil industry and many other assets in the 1970s that were conducive to an enormous web of bribery within the government institutions. He added that the government invested almost $2 million in industrial projects, including about 300 companies. Coronel defined this time as the moment when government, political and economic elites lost control of the graft.

Coronel (2006) goes on to say that in the 1980s corruption continued to be rampant. From 1984 to 1994, about $36 million were "pilfered or stolen mainly through a corrupt exchange control program" (Ruth Capriles as cited in Coronel, p.3).

The Rise of Hugo Chavez
Although Hugo Chavez died in the early part of 2013 from health complications, his influence in the country and region continues. As such, it is important to provide some information regarding his rise to power.

Against this backdrop, the figure of a little known army officer who tried to overthrow President Carlos Andres Perez in 1992, was sent to prison for rebellion, and pardoned two years later by President Rafael Caldera, came to participate in the 1998 presidential elections. Since 1999, Hugo Chavez has been holding the presidency of Venezuela, and he recently was re-elected for six more years beginning in 2013.

But Coronel's (2008) criticism of corruption has continued. In his report he has estimated that in nine years after taking office, the Chavez government has received $700 billion in total revenues, but where that money has gone is uncertain. Coronel said, "This formidable amount of money is nowhere to be seen in terms of public works or effective health and education programs" (n.p.)

Even though Chavez came to power promising to wipe out corruption within the government, during his administration there have been three major areas of corruption: grand corruption, bureaucratic corruption, and systemic corruption (Coronel, 2006).

Grand corruption is the result of many significant policy decisions made by Chavez. Examples of those are, for instance, the acceptance of foreign contributions to support his presidential campaign in 1998 and 1999, promises of oil subsidies and other expenditures made to political leaders in the Americas to gain their loyalty, and the acquisition of a new presidential airplane at the cost of $65 million (Coronel, 2008).

Bureaucratic corruption occurs at the level of government bureaucracy. Examples are the awarding of government contracts without a proper bidding process, accusations of public funds pilfering in the acquisition of a building for the Supreme Tribunal of Justice, and political decisions made by the National Electoral Council that always favor the Chavista groups (Coronel, 2008).

Systemic corruption, according to Coronel (2008), occurs when the government and the private sector cooperate in a way that funds change hands without any control. Examples include private corporations owned by officials in the government that receive preferential treatment from the Chavez administration, the emergence of a new class of individual that is a socialist revolutionary but behaves and act like a capitalist by purchasing goods symbolizing wealth and economic power (Hummers, Rolex watches, etc.), and the drug-trafficking between Colombia and Venezuela, where corrupt border officials allow the crossing without any transgression to international laws.

Summary
Since the early years of an independent Venezuelan nation, the corruption disease has permeated Venezuelan governments. But obviously, the discovery and development of the oil industry has brought to the illness to levels never seen before. The Chavez's promise to end up the corruption of the previous democratic governments made in 1998 during the presidential elections has never been fulfilled.

With Chavez's death in 2013, the coming year looks a difficult one for Venezuelans, according to anecdotal references made by some Venezuelans. Corruption and crime are expected to continue. Is there any hope for Venezuela? The answer is a definite "yes." However, many political scholars, Coronel (2008) and many common Venezuelans believe that eliminating corruption will take more than just a change of president. It will need a government that is willing to prosecute and jail those involved in bribery without any leniency and in strict accordance to the rule of law. Hopefully, the new leaders in Venezuela are going to start with a serious commitment to ethical education of all public servants and the enforcement of all applicable laws.

Chapter 18

Vietnam: Capitalism in the Socialist Republic

Lam D. Nguyen, Bloomsburg University of Pennsylvania

The Socialist Republic of Vietnam, or Vietnam in short, is one of the ten members of the Association of Southeast Asian Nations (ASEAN). Vietnam has a population of about 90.5 million people, of which almost 70% are in the age range of 15-64 years. There are 58 provinces and 5 municipalities (major cities) including Ho Chi Minh City and Can Tho in the South, Hanoi (the capital), Hai Phong in the North, and Da Nang in the Central region. Vietnamese is the official language while English is increasingly referred to as second language. Other commonly spoken languages include French, Chinese, Khmer, and mountain area languages (Mon-Khmer and Malayo-Polynesian). The Vietnamese government is considered as a communist state.

Introduction[9]

Unlike the general perception of the country as a poor, underdeveloped country which was damaged heavily during the war, Vietnam today is a developing country that has been one of the fastest growing and the most promising economies in Asia over the past decade with an average annual GDP growth of 7.6% between 2000 and 2009 (Business Monitor International, 2011, p.13). As a part of the global economy, however, the Vietnamese economy has been negatively impacted by the global recession, which has reduced its GDP growth rate to less than the 7% per annum average between 2009 and 2011 (Central Intelligence Agency, 2012). The IMF has recently projected a 5.1% GDP growth in the coming year for Vietnam (International Monetary Fund, 2012).

Since its adoption of an economic reform called "Doi Moi," or renovation, a shift from a centrally planned economy with a high level of state ownership and frequent government interference to a market economy in 1986, Vietnam has opened up its economy to the world, and attracted a large volume of foreign investment. The business environment has improved significantly as the result of the government commitment to the global integration. With this economic reform and global integration, the author has seen a significantly positive change in

---

[9] Some of the concepts in this chapter come from coauthored publications with Bahaudin G. Mujtaba and Frank J. Cavico, Nova Southeastern University.

Vietnam: steady economic growth, reduced poverty, and more prosperity over the past decade.

Since its formal normalization of diplomatic relations with the United States in 1995, followed by the U.S.-Vietnam bilateral trade agreement (BTA) in 2001, Vietnamese government has achieved several key economic policy goals and attracted many domestic and foreign investors with its large, skilled and low cost workforce (Business Monitor International, 2011, p.23). Trade between Vietnam and the U.S. has grown tremendously. Figure 18.1 shows the U.S. trade in goods with Vietnam from 1995 to 2011. The total trade volume in 1995 was $451.30 million and in 2011, the trade volume reached $21,796.20 million

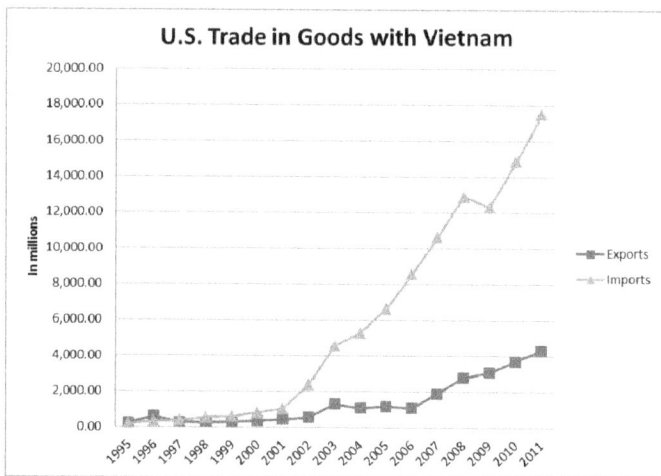

Figure 18.1 - U.S. Trade in Goods with Vietnam
Source: United States Census Bureau (2012)

Vietnam's economic development reached another milestone when it joined the World Trade Organization in January 2007. Vietnam becomes a strategic partner and plays an important role in South East Asian region as well as in the world economy. Facing the global recession, Vietnamese authorities continue their commitment to international integration and an open market economy. At the beginning of 2012, Vietnam has planned a major restructuring of public investment, state-owned enterprises and the banking sector in order to maintain and sustain its macroeconomic stability and strengthen its economic growth (Central Intelligence Agency 2012). In the July 2012 report, IMF has projected a good growth prospect in Vietnam as a result of tightened macroeconomic policies, rapidly declined inflation, increased confidence in the Vietnamese Dong, and recovered international reserves

Vietnamese Culture
Vietnam has an extremely rich and diverse culture. Vietnamese local culture, a "fairly large cultural community," was formed thousands of years ago. Through its long history of being under the control of foreign countries, the culture of Vietnam has also been strongly influenced by the Chinese culture as well as many other cultural features from countries in the region and from the Western cultures. Despite the mix of unique cultures, Vietnamese culture can be referred to as high power distance, high collectivism, moderate uncertainty avoidance, and high context.

Vietnam: Capitalism, Corruption, and Bribery
Vietnam has emerged as a country where big firms are going to take advantage of the educated and available workforce. However, human resources managers and senior managers are often perplexed with the decision of doing business when they see the Transparency International ranking of Vietnam in terms of their Corruption Perception Index scores. In 2011, Vietnam had a CPI score of 2.9 and ranked 112 out of 183 countries. In contrast, China has a score of 3.6 and ranked 75 while New Zealand having the best ranking with a CPI score of 9.5 out of a possible 10 points. Vietnam has a Global Competitiveness Index Score of 4.24 out of a possible 7 points and ranked 65 out of 142 countries.

Vietnamese President, Tran Duc Luong, once said: "Corruption is taking place every day and every hour, at all places, all the time" (as cited in Maitland, 2001). Corruption is nothing new to the world of business, especially in developing and transition economies (Goldsmith, 1995; Ksenia, 2008). It is a global challenge. Vietnam, with its recent economic reform and global integration, is no exception. Vietnam's CPI score of 2.9 out of 10 possible points suggested that it may experience serious issues with corruption. Multiple sources, such as the United Nations Development Program (UNDP) and the World Bank, have confirmed the seriousness of corruption in Vietnam.

Corruption is commonly defined as the misuse of public office for individual gain (Mujtaba, 2011; Maitland, 2001; Svensson, 2005). It happens when an official accepts, solicits, or extorts a bribe (World Bank, 1997). It could be the sale of government property by government officials, kickbacks in public procurement, bribery and embezzlement of government funds (Svensson, 2005). Vietnam's Anti-corruption Law (Clause 2, Article 1) states that "Corruption is the behavior of individuals with status and power who take advantage of their position and power to commit actions against the law in their own interests" (CECODES, 2011).

Corruption is a by-product of capitalism coupled with bad governance; and it has a direct negative impact on economy. According to the World Bank (1997), the causes of corruption rooted in a country's bad policies such as poorly designed economic policies, bureaucracy, political development, weak and inefficient public institutions, and social history. Corruption hinders the economic growth. It can lead to a waste of resources, such as capital, technology, and talent. Corruption negatively impacts ethical standards and civil servants. It can destroy the trust that the people have for the government.

Though corruption is not a new concept in Vietnam, it has been increasingly visible and become more seriously discussed since "Doi Moi" economic reform. In 1995, former Communist Party's General Secretary complained about the rising corruption and deteriorating morality of state officials (Maitland, 2001). According to the 2000 World Bank report, there were approximately 50,000 calls of alleging corruption and government inefficiency made through a complaint hotline established by Prime Minister Phan Van Khai in 1998 in its first year. Most of the corruption cases involved the transfer of public rights to private ownership, which is typical in such a transitional period of time from central planning to a mixed market-economy (Maitland, 2001). Bureaucracy, centralized state management, large control of the SOEs, and ambiguous laws and regulations are among factors that make corruption blossom (Gibson Dunn, 2011). In a survey conducted by the Centre for Community Support Development Studies, two areas that are most vulnerable to corruption are land management and construction projects (CECODES, 2008). Corruption can be seen at any level of the state authority hierarchy, from wards to districts to cities/provinces. It can also be seen in governmental ministries, departments, agencies, and in public sector organizations. A 2005 diagnostic study on corruption in Vietnam found that a third of the public officials and civil servants admitted that they were willing to accept bribes, and half reported that intermediate and higher level offices were involved in corruption (Gibson Dunn, 2011).

The Communist Party, National Assembly and the Government of Vietnam have acknowledged the seriousness of corruption and its threat to the survival of the regime and determined to punish corrupted individuals fairly and strictly regardless of their position and status. Vietnam has taken many specific actions to fight against corruption. In December 2003, the General Inspector of the State of Vietnam, authorized by the Prime Minister, signed the United Nations Convention Against Corruption (UNCAC). This affirmed the determination and the willingness of the Vietnamese government in joining the international community effort to fight against corruption. The UNCAC was approved by the President of Vietnam in June 2009 and became effective in September 2009 (Do, 2010). In November 2005, the National Assembly passed the Anti-corruption Law, which came into effect in June 2006. The new law included measures for preventing and controlling corruption, as well as for detecting and punishing corrupt behavior. Despite the determination of the government and the establishment of legal framework, anti-corruption efforts and laws are poorly carried out and not enforced. Lack of a proper governance mechanism such as a check and balance system is among the top reason. Below are several corruption cases in Vietnam that made national and international headlines.

In 2005, Luong Cao Khai, the head of Vietnam's anti-corruption inspection taskforces to inspect four projects invested in the state-owned oil and gas giant Viet Nam Oil and Gas Corporation (PetroVietnam) and deputy head of the State Inspectorate's Division of Economic Inspect, was arrested and charged with corruption and abuse of his office. He was accused of receiving money and land from some officials of PetroVietnam in exchange of lessening the gravity of wrongdoings committed by the company, and abusing his position to provide relatives with jobs in the sector.

A special political corruption scandal that drew national and international attention was the Project Management Unit 18 (PMU 18) scandal. PMU 18 is a $2 billion internationally funded bureau within the Ministry of Transport whose main responsibility is to manage road construction and other infrastructure projects. In 2007, top officials of PMU were accused of spending public funds for personal reasons. Former General Director Bui Tien Dung was charged with embezzlement, gambling and organizing gambling, bribery, and deliberate violation of the law while other executives were charged with embezzlement, abuse of office, bribery and brokering bribes, and irresponsibility (CSR Asia, 2007). In 2009, Dung and several of his accomplices were further accused of "deliberately acting against the State's regulations on economic management, causing serious consequences" and "abusing positions and power while performing official duties" (Vietnam News, 2011). As a consequence, Dung has to serve 23 years in jail. Transport Minister Dao Dinh Binh was forced to step down and his deputy, Nguyen Viet Tien, was arrested. The charge of corruption against Tien, however, was later dropped due to lack of evidence.

Another corruption case that attracted international headlines was the East/West Highway Project Management Unit within the Department of Transport of Ho Chi Minh City. The case was linked to the corruption case of Tokyo-based Pacific Consultants International (PCI) Company, of which some officials were found guilty of bribing Vietnamese officials and violating Japan's competition law. In 2007, four officials declared that during the implementation of the Official Development Assistance (ODA)-funded East/West Highway Project in Ho Chi Minh City, they gave $820,000 to Huynh Ngoc Sy, Vice Director of the Department of Transport of Ho Chi Minh City and Director of the East/West Highway Project Management Unit, to win a consulting contract. Sy was sentenced to life in prison but was later reduced to 20 years in prison. Sy's bribery case had resulted in a suspension of millions of dollars in ODA loans from Japan to Vietnam in December 2008. Vietnam's reputation in international community, its attractiveness in receiving development loans from foreign countries, and its efforts in the fight against corruption and bribery, were in jeopardy. The ODA loan was, however, resumed the next year.

One of the corruption cases in Vietnam which involved foreign companies was the Nexus Technologies Inc., a Philadelphia-based export company. The U.S. Department of Justice (DOJ) filed charges against Nexus and its four employees-Nam Nguyen, Kim Nguyen, An Nguyen and Joseph Lukas- in a superseding indictment in October 2009, with conspiracy, violations of the Foreign Corrupt Practices Act (FCPA), violations of the Travel Act in connection with commercial bribes and money laundering (U.S. Department of Justice, 2010). According to court documents, based on the needs of the Vietnamese government and other companies operating in Vietnam, Nexus identified U.S. vendors for contracts of a wide variety of equipment and technology. They admitted that "from 1999 to 2008 they agreed to pay, and knowingly paid, bribes in excess of $250,000 to Vietnamese government officials in exchange for contracts with the agencies and companies for which the bribe recipients worked." The bribes were disguised as "commissions" in the company's records (U.S. Department of Justice, 2010).

The most recent case involved Securency International Pty Ltd., an Australian-based company which was alleged to bribe Vietnamese government officials to secure a contract for printing *Dong,* the Vietnamese currency. Australian federal police investigated the allegation that Securency used its agent, a Vietnamese company which employed the son of the Governor of the State Bank of Vietnam, to make unspecified amounts of improper payments to the officials. The case, which is ongoing, has not been recognized by the Vietnamese government (Thomson Reuters Foundation, 2011; Gibson Dunn, 2011).

According to the Inspectorate Deputy Chief Le Tien Hao, inspectors probed 333,000 state organizations and individuals and found violations related to mineral resources, land use management, construction investment management, banking, and the use of capital. They proposed $308.5 million and 3,188 acres of land revoked by the state as well as administrative punishment of up to $12.2 million (Vietnam News, 2012a). Especially in the first six months of 2012, forty-nine cases of corruption in state organizations and companies with a total value of $6.3 million were uncovered. Of the $6.3 million, only $285 million had been recovered. Six heads of state organizations and companies were punished; twenty-seven cases and thirty five people were under criminal investigation; 8 groups and 29 people would receive administrative punishment. The Ministry of Public Security has also found 248 corruption cases involving property worth nearly $32.5 million and 572 people. Only $620,000 of property had been recovered and up to 260 people would be prosecuted.

Implications and Recommendations
With the acknowledgement of the country leaders that corruption is a key constraint on the economic growth and that it imposes a serious threat to the survival of the regime, anti-corruption initiatives have been implemented and a legal framework has been established. A wide range of measures has been introduced to reduce bureaucracy, increase transparency and accountability, and provide clarity to administrative decision making. More rules and regulations have been set to control and prevent corruption and bribery such as the self-declaration of income and assets of cadres or civil servants. Prime Minister Nguyen Tan Dung confirmed positive results from the fight against corruption since the beginning of 2012. According to him, the government inspectors have discovered more corruption cases and they have dealt with these cases strictly (Vietnam News, 2012b). The Vietnamese government has striven a long way in fighting corruption but there are still many challenges ahead.

First of all, corruption in private sector has been unnoticed. Existing laws do provide framework for bribery cases involving government officials. However, private companies cannot prosecute corruption in the criminal court. Though Vietnam had signed the UNCAC, it made some exceptions such as not criminalizing illicit enrichment, not recognizing evidence from overseas, and extradition under Vietnam laws (Thomson Reuters Foundation, 2011). Thus, it is recommended that Vietnam should consider corruption in private sector as seriously as in public sector. The Anti-corruption law should establish bribery and embezzlement of property in the private sector as criminal offense, as well as illicit enrichment.

Secondly, Vietnam lacks effective control mechanism. Under current procedures of legal implementation, the appointed Head of Anti-corruption Steering Committee is also head of the local authority. It is more likely that conflict of interest may happen (CECODES, 2008). Vietnam should have a "checks and balances" system to make sure the anti-corruption efforts are implemented fairly and objectively.

Thirdly, there is a lack of cooperation and control between people and the government in anti-corruption efforts. The general public has not involved much in the measures and enforcement of the laws and legal framework. Though the law has specified the involvement of civil society groups and citizens, the general public still does not cooperate with government because they may worry about the possible negative consequences of their involvement and there may be lack of incentives and encouragement. Fear of the retaliation is among common reasons for not standing up for corruption. Thus, it is very important to provide strong protection and reward measures for whistleblowers.

Fourthly, transparency is the key to "winning the fight" against corruption. Government agencies and administrative offices need to develop and maintain clear communication channels with the general public and among each other, share information and provide guidelines to engage people in the anti-corruption process. Government should make self-declaration of assets and income of public servants a legal requirement.

Fifthly, low wages and lack of monitoring systems are great conditions to nurture corruption and misuse of public resources. This can lead to lack of qualified and motivated personnel in anti-corruption agencies. Though money is not the sole motivator in preventing corruption since corruption also occurs on a larger scale when it comes to high ranking officials and wealthier people, compensating people reasonably and fairly according to their qualifications, skills, experience and costs of living, providing them with proper training and job security, recognizing their contributions and rewarding them accordingly, can help recruit individuals who are qualified for the job.

Sixthly, more international cooperation is recommended. Vietnam needs to promote and take part in the global cooperation in anti-corruption. Vietnam should recognize evidence from overseas and be willing to prosecute its own officials if their corruption threatens the economic relationships with foreign partners. Its law on corruption and bribery should be applied to employees of international organizations.

Summary

The commitment and determination of Vietnamese government toward the war against corruption need to stay firm and strong. Government officials and leaders need to set examples and build strong relationships and trust with the general public, businesses, and the global community if they are to benefit from a transition toward a mixed economy and capitalism.

The fight against corruption and bribery needs concerted efforts and cohesive collaboration at all levels, and the best way to initiate anti-corruption efforts is by having all public employees attend ethical education and development workshops.

Chapter 19

Immorality's Impulsiveness and the American Healthcare

Mario E. Delgado, Rural Development Specialist/USDA

Capitalism is likely to bring changes quickly to any society. The first part of this chapter explores how people must adjust their perspectives and conduct towards life to adapt to significant changes in their environments. People of a country and the society in general must accommodate unexpected changes and unintended consequences in order to progressively move forward.

The second part of this chapter explores how nations, the same as individuals, will never cure health failures by addressing symptoms instead of the underlying root causes. The American health sector offers a clear example of how challenging capitalism can be when some people depend on work insurance, others pay their own costs, and some depend on the hospitals to treat them for free as the costly expenses cannot possibly be repaid. The author explores some of the causes for such challenges and offers practical solutions to these underlying issues.

Immorality's Impulsiveness: An Inevitable Outcome

Historical evidence shows that individuals as well as societies can adjust their perspectives and conduct towards life to adapt to significant changes in their environments. Both can accommodate not only to planned, but also to unexpected changes and to unintended effects, which can be positive and negative. They may not capture net benefits at all, but adapt, justify and even resign they do.

For example, individuals and societies have adapted to the transition from environments of economic self-sufficiency with limited product specialization; small and semi-isolated communities and limited physical mobility, to intensive and extensive products specialization; large and mega-large urbanizations and expansive mobility. Moreover, in today's rapidly expanding dependency on computer technologies with their continuous updates; the Internet; mechanization / "robotization," and global social and economic networking and integration, they're shifting their tolerance for change and adaptability to a new dimension - a dimension requiring a revision not just in perspectives towards life, but also to its intrinsic meaning as well.

No change is free of trade-offs or foregone opportunities and some trade-offs may even have higher benefits than the chosen alternative. Moreover, change could even generate net losses relative to the original conditions. But in all possible scenarios, and as long as the motives and methods are well intentioned and constructive, the participating individuals and societies will ultimately adapt if not thrive. Yes, instability derived from an honest mistake in alternative selected is adaptable to. However, if attempted changes are rooted on immoral principles and processes the whole scheme won't survive unscathed and will ultimately implode. Initially the damages may fall exclusively on the intended victims and impact just the scheme in question, but ultimately immoral conduct will spread like a contagion throughout the entire society victimizing the instigators as well. There will be no adaptation, only relentless disintegration through exponential cultural contamination.

For example, compulsive materialism, cultural, military and economic imperialism, slavery, discrimination and exploitation of populations, physical and psychological abuse of family members and the elderly, and environmental degradation that we face today, all are cases in point. They embody the spread effect of individual and social immoral decisions made in the past. Decisions disguised more than likely under banners of competitiveness, market needs and national interests, but with immoral underpinnings from the start.

Let us elaborate on some of their underlying evolutionary principles by addressing a couple of these issues on the next few pages.

Urban Congestion and Suburban Sprawl
These conditions originate out of the excessive production and product specialization fueled by the drive of entrepreneurs to concentrate resource so as to capture the required economies of scale for maximum profitability. Entrepreneurs and producers at the start of the innovation era (circa 1700s) in production technologies (e.g. iron-ore foundries) weren't satisfied with a moderate amount of surplus output to trade with. Instead, greed led to the production of unlimited levels of output and to as wide an access to new products and resources as possible. This push for an insatiable expansion of markets at any social cost spread urban concentrations and ultimate congestions nationwide.

After the advent of the car, the participating economic agents began rejecting the negative quality of life from congestion. They started to move away from the urban centers and into outlaying suburbs creating in turn traffic congestion, extended commuting time and stress related responses such as road rage and generalized states of anxiety. Also the improvements in the quality of life from access to affordable substantive products became negated once consumerism became focused on waves of superfluous/ephemeral products. All along, the environment, the participating labor and affected families, as well as the directing economic agents became victims in return. To these effects we may add an endless circle of frauds, scams, markets manipulations, and political opportunism, all under the cover of progress.

Slavery

So as to maximize agricultural output, minimize their physical labor and maximize their socio-economic power and prestige, large landowners during the early colonial days bought and exploited slaves. Along the way and also to maximize their returns, the owners readily divided enslaved families by selling their members together or separate, including the children. Further, when slavery was abolished, no real efforts were made to upgrade the skills and open meaningful opportunities to the now free families. They were instead segregated, discriminated, and economically exploited under different disguises.

Today the "minority" classifications and the "affirmative action" programs have continued to serve as tools for discrimination through "accepted stereotypes" and employment based on "token" opportunities. These hypocritical approaches have left growing segments of the population disenfranchised and despondent towards the culture in general. This in turn continues promoting cultural instability, racial and ethnic anger with escalating immoral conduct justified under rationalizations of redress, catch-up and political "responsibilities". The spread effect and contagion like impact of immorality makes its presence extend well beyond its initial application. It ripples into the general culture through a "social multiplier" like effect.

Adaptability is a Moral Imperative

Adaptability to immorality is impossible because it automatically promotes an escalating decay in values and conduct that are never satiated. It engenders by its nature, an endless perpetuation of abuses and excesses focused on short term and short sighted selfish ends. Immorality by implication and as it spreads, leads to an exponential growth in the number of socio, economic and political agents exploiting in increasingly creative ways everyone within reach. Ultimately, the majority of a nation's population for lack of trust in others and from survival needs becomes, the termites demanding from and consuming the existing institutions and structures until the entire national frame collapses on itself.

Immoral values and behavior, by nature and design, promote in all participants a generalized lack of trust that undermines the faith not only for each other, but towards human nature as a whole. If on top of these dynamics, the cultural ethos becomes dominated by materialism, which by nature is never satisfied or satisfying; the downward social spiral is precipitous and ultimately final. There is in this disastrous mix no ultimate acceptance and adaptability to normal change. Every conduct is relativized and rationalized to meet the next impending escalation in greed and mistrust. There is no long term perspective, because only the things close at hand and rapidly attainable can be counted with. In individual materialistic pursuit for fulfillment under a materialistic and immoral framework, there's no letup in the rate of detrimental change until there is nothing else to compromise and no one else to scam. And as the predominant values and conduct go, so goes the nation.

"Every system brigs the seeds of its own destruction" so a communist proverb goes. These "seeds" however aren't particular to specific system, but universal and uniform to human immoral conduct. They originate from the drive by mankind towards an unbounded individual search for power and wealth. They generate a headlong dash that engenders immoral values and conduct with their inevitable destructive implosive outcomes for both the innocent and the guilty.

Let us not shape our conduct to fit a superimposed molds derived from immoral justifications and premises. Immoral conduct is unreliable, opportunistic and without boundaries, in other words, un-trustworthy at any level or application. Instead let's orient our path in consonance with our intrinsic moral light so that our independently derived behavior converges autonomously into constructive and stable human development paths. Further, errors resulting from intentions framed within moral guidelines lead to corrections and adaptations in due time. Errors derived from immoral principles and processes lead to generalized social decay and the ultimate destruction of cultures in general. Such is the path where we find ourselves today.

The Unhealthy Health Sector: The Patient and not the Potions
Nations, the same as individuals, will never cure health failures by addressing symptoms while leaving untouched, if not reinforcing, the underlying real causes (e.g. diabetes and insulin vs. changes in lifestyle to include diet and exercise). Addressing symptoms as causes not only wastes scarce resources, but also complicates the dynamics of the problems and contributes to disguise their genesis. Our health sector offers a clear example of such misguided attempts and the resulting failures. Even after all our scientific advances on health matters, and the large investments by both the public and private sectors in containing and eradicating health risks, we remain on a deteriorating downward spiral. We continue suffering without abatement from a host of cardiovascular diseases, obesity, cancer, drug addiction, depression, diabetes, and complications from teen pregnancy and abortion, among others.

Further, in the health sector as well as in other national systems such as the political, social and economic, the fundamental causes and ultimate solutions rest in deeper terrain. They reside with individual and cultural determinants and not in monetary, fiscal and regulatory measures. For our health sector in particular, if not also for the remaining national systems, the three overarching causal forces behind its dire and deteriorating conditions must be discussed. First, there is an overall lack of individual moral values which promotes a permissive, relativistic and opportunistic stance towards life's challenges. This perspective leads individuals and groups to incoherent and destructive behavior, both mental and physical, towards the self and others. Second is the demise of the integrity and strength of the intact family unit, which leads to individual dysfunctional behaviors within a permeating state of latent anger and frustration in its members. This condition also destroys the availability of constructive role models of behavior for present and future generations. Third, there is a pervasive materialistic culture where economic wealth and not well-being frames most social, economic and political contexts.

Where "power grabs" trumps principle, show stances supplants substance and existential anxiety if not despair, color most daily activities.

The following sample of symptoms afflicting the health sector puts in perspective both the magnitude of their negative impact on the overall economic growth of the nation, and the failure of attempting to cure a disease by addressing symptoms instead of the underlying causes. Some of the main symptoms can include the following:

1. Health care expenditures growing very rapidly in and of themselves and as a share of Gross Domestic Product (GDP). Accounted for 5% of GDP in 1960 and jumped to 18% of GDP in 2011. Since 1980 it has been growing by 1.4% a year and if this rate is maintained it will account for 62% of national income by 2105 (The Economist; "An Incurable Disease", p.82, Sept.29, 2012).
2. Demand for health workers and facilities outstripping their existing supplies.
3. An ever expanding use of expensive tests utilizing advanced medical technologies and procedures to include surgical ones. This is in an attempt by doctors and hospitals to limit their exposure to expensive litigations and to expand profits.
4. Hospitals obliged to treat emergency cases even if patients cannot pay.
5. Entitlement attitude by unable to pay patients contributing to a "moral hazard" condition. Such condition promotes a riskier unhealthy lifestyle that adds to the cost crisis.
6. Expansion of insurance coverage generating not only a "moral hazard" effect on life style but also on demand for unnecessary medical services.
7. Since 1980 costs have risen by 440% for a university education and by 250% for medical care. In turn the average of consumer prices rose by only 110% and the average for wages by 150% (The Economist; "An Incurable Disease", p.82, Sept. 29, 2012).

As it can be observed from this list of symptoms, the cost crises also belongs not just to the demand, but to the supply side of the health market as well. It is also plain to see the contribution from government regulations to the escalation of costs. Fortunately, individual choices and conduct ultimately determines the size of government and its degree of interference with market forces. Hence the latter does not become an inevitable condition if the individual takes a constructive and responsible hold of life choices.

The key causal variables behind the ever-expanding health costs can be classified into a set of five major factors. These factors are interdependent and also correlate in a positive direction. The factors and some of their most prominent component variables are environmental, institutional, cultural, materialism, and family-related.

1- Environment factor includes:

- All categories of health damaging spillover costs such as air, water, noise and visual pollution.
- Health damaging food growing and processing practices through the application of pesticides, fertilizers, hormones, antibiotics, and preservatives.

Hence, the private gains captured by individual producers are ultimately negated through widespread damages to the natural and human resources in the eco-system. All of society ends up paying and exponentially, as the damages accumulate and spread directly and indirectly to unrelated products and producers both private and public.

2- Institutional factor includes:

- Medical fraud, malpractice, and incompetence.
- Limited supply of providers and facilities from licensing and higher education restrictions on numbers.
- Immigration quotas and restrictions.
- Incompetent and negligent oversight from the U.S. Congress and from responsible federal and state regulatory and systems compliance bodies.

Hence, protectionism from competition limits the available supply of health products and services, increasing their cost and limiting their geographical availability. Moreover, lax public auditing and lack of preventive controls from oversight bodies including Congress, adds to the negative impacts from Factor No.1 above.

3- Cultural factor includes:

- Chronically depressed citizenry from an over stressful lifestyle.
- Absence of unifying common cultural values and goals. Nation's mood is more representative of a "boiling" pot than a melting one.
- Unhealthy school cafeteria menus and the prevalence of both processed and fast food nutrition in the typical family diet.
- Very short school days leading to unsupervised latch-key children and/or inadequate family/adult supervision after school.
- Discriminatory hiring and promotion practices hindering economic opportunities and depressing the self-concept in members of the afflicted groups.

Hence, the aforementioned factors contribute to a self-destructive lifestyle including health and mental deteriorations. Diets compromised for lack of parental and school supervision, from budgetary priorities and short-cuts and from adult negligence.

4- Materialism factor includes:
- Individual dissatisfaction with the cultural compulsion over consumption and emphasis on the acquisition of superfluous products.
- Generalized anxiety from the endless increase in the rates of change in technological innovations, production processes and communication networks.
- Job instability and businesses/industries fragility from exploding and unmanaged global competition.
- Supersizing of "junk" food offerings at most fast food outlets.

Hence an unfulfilling and unsettling "consumption-driven" life misallocating budgets, time and natural resources. It also engenders pervasive feelings of dissatisfaction with life in general, while propitiating the neglect of self, family and community gestalts.

5- Family factor includes:
- Dysfunctional family environments from parental absence and/or immaturity and incompetence in child rearing practices.
- Relegation of acculturation to the advertising industry, sit-coms and social media all appealing mostly to the lowest common denominators in the culture.
- Delegation of fitness to video games.
- Pugnacious cognitive conflicts between youth and adults as well between real and virtual worlds.
- Unsupportive if not destructive families diluting the motivation and ability of children to succeed academically and socially, plus destroying their sense of worth and self-respect.

Hence, lacking the stability and ability to provide the constructive examples needed by children to model after and to approach life with confidence and purpose. Families have become the biggest and more noxious polluters to society by dumping into the national "commons" immature, frustrated, and destructive individuals, generation after generation.

As it can be determined from these causal factors, the detrimental conditions of the health sector will not be resolved or even mitigated through mere financial and regulatory measures. These palliatives are only capable at best to cover up with layers of distraction the real determinants, while also throwing good money after bad. At a more immediate and accessible level, it is important to note that many of the variables within these factors are found, not just on the demand side of the markets, but on the supply side as well. Therefore, if the determinants of supply, such as the number of available medical facilities and the variety of medical imports were less regulated and allowed to grow more naturally, the resulting additional competitive pressure would reduce prices and costs. This reduction would make the health related products and services more affordable to a larger number of users currently dependent on public largesse, while also making the required public share of the costs less expensive.

Summary

The negative symptoms afflicting the health sector have to be addressed head-on. Resources must be allocated to obstruct their progress and prevent them from becoming of greater endemic proportions than they are already. However, their permanent eradication isn't a function of additional funds or external control of symptoms (e.g. medicines, advertising campaigns, research, etc.). The solution lies in revamping the individuals,' the families,' and the culture's underlying values, structures and conduct toward a moral and not a materialistic order. Further, to be permanent it must be done not for the obligation of it, or for survival or evolutionary reasons, but for the pure and superior heartfelt pleasure it engenders. The current overwhelming emphasis in a consumption-"stuff"-oriented and "more-of-it-is-better" lifestyle are creating the conditions listed in the section on causes above, and precipitating the continued deterioration of health with no abatement in sight. Moreover, as long as we confront just symptoms, the entrenched economic interests benefiting from the ensuing misguided expenditures will continue directing our attention to the expenditures that benefit them.

One solution lies in promoting the implementation of approaches that secure a moral answer for each of the five factors above. Practices and processes that endorse emotional well-being as the main cultural goal; that promote achieving the level of skills-preparedness required for real access to economic and social advances for all; that support the maintenance of intact and constructive families; that eliminates industrial fraud and political corruption; that promotes spiritual well-being over material wealth and that allows the private sector under a competitive regime, to provide as many as possible of the products and services required to reach and maintain a holistic life style.

Any approach less comprehensive misses the mark and leaves the nation dealing with symptoms while descending into an abysm of physical and emotional deterioration as we are experiencing today. Because of the cultural unwillingness to address causes, more and more public expenditures and controls are being exacted for less and less returns. This is the case with the healthcare as well as the remaining national systems. If we look closely at the history of the downfall of not only powerful empires but also of countries, religions and even tribes, we would come to a similar conclusion. That is, that generalized immoral perspectives and conduct and their deleterious impact on the general culture and the institution of the family were at the roots of their demise. The rest of their arguments as well as ours today are mere potions addressing symptoms, while the real health of the patient is held in a fatal denial.

Chapter 20
Case Studies for Discussion

Capitalism is not necessarily a new system and it is not a western success phenomenon as it has been used for trade across the globe for thousands of years. The countries of China and Vietnam are two examples of a mixed economy as their policy makers believe that a centralized control system combined with some aspects of modern capitalism are most appropriate for their culture and society. While there are many examples of successful joint ventures between the public and private sectors, this chapter provides several cases for discussion and reflection purposes.

The first case is the Virtual University of Pakistan, which is over one decade old now. Another case is related to the discussion of trade along with its benefits and challenges in today's global forum. Other cases deal with the recent Bangladesh garment factory tragedy and the presence and business dealings in Haiti of a large cruise ship company. Included are also case studies dealing with bribery and corruption, as well as globalization. Each case ends with discussion questions for individual and group reflection exercises.

Case 1 - The Virtual University of Pakistan
The Virtual University of Pakistan[10] (VUP), which was started through government funding and is now successfully operating mainly on its own tuition revenues, is considered to be one of the world's success stories where the public and private sectors can partner up to make education more affordable to people throughout a country. This is a socially responsible way of strategically spending public resources to make the world a better place for everyone.

There are no stockholders benefiting from the VUP initiative. However, it is a worthy project that was founded to strategically help millions of young minds become better educated for the globalized world. This case provides an overview of the Virtual University of Pakistan, along with some discussion questions at the end for reflection purpose.

---

[10] Bahaudin G. Mujtaba, Nova Southeastern University; Talat Afza and Mahmoud Bodla, COMSATS Institute of Information Technology, Pakistan.

The Founder of VUP

During an interview with the authors in December of 2012, the founder of VUP, Dr. Naveed Malik, mentioned that he was contacted by the Ministry of Science & Technology of the Government of Pakistan to spearhead the challenging education project over eleven years ago. He continued to mention that the major problem facing Pakistani higher education program at that time, and in fact currently still valid, is that we had a steadily increasing strength of students ready to go to colleges and universities, while the existing colleges and universities were already full and had no capacity to absorb all of the eligible graduates from higher secondary institutions. Besides the capacity problem, another major challenge was finding qualified faculty, even if we could accept more students into the existing colleges and universities. It was obvious that an organic solution to these challenges would not work as it would take about one to two decades to educate enough qualified faculty members for such positions. Hence a technological intervention was a necessity in order to educate the eligible population.

According to Dr. Malik, if we visualize all of the country as one university system, then we would have enough professors to develop courses which could then be used to educate additional students. As such, the idea of having a virtual university became more attractive as we could ask the existing professors to develop the course materials for their areas of expertise without actually stealing them away from their institutions. These qualified gurus would develop the right content for each course in their areas of expertise in the curriculum without necessarily leaving their institutions; and then the virtual university administrators and staff would be responsible for the management of the school.

The first four courses developed at VUP, mentioned Dr. Malik, were for the B.S. Program in computer sciences. The original target was 500 students in 18 cities and these numbers were quickly met. Initially we went into a partnership with 28 private educational institutions around the country so they could offer their infrastructure to the virtual university in exchange for a percentage of the fees collected. Now, in 2013, the Virtual University of Pakistan (VUP) operates in over 110 cities around the country, in more than 200 campuses with an enrollment of over 100,000 students living nationally and in 52 other countries around the globe.

Motivation, says Dr. Malik, is something that students have to bring with them in distance or virtual education. While many distance educational programs tend to keep students isolated, VUP does provide them regional and local campuses where students can come to study collectively and interact socially. As such, students can connect with others based on their preferences and learning styles. During the first few semesters, new students can even find mentors from among their seniors. According to Dr. Malik, some traditional students are used to the "spoon-feeding" process of professors lecturing and giving them solutions. However, in the virtual university environment, the student has to be self-disciplined and take responsibility for his or her learning, time management, and project completion. We find that virtual students tend to be self-motivated based on necessity as they have to be in order to be successful.

Regarding plagiarism, Dr. Malik explains that VUP has a policy of "zero tolerance" for it. All examinations are proctored in our regional centers, campuses or through updated technologies for overseas students. The faculty and administration also understand that this is the age of internet; and this means anyone can look up the materials and papers over the cyberspace highway. At times, this can make plagiarism a high temptation for traditional and virtual students alike. With VUP, all submissions are done online and all assignments are put through specialized software to see if any portion of the assignment is plagiarized. With such a system, plagiarism detection is higher than conventional submissions at other universities, since our online learning management system is designed for it. Overall, Dr. Malik thinks the rate of plagiarism is probably the same across virtual and traditional formats but the detection of such forms of cheating is easier and higher in the virtual world as we can easily run all submissions through various software programs which automatically provide information regarding cheating and plagiarism. Of course, one problem with software detection programs is the rate of "false positives" and it needs human oversight in order to reduce the possibility of wrongly accusing students of plagiarism. For example, properly cited materials are usually reported as plagiarism by the software and this must be reviewed by a human as it is not cheating. Overall, technology can be effectively used to enable quality students to graduate who then create value for themselves as well as their employers and society.

History of Virtual University

The Virtual University of Pakistan, which is one of the first universities around the world that is based on modern communication technologies,[11] was established by the Pakistani government as a public sector, not-for-profit institution with a mission "to provide extremely affordable world class education to aspiring students all over the country." As part of its education process, VUP uses free-to-air satellite television broadcasts and the Internet, which allow students to follow its rigorous course and programs regardless of their ability to attend face-to-face sessions or their physical locations. This process alleviates the lack of capacity in the existing universities while simultaneously tackling the shortage of qualified professors in each field of study. By identifying the best professors within the country or outside of the country in various subjects, regardless of their institutional affiliations, and requesting them to develop and deliver hand-crafted courses, VUP aims at providing the very best courses to students around the country.

VUP's degrees are recognized and accepted all over Pakistan as well as overseas. VUP opened its virtual doors in 2002 and in a short span of time its outreach has reached throughout the country serving over 100,000 students. Furthermore, VUP is associated with more than a hundred institutions providing infrastructure support to students across the country at a fraction of the cost of traditional educational organizations.

---

[11] Retrieved from Virtual University of Pakistan website: http://www.vu.edu.pk/

VUP delivers education through a thoughtful combination of broadcast television and the Internet. VUP[12] courses are designed and delivered by knowledgeable and published experts in the field. For each course's topics, professionally developed lectures are recorded at the school's studio environment and they are accompanied by relevant slides, video clips and other materials for broadcast to students. Besides being broadcasted over the television networks, course lectures are also made available in the form of multimedia CDs which are sent to registered students. These course lectures are also be made available as streaming media from the Virtual University's servers to their students.

The multiple formats allow flexibility for students who may view the lectures at a time of their choosing. In addition, comprehensive reading materials, lecture notes and other help learning tools in the form of web-enabled content are provided through a comprehensive Learning Management System (LMS) hosted on the VUP Web Servers that accessible over the Internet at any time. The LMS also provides an e-mail facility to each and every student as well as asynchronous discussion boards for interaction within the VUP community. An important feature of the LMS is a Question/Answer board where VUP faculty provides answers to questions posed by students on the subject matter covered in the lectures. The question/answer board, moderated to enhance learning, provides separate sessions for each lecture of the course. In addition, read-only access is made available to previous question/answer sessions and this constitutes an extremely useful study resource for students. VUP faculty monitors this board on a continuous basis and answers to student questions are provided regularly within a short space of time. Assignments are submitted through the LMS and graded within a short span of time so students can receive feedback as quickly as possible.

Pop-quizzes and practice tests are also conducted through the LMS. Examinations are conducted in a formal proctored environment at exam centers throughout the country. The formal examination atmosphere assists in critical quality assurance of the student assessment system. Such comprehensive learning programs and detailed focus on learning has enabled VUP's enormous success in less than a decade.

VUP Milestones

One critical point is that VUP provides an identical education to all its students regardless of their geographical location. A student can live at home to help his/her parents and work on a full-time basis, and still complete his or her educational degree in a realistic time-frame.

All Virtual University students, regardless of whether they live in large cities or small towns or even remote areas, are taught by the same professors, receive the same study materials and master the same course competencies. All

---

[12] See: Afza and Mujtaba's (2014) case entitled *"Establishing and managing a virtual university"*, Case 13, pages 285-287, in Bahaudin G. Mujtaba's 2014 book entitled "*Managerial Skills and Practices for Global Leadership*", ILEAD Academy, LLC.

these proctored examinations are identical throughout the country. This process ensures that every graduate has the same credentials and qualifications upon obtaining his/her degree.

Graduates of VUP have gone on to be accepted at masters and doctoral programs throughout the world. Many of these graduates are working in great professional jobs in Pakistan or other countries across the globe. VUP is a great success story of human intellect combined with modern technology to make learning more flexible and affordable to the general population. Some of the main milestones are presented in Table 20.1.

Table 20.1 – VUP Milestones

Important Milestones	*Year*
Inauguration & launch of BS(CS) & BS(IT) programs	March 2002
Federal Charter granted by Government of Pakistan	September 2002
Virtual University starts broadcasts of its own channels	June 2004
Selected to lead DE Research project by IDRC	March 2005
Launch of MCS, MIT and MBA programs	February 2006
Launch of 2-year Bachelor programs	September 2007
Launch of MS program in Computer Science	September 2007
MoU with University of Veterinary & Animal Science, Lahore	May 2007
Launch of VU's unique Examination System	May 2008
VU goes global – all video lectures placed on youtube.com	June 2008
Launch of VU's new e-Examination System	October 2008
MoU with MIT (USA) for BLOSSOMS project	January 2009
MoU with University of Bradford – UK	March 2009
MoU with University of Huddersfield – UK	March 2009
MoU with National University of Science & Technology, Islamabad	May 2009
Launch of Web Radio	August 2009
MoU with Karakoram International University, Gilgit / Baltistan	January 2010
First Convocation	May 2010
Lauch of Virtual University Open Course ware site	October 2011
VU's Open Courseware website declared best new OCW website of year by OCW Consortium	Aril 2012
Students based in 52 different countries	December 2012
Over 100,000 students enrolled	July 2013

Questions for Discussion

1. What is the role of government for education in a capitalistic society?
2. How can government help enhance creativity, innovation and productivity through various economic systems?
3. Should governments help universities or should universities operate only on tuition revenues from students? Discuss the advantages of each system.

4. Are virtual universities becoming the norm for learning and education? Discuss.
5. What are some challenges that virtual universities face as they try to educate students across borders and continents?
6. What challenges do the administrators face as they start virtual programs?
7. Should education be privatized in any economic structure so entrepreneurs can make a profit out of the traditional school systems? Discuss.

Case 2 - The Benefits and Costs of Free Trade[13]

Since 1980, the orthodox recipe for economic growth has been the reduction of barriers to the free flow of commerce and capital. International institutions such as the International Monetary Fund (IMF) and the World Bank have contended that the free market approach to development will create faster levels of economic growth and alleviate poverty. The integration of markets has been largely achieved through regional free trade agreements and unilateral liberalization. It has also been facilitated by deregulation, the shrinking costs of communications and transportation and the IT revolution.

Some developing countries benefited from trade liberalization. China's ratio of trade to GDP doubled. Brazil, Mexico and other middle-income countries registered large increases in their volume of trade. They managed to export a range of manufactured goods, often as part of global production networks. In China, the number of poor people (earning less than $0.70 a day) went down from 250 million (1978) to 34 million in 1999. Similarly in India, the number went down from 330 million in 1977 to 259 million in 1999.

In the case of many other nations, however, the laissez-faire approach appears to have worsened growth rates and income distribution. In 1980, for example, the medium income in the richest 10 percent of countries was 77 times greater than in the poorest 10 percent. By 1999, this gap had grown to 122 times. Many studies have shown that trade liberalization in Latin America, for example, led to widening wage gaps, falling real wages for unskilled workers, and rising unemployment. In many countries, trade liberalization, deregulated markets have induced rapid structural changes often leading to declining wages, working conditions and living standards. The challenge today is to make trade liberalization work for the poor. This requires a wide-ranging reform in national institutions and policies.

Discussion Questions

1. How can trade liberalization be made to work for the poor?
2. What can world leaders do to reduce poverty?
3. Why is the rich getting richer?
4. Is trade related to capitalism or can trade happen under any economic system?

---

[13] Contributed by Belay Seyoum, Nova Southeastern University. Initially published in Bahaudin G. Mujtaba's book entitled *"Managerial Practices and Skills for Global Leadership,"* 2014.

Discuss.

5. How long has trade between countries been around and where? Research the history of trade and provide some examples.

6. Select a country or region and evaluate its performance (GDP per capita, distribution of income, etc.) before and after trade liberalization.

7. Which countries have benefited the most from the NAFTA agreement and why? Discuss.

8. Which countries have benefited the most from the European Union agreement and why? Discuss.

9. Which countries are more likely to benefit from the ASEAN agreement and why? Discuss.

Case 3 - The Paradox of the Bangladesh Garment Industry[14]

On April 24, 2013, an eight-story garment factory building in Dhaka, Bangladesh collapsed, killing over 1000 workers, thereby bringing stark attention to the hazardous working conditions in that country, where workers for low wages sew low-cost clothing that ends up in stores around the world, including the U.S. and Western Europe. The tragedy came only months after a fire at another garment factory in Bangladesh where over 100 workers were killed.

However, the garment industry in Bangladesh is an $18-20 billion one, which provides jobs for millions of poor illiterate women, but which also, as noted, places them in danger of physical harm. The Prime Minister of Bangladesh, Sheikh Hasina, who is a woman, has stated that the garment industry is the only way out of poverty for many poor women in Bangladesh. *Bloomberg Businessweek* quoted a professor at Georgetown University who stated that Bangladesh today resembles "for better or worse...what the early industrial revolution looked like." The professor added that Bangladesh is "still a desperately poor country and we shouldn't minimize what a job with a steady paycheck means to a poor woman."

The garment industry is clearly a growth industry in the country. Bangladesh's exports of garments tripled between 2005 and 2010; and they are expected to triple again by 2020 to about $50 billion a year. One of the main reasons is low wages. To illustrate, the average monthly pay in Dhaka was $47 vs. $235 in Shenzhen, China, and vs. $100 in Hanoi. By 2010, Bangladesh had about 5000 garment factories, second only to China, and more than in Vietnam and Indonesia. By 2011, about 12% of the women in Bangladesh between 15 and 30 years old worked in the garment industry. And the pay was 13% higher than in other industries. Moreover, the garment factories favor women, who are better at sewing, and who are perceived as being more compliant. Furthermore, a Yale researcher found that many of the women of Bangladesh in the garment industry viewed their sewing jobs to be the means of getting better jobs, such as a secretary or a manager; and these ambitions are motivating more of these women to pursue studies. However, in another survey, 70% of the women workers said they were verbally

---

[14] Contributed by Frank Cavico, Nova Southeastern University.

abused by their bosses; and with mostly female workers being overseen by male bosses, reports of sexual harassment were commonplace; and actually 1/3 of the women in the survey said they had been inappropriately touched. Moreover, one-half the women surveyed said they were not allowed to take their legally guaranteed 100 day maternity leave. Some women worked right up to the last weeks of their pregnancy, and then some were fired too when they gave birth. And "breaks" to the bathroom are usually rare; and factory bathrooms are typically very dirty too. Is this what local people in poorer countries can expect from capitalism?

As a result of the recent tragedies as well as the poor working conditions, several of the world's largest fashion retailers, including H&M (which is a Swedish company and the largest purchaser of garments from Bangladesh), Zara (which is owned by Inditex, the world's largest clothing retailer, which also owns Calvin Klein and makes clothes under the Izod and Tommy Hilfiger labels), British companies, Primark and Tesco, and German retailer, Tchibo, announced shortly after the Bangladesh worker tragedy that they would support and sign an agreement designed to prevent a repeat of the tragic collapse of the Bangladesh clothing factory that killed over 1000 people. The agreement consists of standards on fire and building safety, improving worker's rights, and strengthening worker training and inspections. It is a five-year agreement that imposes strict safety requirements for suppliers and requires that regular reports be made on factory conditions. The agreement also permits the workers to refuse dangerous work. Furthermore, the agreement requires the companies to stop doing business with any factory suppliers that refuse to make the necessary improvements. The impetus for the agreement is being led by the United Nations International Labor Organization as well as trade union and other organizations. The agreement covers between 500-1000 of the 5000 factories operating in Bangladesh. The agreement calls for a governing board consisting of three labor representatives and three retailer representatives and a chairperson chosen by the United Nations International Labor Organization. The board will conduct safety inspections and make the results public. The board will also oversee disputes between retailers and union representatives, which will be subject to arbitration with decisions enforceable in the courts of law in the country of the retailers. The board will also have the power to determine which companies should pay for the repair and renovation of certain factories, which could be complicated since retailers use different factories, parts of factories, and move production around. To implement the agreement each company that signs it will pay an amount based on how much they produce in Bangladesh (but with a maximum of $2.5 million over a five-year period). H&M, it should be noted, is a major purchaser of garments from Bangladesh, but the company did not use any of the suppliers operating in the collapsed building. Nonetheless, a company spokesperson said the agreement was a "pragmatic step" and urged more companies to sign the agreement. The agreement, though, is viewed as a "first step," and many details have to be worked out, but if the agreement is to work at all, many more companies must sign it, experts and activists say.

However, other big companies and brands, such as Wal-Mart, which is the second-largest producer of clothing in Bangladesh, and the Gap, said they would establish their own safety programs. Wal-Mart plans to hire an outside auditor to inspect its 279 factories in Bangladesh and publish the results on its website. And if any fire or safety issues are found, the company will require factory owners to make the necessary renovations or risk being removed from its list of authorized factories. Furthermore, the company will set up an independent call center for garment workers to report unsafe conditions, child labor, human rights abuses, bribery, and other wrongs; and the company will also institute fire and safety training for every worker in its Bangladesh factories. Wal-Mart said that the key point is for a company to be "transparent" about its product sourcing. Also, it should be noted that Wal-Mart recently gave $1.6 million donation to a U.S. organization to start an environmental health and safety academy in Bangladesh. Wal-Mart also has a director of Ethical Sourcing who recently attended a meeting in Germany of retailers, worker's rights groups, labor unions, and non-governmental organizations to discuss industry-wide safety standards.

However, Wal-Mart did not want to take part in the aforementioned agreement that other companies have made in order to improve working conditions in Bangladesh because the company was concerned that the agreement was a legally binding one. Wal-Mart and other retailers are fearful that if they signed the agreement they could be sued in U.S. courts if the terms of the agreement were not fulfilled. So, JC Penny's and Sears are also drafting their own safety plans for Bangladesh. Yet some commentators fear that too many competing plans and programs for Bangladesh could undermine their effectiveness. Different plans and different standards could complicate efforts to determine which factories are safe. For example, confusion arises when there are different standards to where fire extinguishers have to be placed. Moreover, some commentators say that voluntary efforts to improve working conditions have a poor track record.

The Walt Disney Company, however, has decided to stop all production in Bangladesh; but the Georgetown professor said that the decision by Disney was "wrongheaded" because any improvement in working conditions in Bangladesh will depend on large multinational companies working with the Bangladesh government. Yet a Disney spokesperson, as quoted in *Bloomberg Businessweek*, said that Disney is a publicly traded company accountable to its shareholders, and as such the company believed that its decision not to make garments in Bangladesh was the "most responsible" one.

The government of Bangladesh, moreover, also agreed to allow garment workers to form unions without permission from factory workers. The government is also planning to raise the minimum wage of workers as well as institute more protections for workers. However, some critics say the government, as well as some of the companies, are just "paying lip-service" to improving standards, and consequently will really do nothing once the adverse publicity over the recent tragedies fades.

Finally, some activists, such as the Amsterdam-based Clean Clothes Campaign, want Western retailers to contribute $70 million to a fund that would compensate the victims and their families of the recent garment factory collapse.

Bibliography: Alam, Julhas and Hossain, Farid, "Retailers Pledge to Improve Conditions," *The Miami Herald*, May 14, 2013, p. 8B; Al-Mahmood, Syed Zain, "Bangladesh to Raise Workers' Pay," *The Wall Street Journal*, May 13, 2013, p. B4; Banjo, Shelly and Passariello, Christina, "Promises in Bangladesh," *The Wall Street Journal*, May 14, 2013, pp. B1, B7; Banjo, Shelly, Zimmerman, Ann, and Kapner, Suzanne, "Wal-Mart Crafts Own Bangladesh Safety Plan," *The Wall Street Journal*, May 15, 2013, pp. B1-2; Ek, Veronica and Kane, Clare, "Fashion chains agree to Bangladesh Reform," *Sun-Sentinel*, May 14, 2013, p. 3D; Passariello, Christina, Banjo, Shelly, and Fairclough, Gordon, "Standards Clash in Bangladesh Reforms," *The Wall Street Journal*, May 17, 2013, pp. B1-2; Srivastava, Mehul and Devnath, Arun, "The Paradox of Bangladesh," May 13-May 19, 2013, *Bloomberg Businessweek*, pp.15-16.

Discussion Questions

1. Should the government of Bangladesh institute uniform legal working standards for all the garment factories in the county? Why or why not? What should the government of Bangladesh be doing to improve legally the working conditions in the garment industry? And to what extent? Why?
2. How should an ethically egoistic company proceed when it comes to making garments in Bangladesh – sign the agreement to improve conditions (even if it is a legally binding pact), proceed on its own like Wal-Mart, or just pull out like Disney? Why?
3. Is the garment industry in Bangladesh a good example of capitalism? Why or why not?
4. Should maximization of profit always come at the cost of safety to workers? Discuss.
5. What should a "socially responsible" company be doing when it comes to making garments or buying from suppliers in Bangladesh? Why? Is Wal-Mart a socially responsible company when it comes to Bangladesh? Why or why not?
6. Are Western retailers morally obligated to contribute to the fund to compensate the victims of the recent factory tragedy? Why or why not? Even if they are not morally obligated to do so, should they do so regardless? Why or why not?

Case 4 - Haiti and the Cruise Ship Industry[15]

An issue with legal and moral ramifications arose out of the Haiti earthquake tragedy. Passengers who booked cruises with the Royal Caribbean cruise lines are now confronting a dilemma since the cruise line plans to continue to stop in its private island resort in Haiti. The problem is that many people feel it is not "quite

---

[15] Contributed by Frank Cavico, Nova Southeastern University.

right" for people to party on an island where about 100 miles away many thousands of people are still suffering from the aftershocks – literally and figuratively – from the earthquake. As one potential passenger was quoted in an CNN.com article, how could one order a drink and party when people are dying 100 miles away. Royal Caribbean, soon after the earthquake which killed almost 200,000 people in Haiti and devastated its capital of Port-au-Prince, resumed depositing its tourist cruise ship passengers on the very picturesque peninsula of Labadee, which was unaffected by the disaster, and where the company has spent millions in developing what it markets as its own "private paradise." This "paradise" is heavily guarded, and the cruise ship passengers do not spend the night; but, according to the Royal Caribbean website, they do enjoy Labadee's "pristine beaches, breathtaking scenery and spectacular water activities."

However, CNN.com reported that the reaction of many people to the continued use of Labadee has been one of "disgust" and "outrage," since the tourists are "frolicking in the sun while bodies pile up in Port-au-Prince and quake survivors struggle to stay alive." CNN also reported that one person deemed the cruise ship company to be performing a "sickening act" by taking tourists to Haiti.

Yet other people say that there are benefits to tourism, to Haiti, and its people by the cruise line company continuing to visit Haiti. Money surely will come into the local economy by the cruise ships stopping in Haiti and the tourist spending their money there; and, as one commentator noted, this is the time that Haiti needs tourism and tourism dollars the most. Visitors can thus have a positive effect economically. CNN reported that the United Nations World Tourism Organization stated that tourism can be a "useful instrument for the necessary reconstruction of Haiti." One commentator also stated that tourism can be particularly important to an area after a disaster, and used the examples of New York City after "9-11," as well as New Orleans after Hurricane Katrina, where both cities sought tourists to help them rebuild.

Royal Caribbean also stated that it would donate at least $1 million in humanitarian aid to Haiti, and also would contribute all of its net revenue from its Labadee operations to the relief effort. The cruise ships are also delivering supplies, including rice, beans, powdered milk, water, and canned goods – to the region. The company has been trying to reassure its passengers that it is appropriate to still stop at Haiti, and that to stay on the ship or go to alternative destinations are not viable options. The company emphasizes that it substantially helps the local economy by generating economic activity for the local populace, for example the straw market vendors and the hair-braiders; and moreover, the company noted that while its ships are in port over 200 of its personnel are helping with earthquake relief. One commentator noted that Haiti's plight would not improve if the cruise ships were diverted to another island. This commentator said the cruise ships are not hurting anyone, and they are doing some good by bringing help and generating money into the local economy. To the accusation that it is disrespectful to the Haitians for the tourists to come there and to have fun so close to a horrible disaster, one commentator countered by stating that the alternative of avoiding the area would not be more respectful. One said that the proximity to the disaster sets off a "gut reaction," but should not make any difference morally. Another commentator noted that Haiti's neighbor on the island of Hispaniola, the Dominican Republic, is very close to the disaster but is still functioning as usual. Yet another person contended that if a person does not feel at the least "a bit of awkwardness at the thought of playing beach volleyball" in Haiti right now does not have "normal moral intuitions." However, another commentator said that business must send a "hopeful" message to Haiti, and not treat it as a "fenced-off" and quarantined place that one can never invest or do business in; but rather one should treat Haiti, especially now, as a place that is still, to some extent, "open for business."

Bibliography: Pawlowski, A., "Haiti cruise stops draw ire, support". CNN.com, retrieved January 21, 2010 from: http://cnn.site.printthis.clickability.com.

Discussion Questions
1. What are some of the legal issues that might arise from this Haiti cruise ship situation? For example, what are some of the legal or ethical issues if the company cancels the stop and diverts the passengers? Conversely, what are some of the legal or ethical issues if the company decides to continue with the Haiti stop? How should these issues be resolved?
2. Is it moral for the company to continue stopping in Haiti? Why or why not?
3. Is Royal Caribbean being a sufficiently "socially responsible" company? Why or why not? If not, what else should they be doing?

Case 5 - Bribery and Wealth in the ASEAN[16] Community
Corruption is a reality of life in all countries and the ASEAN Community is no exception (Mujtaba, Cavico, Williamson and McClelland, 2013). This case proposes that the wealth of a country can be a determinant of corruption. The goal is to ascertain if there is a relationship between gross national product (GNP) per capita and the corruption perception index (CPI) of ASEAN countries. The main question is: "Is there a relationship between GNP and CPI in the ASEAN community?" And if so, then "why" is there a relationship between GNP and CPI in these ten ASEAN countries?

A study conducted by Mujtaba, Cavico, Williamson, and McClelland (2013) demonstrates that there is a significant linear relationship between wealth generation and a country's level of corruption. Wealth, or lack of it, emerges as a significant determinant variable in understanding the corruption pattern.

---

[16] This section is coauthored with Bahaudin G. Mujtaba and Frank J. Cavico, Nova Southeastern University; Peter Williamson and Bob McClelland, Liverpool John Moores University.
Also see: Mujtaba, B. G., McClelland, B., Cavico, F. J., Williamson, P. (January 2013). A Study of Bribery and Wealth in the ASEAN Community Based on the Corruption Perception Index Scores and GNP per Capita. *International Journal of Management, IT and Engineering*, 3(1), 576-597.

"ASEAN" refers to the Association of Southeast Asian nations, which was established in 1967 in Bangkok, Thailand. The five original members were Indonesia, Malaysia, Philippines, Singapore, and Thailand; and in 1995, Vietnam joined the organization. Today, ASEAN also includes the countries of Brunei, Laos, Cambodia, and Myanmar. The major purposes of ASEAN, as set forth in its declaration, are two: 1) to promote economic growth, social progress, and cultural development in the region by means of partnerships, joint ventures, accords and agreements; and 2) to promote regional stability and peace by adherence to the principles of the United Nations charter. Joint efforts to fight crime and combat corruption are certainly within the "jurisdiction" of ASEAN.

In answering the aforementioned research questions for the ASEAN countries, the authors relied on data from Transparency International (TI). TI, which was founded in 1993, is a non-governmental international organization whose objectives are to reduce corruption and bribery in politics, public affairs, and the private sector, and to promote economic development. Transparency International accomplishes these objectives primarily by conducting in-depth economic studies and disseminating the results of these studies as publicly and broadly as possible in order to improve societal awareness of corruption and bribery and the harm that these types of misconduct inflict on societies]. Two important aspects of TI's work for the purposes herein are: 1) the Corruption Perceptions Index (CPI), which is an annual report that as of 2011 ranks 183 countries by their perceived levels of corruption; and 2) the Bribe Payers Index, which is a listing of the 28 "leading economies" based on the likelihood of businesses from those economies paying bribes abroad. The Organization of Economic Cooperation and Development has an international treaty specifically combating bribery, called the Convention on Combating Bribery of Foreign Government Officials in International Business Transactions. This treaty is patterned after the primary U.S. statute prohibiting bribery abroad, the Foreign Corrupt Practices Act (FCPA). For the U.S. business person, the key statute is the Foreign Corrupt Practices Act, which has also extraterritorial reach, and which is enforced by the Justice Department. The FCPA makes the payment of a bribe, or the transfer of something of value, directly or indirectly, to a foreign government official, by a business person, in order to wrongfully secure a government contract with the host county a serious criminal wrong. Although it is beyond the purposes of this case to examine in detail the FCPA, the authors must emphasize that in order for there to be legal liability pursuant to the statute, the government must possess evidence of wrongful intent, that is, the bribe-giver must have had an "evil mind" and the corrupt motive, to, in essence, wrongfully direct the business to his or her firm, that is, to "purchase" the contract. Internationally, moreover, there is a treaty in the form of a convention by the Organization for Economic Cooperation and Development (OECD) which bans bribery. This treaty sets out criteria for national anti-bribery legislation, some of which provisions are very similar to the FCPA. However, in the FCPA as well as the OECD convention there is an exception, that is, a legal "bribe," called the "facilitating and expediting" exception. This legal exception bears direct relevance to the central issue on examination for this paper. Pursuant to the "facilitating and expediting" exception, a business person can make relatively small payments or "gifts" to lower level foreign government officials, who possess merely ministerial clerk-like authority, to facilitate, that is, to make things go more smoothly, and expedite, that is, to make to go more quickly, routine government actions, such as the processing of visas, custom forms, obtaining permits, licenses, and documents, and other "paperwork," that the business person is legally entitled to. Yet the greater the sum of money paid to the foreign government official, and the higher his or her position is, and the more discretionary power he or she has, and the less "routine" the government actions, the risk is that the payment will be transformed, at least in the eyes of the Justice Department, from a legal "bribe" to an illegal and perhaps felonious one. Nevertheless, the "facilitating and expediting" exception was placed in the law by Congress to reflect a "real-world" view that in many countries, especially less developed and poorer ones, these payments are considered normal, and culturally acceptable, business practices, in order to afford additional compensation to inadequately paid lower level government officials (that is, "petty bureaucrats").

The Asian Development Bank as well as the World Bank have promulgated anti-corruption policies and integrity principles and also are engaged in monitoring activities to encourage national governments to implement strategies to combat bribery and corruption. The Asian Development Bank's efforts are based on certain fundamental understandings, to wit: corruption is widespread; corruption raises serious ethical and political concerns; corruption has a deleterious effect on good government and the rule of law, impedes economic growth and efforts to reduce poverty, and distorts competition; yet nonetheless the fight against corruption is a complex undertaking that will require involvement by all parts of a society. Emphasis also must be made on a policy statement by the World Bank, pertinent to the purposes herein, which relates economic development to corruption. The World Bank believes that anti-corruption efforts are based on, and must be integrated with, a country's attempt to reduce poverty and increase economic development since creating economic opportunities and reducing poverty make a state more transparent and accountable.

Put simply, the poor are perceived, correctly or incorrectly, as being more corrupt; and, as a corollary, the perception of corruption decreases as countries become wealthier.

The Asian Cultural Orientation

Culture is generally defined as the common values, beliefs, ideas, practices, symbols, and artifacts of a distinct group of individuals. Organizational cultures can influence interpersonal relationship and behaviors in the department. Societal cultures influence people through their socialization in it, especially so during their upbringing. Culture is acquired knowledge that people of a country or region use to interpret experience in a common manner and generate social behavior. This knowledge forms values, creates attitudes, and influences behaviors. Culture can form the foundation for ethics and ethical behavior by determining what is moral or immoral. The norms and practices of one culture, including moral beliefs and precepts, may not be the norms and practices of another. Generational and gender differences and discrimination naturally affect the employment setting, but cultural differences are also an important reality of today's workforce. Cultural differences, such as languages spoken, clothing designs, and music played, are often apparent among people living in different cities, countries, or continents. Yet certain cultural differences, such as beliefs, values, and morals, are not always apparent at the "surface" level, but they are adhered to and practiced among different human groups.

Forming and sustaining personal relationships are important aspects of Asian culture. Of course, developing a personal relationship is critical in Asia before business can be even discussed; and the establishing and maintaining of this personal relationship is the key to any successful business transaction.

The Asian cultures represented by the ASEAN nations have had strong influence from two different philosophical schools – Taoism and Confucianism. Taoism underscores selflessness as an essential quality of life; altruistic ideals are thus an integral part of the teachings of Taoism. The goal is to perfect oneself by the self-cultivation of virtue and also to benefit others in a selfless manner. Confucianism's main concern is to cultivate the living humanity of the individual and society in harmony. Harmony and balance are exemplified by the superseding forces of Ying and Yang, which govern and hold together every aspect of life, including business, particularly negotiations where the Ying-Yang principle is viewed as a fundamental principle. A central tenet of Confucianism is the belief that "man" is essentially good. A person, therefore, should learn, reflect on, and attain moral ideals. Another important principle of Confucian principle is proper role relationships, for example, between father and son, and husband and wife; and if everyone plays his or her role properly, for example, the father is kind to the son, and the son is dutiful to the father, then the entire society will remain in a harmonious state.

Culture and Corruption
Culture has a relationship to corruption; many forms of corruption are intrinsically bound up in the social norms and practices of a society. Corruption has many forms, encompassing ballot-stuffing, extortion, embezzlement, tax evasion, smuggling, currency manipulation, money laundering, a conflict-of-interest, insider-trading and -dealing, "kick-backs," expense account "padding," over-invoicing, favoritism, and nepotism. However, bribery, particularly of government officials to secure government contracts, is a major and highly deleterious type of corruption. Many forms of corruption are intrinsically bound up in the social norms and practices of a society. Moreover, bribery is a common way of doing business in many societies; and it is in many places an engrained, and perhaps acceptable, cultural practice. Some business executives may view bribery as just a "routine" way of doing business and the "price of entry" in today's highly competitive global economy.

Bribery, furthermore, is not "merely" a Western or Eastern problem, but rather a universal concern that impacts countries, societies, and people around the world. Nonetheless, bribery is typically viewed as being more prevalent in less developed countries and poorer countries, where jobs do not pay well, and thus it is considered to be customary and appropriate for local government officials to "supplement" their typical "meager" incomes by taking such payments. Of course, there may be legal issues involved in the making of these payments pursuant to the Foreign Corrupt Practices Act as well as a country's own "domestic" law. A country may have laws that prohibit its government officials from taking bribes; yet whether these laws are enforced is another question. Anti-corruption efforts cannot be divorced from good governance and honest and efficient law enforcement. Internationally there is also a treaty in the form of a convention by the Organization for Economic Cooperation and Development (OECD) which bans bribery. This treaty sets out criteria for national anti-bribery legislation. Of course, it is problematic whether the signatories of the treaty enforce it against their business people doing business globally. Despite the laws and regulations and government agencies, corruption continues. Furthermore, despite the prevalence of corruption in many countries and despite the existence of a major statute and treating outlawing a principal form of corruption - bribery, surprisingly, there is very little in the literature as to the specific effect of wealth as a discrete cultural component influencing corruption, particularly bribery, and especially concerning bribery in the form of "facilitating and expediting" payments.

Discussion Questions

1. Should trade agreements be practiced in various communities? What are their advantages and disadvantages? Discuss.
2. What are the various forms of corruption in any given society? Discuss the common ones.
3. Is bribery a beneficial element for a society that has huge amounts of red tape? Discuss why or why not?
4. An alternative perspective might suggest that as a country's wealth increases, and its tax revenues rise, its ability to police and enforce anti-corruption measures improves, and hence the level of corruption falls due to legal intervention. Can this assumption be true? Why or why not?
5. Corruption plainly is a multi-faceted problem; and consequently there may be a number of factors, which once combined together, can lead to greater or lower levels of CPI. Discuss two factors that can reduce corruption in any developing country?
6. Wealth creation is an objective and expectation for countries since obviously wealth is important for each citizen's quality of life. So why is it that certain countries in the ASEAN Community seem to have more wealth than others? Discuss.

Case 6 - Globalization and Capitalism

Let us think about the diversity of different cultures, organizations, contributions of different countries and regions to modern society, and various practices that today's global firms use to achieve their objectives by understanding the origins of globalization. The key is to reflect upon what has caused globalization. Globalization has impacted people both positively and negatively throughout the world. Globalization has been spread, to some extent, by many of today's large multinational corporations in their drive to maximize profitability and their stockholder's wealth. The more risk that multinational corporations take as they serve new markets around the globe, the more rewards they are likely to enjoy when they are successfully serving an emerging base of prospective customers. So, multinational corporations are one driver of globalization. Is globalization a Western or an Eastern phenomenon? How did it get started and who should claim credit for its innovation or rise? Contrary to the popular perceptions, many claim that such questions do not have a simple answer as globalization has many sources of origin. Some writers claim that popular sentiments against globalization have often been directed at one of its "perceived" vehicles or engines — a Western consumer culture of fast food, gadgetry and cinema imposed on the entire world. But is globalization itself truly a creation of the West to benefit the West? Amartya Sen, Nobel Prize Winner in Economics, argues that "globalization's fruits" and even its origins can be claimed by East and West alike.

Experts, such as Amartya Sen and other economists, agree that globalization is often seen as global Westernization. On the other side, experts also state that Western dominance or imperialism is the devil of the piece. In this view, many claim that rules of trade and business relations that do not necessarily serve the interests of the poorer people in the world. Globalization is not necessarily a Western phenomenon since for thousands of years, globalization has been around. So there are many roads and avenues that have led to what is today termed as globalization.

Discussion Questions

1. What is globalization? Define it as you or other experts see it.
2. What are the main drivers, vehicles or engines of globalization? What forces are impacting or driving the trend toward globalization?
3. Is globalization good or bad? First, give a specific example from your perspective (or your culture) and then provide one more point of view (from another expert or culture).
4. Is globalization good for capitalism or is capitalism good for globalization? Discuss.
5. Will globalization speed up the divergence or convergence of cultures around the world? How and why? Discuss.

Bibliography

Abe, N. and Shimizutani, S. (2005). "Employment Policy and Corporate Governance: An Empirical Analysis on the Stakeholder Model in Japan," *ESRI Discussion Paper Series*, 136, Economic and Social Research Institute, Cabinet Office, Tokyo, Japan.

Abegglen, J.C. (1958). *The Japanese Factory: Aspects of its Social Organization*. Glencoe, IL: Free Press.

Abegglen, J.C. and Stalk, Jr., G. (1985). *Kaisha, the Japanese Corporation*. New York: Basic Books.

Adusei, L.A. (2012). Ghana, cocaine, corruption and the coming Armageddon. Retrieved from: http://www.modernghana.com/news/370709/1/ghana-cocaine-corruption-and-the-coming-armageddon.html

Agence France-Presse. (2012). War and neglect leaves 500,000 Afghans homeless: Amnesty. Retrieved from http://www.rawstory.com/rs/2012/02/23/war-and-neglect-leaves-500000-afghans-homeless-amnesty/ on December 8, 2012.

Ahmed, Mohammed, R. (2012). An Analysis of Leadership Style during the Mughal rule of India. Leadership Development Conference, Hyderabad, India.

Ahmed, Mohammed, R. (2009). An Analysis of U.S. Financial Service Industry's Crisis In Relation to Market Efficiency, Bankruptcy, and Regulation. Annual Global Finance Conference, Honolulu, Hawaii.

Ahmed, Mohammed, R. (2011). An Investment Performance of High-Intensity Firms In Relation to New Product Information. Annual Global Finance Conference, Bangkok, Thailand.

Ahmed, Mohammed, R. (2010). How do we Jump Start Our Economy. Annual Global Finance Conference, Poznan, Poland.

Ahmed, Mohammed, R., & Pellet, Pedro, F. (2010). A Model for Sustainable Economic Growth and Technological Development in Africa. Annual Global Finance Conference, Poznan, Poland.

Ajzen, I. (1987). Attitude, traits and actions: Dispositional prediction of behaviour in personality and social psychology. In L. Berkowitz (Ed.), *Advances in experimental social psychology* (pp. 1-63). San Diego, CA: Academic Press.

Ali, I.; Rehman, K. U.; and Akram, M. (2011). Corporate social responsibility and investor satisfaction influences on investor loyalty, *Actual Problems of Economics*, 8(122):348-357.

Anonymous. (2007). The dragon awakens: What foreign investors need to know about doing business in China. *Strategic Direction, 23*(3), 6-9.

Asahi Shimbun (Ed.). (2009). *The Lost Two Decades*. Tokyo: Iwanami Syoten (in Japanese).

Associated Press, (2012). *3 bank failures bring US 2012 total to 46*. Retrieved from http://news.yahoo.com/3-bank-failures-bring-us-2012-total-46-232728798--finance.html

Baker, W. R. (2005). Capitalism's Achilles Heel. John Wiley & Sons Inc. Hoboken, New Jersey.

Ballantine, L. (2012, September 09). *infrastructure key to giving properly*. Retrieved from cnn.com: http://globalpublicsquare.blogs.cnn.com/2012/09/12/infrastructure-key-to-giving-properly/?iref=allsearch

Bate, R. (2012). Combatting corruption. Retrieved from: http://www.american.com/archive/2012/october/combatting-corruption

Berteaux, J. (2005). What Are the Limits of Liberal Democratic Ideals in Relation to Overcoming Global Inequality and Injustice? *Human Rights Review*, 6(4) pp. 23-33.

Bhadwaj, A., Dietz, J., & Beamish, P. W. (2007). Host country cultural influences on foreign direct investment. *Management International Review, 47*(1), 29-50.

Bhasin, B. B. (2007). Succeeding in China: Cultural adjustments for Indian businesses. *Cross Cultural Management: An International Journal, 14*(1), 43-53.

Black, R. (2003). *Organizational culture: creating the influence needed for strategic success*. USA: Universal Publishers.

Bond, M. H. and Wang, S. H. (1983), 'China: Aggressive behaviour and the problem of maintaining order and harmony', In A. P. Goldstein and M. H. Segall, (Eds.), Aggression in Global Perspective, New York: Pergamon Press.

Boyer, R. (2004). *Une Theorie du Capitalisme Est-Elle Possible?* Paris: Odile Jacob.

Brewer, P., & Sherriff, G. (2007). Is there a cultural divide in Australian international trade. *Australian Journal of Management, 32*(1), 113-134.

Busenitz, L.W., Gomez, C., & Spencer, J.W. (2000). Country institutional profiles: Unlocking entrepreneurial phenomenon", *Academy of Management Journal, 43*(5), 994-1003.

Busse, A. (2010). The Best Laid Plans: The Impact of Informal Rules on Formal Institutions in Transitional Regimes. *Studies in Comparative International Development. 45,* 311-333. DOI 10.1007/s12116-010-9071-y

Business in Haiti. (2009, October 7). *Why Haiti; Haiti at a Glance.* Retrieved from Business in Haiti Website: http://businessinhaiti.com/index.php/whyhaiti

Business in Haiti. (2010, August 9). *Key Sectors; List of Apparel and Textile Manufacturers in Haiti.* Retrieved from Business in Haiti: http://businessinhaiti.com/index.php/keysectors

Business Monitor International. (2011). Economic outlook. Vietnam Business Forecast Report. Retrieved from http://web.ebscohost.com.library3.webster.edu/ehost/pdfviewer/pdfviewer?hid=15&sid=5e54 5774-ca33-46fe-af46-d79f69fd73eb%40sessionmgr12&vid=6

Cabinet Office, Government of Japan (2012). Annual Reports on National Accounts, available at http://www.esri.cao.go.jp/jp/sna/menu.html (accessed September 18, 2012).

Cañizares, S. M. S., & García, F. J. F. (2010). Gender differences in entrepreneurial attitudes. *Equality, Diversity and Inclusion: An International Journal,* 29(8), 766-86.

Aimkij, N., Mujtaba, B. G., and Kaweevisultrakul, T. (May 2013). Green Management Sustainability and its Economic Impact. *Journal of Economics and Sustainable Development,* 4(6), 104-115.

Cavico, F. J., Mujtaba, B. G., Muffler, S. C., and Samuel, M. (May 2013). Social Media and the Workplace: Legal, Ethical, and Practical Considerations for Management. *Journal of Law, Policy and Globalization,* 12(1), 1-46.

Cavico, F. J. & Mujtaba, B. G. (2013). *Business Ethics: The Moral Foundation of Leadership, Management, and Entrepreneurship (3rd edition).* Pearson: Boston.

Cavico, F. J. and Mujtaba, B. G. (2012a). National and Global Perspectives of Corporate Social Responsibility. *International Journal of Management Sciences and Business Research,* 1(3), pp. 1-24.

Cavico, F. J. and Mujtaba, B. G. (2012b). Social Responsibility, Corporate Constituency Statutes, and the Social Benefit Corporation. *International Journal of Management and Administrative Sciences,* 1(7), pp. 21-25.

Cavico, F. J., and Mujtaba, B. G. (2011). *Baksheesh or Bribe: Cultural Conventions and Legal Pitfalls.* ILEAD Academy Publications; Davie, Florida, United States.

Cavico, F. J. and Mujtaba, B. G. (2011). *Business Law for the Entrepreneur and Manager (2nd edition).* ILEAD Academy Publications. Florida.

Cavico, Frank J., and Mujtaba, Bahaudin G. (2008). *Legal Challenges for the Global Manager and Entrepreneur.* Dubuque, Iowa: Kendall-Hunt Publishing Company.

CBS News. (2012). Afghan Bank Sent Millions Abroad in Fraud. Retrieved on December 9, 2012 from http://www.cbsnews.com/8301-202_162-57555636/report-afghan-bank-sent-millions-abroad-in-fraud/

Central Intelligence Agency (2011), World Factbook: East & South East Asia: Vietnam. Washington, DC: US Central Intelligence Agency. Retrieved from https://www.cia.gov/library/publications/the-world-factbook/geos/vm.html

Central Intelligence Agency (2012), World Factbook: East & South East Asia: Vietnam. Washington, DC: US Central Intelligence Agency https://www.cia.gov/library/publications/the-world-factbook/geos/vm.html

Center for Economic and Policy Research. (2011, November 30). *Investigation Finds Evidence of Violations of Union Rights in Garment Industry.* Retrieved from Center for Economic and Policy Research Web site: http://www.cepr.net/index.php/blogs/relief-and-reconstruction-

Centre for Community Support Development Studies CECODES. (2008). Anti-corruption in Vietnam: The situation after two years of implementation of the law. Retrieved from http://www.finland.org.vn/public/download.aspx?ID=38961&GUID=%7B96721A6B-F87E-4B53-9342-5FDACC26B097%7D

Chang, H-J (2003). Kicking away the ladder: The real history of free trade. Foreign Policy in Focus (FPIF) special report.

Chatterji, Aaron K., and Richman, Barak D. (Summer, 2008). Understanding the "Corporate" in Corporate Social Responsibility. *Harvard Law and Policy Review*, Vol. 2, pp. 33-48.

Chen, C. C., Chen, Y. R., & Xin, K. (2004). Guanxi practices and trust in management: A procedural justice perspective. *Organization Science*, 15(2): 200-209.

Cheng, Y.-M. (2006). Determinants of FDI choice: Acquisition, Brownfield, and Greenfield entry in foreign markets. *Canadian Journal of Administrative Sciences, 23*(3), 202-220.

China Country Review (2010). *Country Watch Inc.* Available at: www.countrywatch.com [Accessed 04 September 2012]

Chomsky, N. (2004, March 9). *Getting Haiti Right This Time.* Retrieved from The "Noble Phase" and "Saintly Glow" of US Foreign Policy: http://www.thirdworldtraveler.com/Haiti/NoblePhase_GHRTT.html

Chomsky, N. (2004, March 9). *US-Haiti.* Retrieved from Chomsky Web site: http://www.chomsky.info/articles/20040309.htm

Chomsky, N. (2010, March 9). *Chomsky on Haiti.* Retrieved from Chomsky Info Web site: http://www.chomsky.info/interviews/20100309.htm

Christian Education Development Co. (2012, October 10). *Haiti Training Center & Trade School.* Retrieved from Extollo International Web site: http://www.extollointernational.org/our-projects/training-center

CIA. (2012, September 22). *Haiti.* Retrieved from CIA World Factbook: https://www.cia.gov/library/publications/the-world-factbook/geos/ha.html

Coase, R. H. (1937). The nature of the firm. *Economica, New Series, 4*(16), 385-405.

Cook Ross Inc. (2010). *Background on Haiti & Haitian Health Culture.* Retrieved from Cook Ross Website: http://www.cookross.com/docs/haiti.pdf

Coronel, G. (2006). *Corruption, Mismanagement, and Abuse of Power in Hugo Chavez's Venezuela.* Washington, D.C.: Cato Institute.

Coronel, G. (n.d.). *The corruption of democracy in Venezuela.* Retrieved December 31, 2013, from Cato Institute: http://www.cato.org/publications/commentary/corruption-democracy-venezuela

CSR Asia (2007). Police finished the PMU-18 scandal case. Retrieved from http://www.csr-asia.com/index.php?id=8934

DeJong, E., Smeets, R., & Smits, J. (2006). Culture and openness. *Social Indicators Research*(78), 111-136.

Department of Regulatory and Economic Resources. (2012, October 10). *Economic Development & International Trade.* Retrieved from Miami Dade County Web site: http://www.miamidade.gov/oedit/news.asp

Development Indicators: Singapore *World Bank 2010.* Available at: http://data.worldbank.org/country/singapore?display= default

Development Indicators: Australia, *World Bank, 2010.* Available at: http://data.worldbank.org/country/Australia.

Devex Inc. (2012, May 04). *Workforce Development Haiti.* Retrieved from Devex Inc. Web site: http://www.devex.com/en/jobs/workforce-development-wfd-capacity-building-expert-haiti-142

Diaz, C.B. (2012). U.S says BizJet settles foreign bribery charges. Retrieved from: http://www.reuters.com/article/2012/03/14/us-mexico-lufthansa-idUSBRE82D1H220120314

Dimitrov, M., 2009. Capitalism without Democracy: The Private Sector in Contemporary China. *Political Science Quarterly, 123*(4)

Do, P.T. (2010). Anti-Corruption in Vietnam. *The 13th International Training Course on the Criminal Justice Response to Corruption.* Retrieved from http://www.unafei.or.jp/english/pdf/RS_No83/No83_23PA_Phuong.pdf

Dong, L., & Glaister, K. W. (2007). National and corporate culture differences in international strategic alliances: Perceptions of Chinese partners. *Asia Pacific Journal of Management*(24), 191-205.

Dore, R. (2000). Stock Market Capitalism: Welfare Capitalism: Japan and Germany Versus Anglo-Saxons. New York: Oxford University Press.

Dunne, M. J. and Mujtaba, B. G. (May 2013). Employee Engagement and Change Management Programmes: a Comparative Study of Organisational Commitment between Thai and Irish Cultures. *International Affairs and Global Strategy*, 9, 01-22.

Fan, P. K., & Zigang, Z. K. (2004). Cross-Cultural Challenges When Doing Business in China. *Singapore Management Review, 26*(1), 81-90.

Fei Xiaotong (1985). *From the Soil, the Foundations of Chinese Society*. SDX Joint Publishing Company: Beijing, China.

Filatochev, I., Strange, R., Piesse, J., & Lien, Y.-C. (2007). FDI by firms from newly industrialised economies in emerging markets: Corporate governance, entry mode and location. *Journal of International Business Studies*(38), 556-572.

Fox News. (2012). Nearly $900M Kabul Bank fraud Reportedly included smuggling money out on airline food trays. Retrieved from http://www.foxnews.com/world/2012/11/27/report-kabul-bank-sent-hundreds-millions-dollars-out-afghanistan/?test=latestnews#ixzz2DalaV67W on December 8, 2012.

Fowom Ouvriye. (2008, February 13). *The Struggle For A Minimum Wage Adjustment In Haiti*. Retrieved from Fowom Ouvriye: http://fowomouvriye.org/index.html

Fraser Institute, 2011. *Index of Economic Freedom*. Available at: http://www.freetheworld.com/release.html [Accessed 04 September 2012]

Freedom House, 2010. *Freedom in the World*. Available at: http://www.freedomhouse.org/report/freedomworld/2010/singapore?page=22&year=2010&country=7915

Free Market Economy. (2010, October 14). Retrieved from Economy Watch: http://www.economywatch.com/market-economy/free-market-economy.htm

Free Market Economy vs State Driven Economy. (2010, Septeber 11). Retrieved from Care2: http://www.care2.com/c2c/share/detail/2345298

Frontline: The Dancing Boys of Afghanistan (2010). Retrieved from http://www.kpbs.org/news/2010/apr/16/frontline-dancing-boys-afghanistan/ on December 2, 2012.

Fu, P. P., & Yukl, G. (2000). Perceived effectiveness of influence tactics in the United States and China. *Leadership Quarterly*, 11(2): 251-266.

Gable, W., and Ellig, J. (1993). *Introduction to Market-Based Management*. Fairfax, VA: Center for Market Processes.

Galeano, E. (1997). *The Open Veins of Latin America*. New York: Monthly Review Press.

Gboyega, A., Soreide, T., Le T. M., & Shukla, G.P. (2011). *Political Economy of the Petroleum Sector in Nigeria* (Report No. 5779). Retrieved from World Bank website: http://www-wds.worldbank.org/external/default/WDSContentServer/WDSP/IB/2011/08/24/000158349_2 0110824134316/Rendered/PDF/WPS5779.pdfHamel

Gary (2007). *The future of management*. Boston: Harvard Business School Press.

Gerring, J., & Thacker, S.T. (2004). Political institutions and corruption: The role of unitarism and parliamentarism. *B.J. Pol, 34, 295-330.*

Ghazanfar, S. M. and May, K. S. (2000). Third world corruption: A brief survey of the issues. *The Journal of Social, Political, and Economics Studies*, 24(3), 351-368.

Gibson Dunn. (2011). Vietnam-An Update. Retrieved from http://www.gibsondunn.com/publications/pages/vietnam--anupdate.aspx

Global Integrity Report (2009). *Global Integrity Report: Complete 2009 Results*. Retrieved on November 05, 2012 from: http://report.globalintegrity.org/globalIndex/results.cfm

Goldsmith, A.A. (1995). Democracy, property rights and economic growth. *Journal of Development Studies, 32*(2), 157-175.

Graham, C., & Chattopadhyay, S. (2009). Well-being and public attitudes in Afghanistan. World Economics, 10(3), 105-146.

Greenhouse, S. (2010, 07 17). *Factory Defies Sweatshop Label, but Can It Thrive?* Retrieved from NY Times Web site: http://www.nytimes.com/2010/07/18/business/global/18shirt.html?pagewanted=all

Griffin, T. M. (2005, January 14). *Haiti Human Rights Investigation*. Retrieved from Institute for Justice and Democracy in Haiti Web site: http://www.ijdh.org/CSHRhaitireport.pdf

Gyimah-Boadi, E. (2009). Another step forward for Ghana. *Journal of Democracy, 20(2), 138-152.*

Hall. M.A. (2002), Measuring patients' trust in their primary care providers. *Medical Care Research,* 3(59):193-318.

Hall, P. and Soskice, D. (Eds.) (2001). *Varieties of Capitalism: The Institutional Foundations of Comparative Advantage.* Oxford: Oxford University Press.

Hall, E.T. (1976). *Beyond Culture,* New York: Anchor Books.

Harris, L. (2002). Achieving a balance in human resourcing between employee rights and care for the individual. Business & Professional Ethics Journal, 21(2), pp. 45-60.

Haynes, J. (1991). Human rights and democracy in Ghana: The records of the Rawlings' regime. African Affairs, 90, 407-425.

Hill, W. L., (2009). *Global business today.* New York, NY: McGraw-Hill

Hill, Charles (2011). *International Business: Competing in the Global Marketplace,* 8th edition. New York: McGraw Hill.

Gary, H. (2004). The network structures of East Asian Economies in Capitalism in contrasting cultures. Berlin: Walter de Gruyter.

Gittins, R. and Tiffen, R. (2009). *How Australia Compares.* Melbourne: Cambridge University Press.

Hofstede, G. (2012). National culture dimensions. Retrieved from: http://geert-hofstede.com

Hofstede, G., 2012. National culture dimensions: Singapore. Available at: http://geert-hofstede.com/singapore.html [Accessed 05 September 2012]

Hofstede, G. (2001). *Cultural consequences: Comparing values, behaviors, institutions, and organizations across nations.* Beverly Hills, California: SAGE Publications.

Hofstede, G. (1980). *Culture's Consequences: International Differences in Work-Related Values.* Beverly Hills, CA: Sage.

Hofstede, G. (1991). *Culture and Organizations: Software of the Mind.* New York: McGraw-Hill.

Hofstede, G. (1984). Cultural Dimensions in Management and Planning. *Asia Pacific Journal of Management,* 81-99.

Hofstede, G. *Culture's consequences: International differences in work-related values.* Beverly Hill, CA: Sage, 1980a.

Hofstede, G. (1991). *Cultures and Organizations: Software of the Mind.* McGraw-Hill, New York.

Hors, I. (2000). Fighting corruption in the developing countries. *Organization for Economic Cooperation and Development,* 220, 43-45.

Husted, B. W. (1999). Wealth, culture, and corruption. *Journal of International Business Studies,* 30(2), 339-359.

Hussain, A. (1988). "Land Reforms in Pakistan", in Hussain, A. (ed.) *Strategic Issues in Pakistan's Economic Policy,* p. 178, Lahore: Progress Publishers.

Hussain, I. (1999). Pakistan: Economy of an Elitist State. Oxford University Press.

Hussain, I. (2009). The role of Politics in Pakistan's Economy. *Journal of International Affairs,* vol. 63, No. 1, Fall/Winter 2009, pp. 1-18.

Ibukun, Y. (2012, January 13). Strike could halt Nigeria oil output. *USA TODAY.* Retrieved from http://www.usatoday.com/USCP/PNI/MONEY/2012-01-13-BCAFNigeriaFuel-SubsidyOil10th-LdWritethru_ST_U.htm

Immanuel, W. (2003). *The Capitalistic World Economy.* Cambridge: Cambridge University Press

Institute of Developing Economics. (1994). Tokyo, p. 324.

International Institute for Management Development IMD (2010). World Competitiveness Yearbook, 2010. Available at: http://www.worldcompetitiveness.com/ [Accessed 05 September 2012]

International Monetary Fund. (2012). World Economic Outlook, October 2012: Coping with High Debt and Sluggish Growth. Retrieved from http://www.imf.org/external/pubs/ft/weo/2012/02/pdf/text.pdf

International Monetary Fund, Nigeria. (2008). Staff Report for the 2007 Article IV Consultation (IMF Country Report No. 08/64). Retrieved from http://www.imf.org/external/pubs/ft/scr/2008/cr0864.pdf

Isomura, K. and Huang, P.Y. (2012, in press). Exploring the Future Direction of Japan's MBA Education. *Asia Pacific and Globalization Review,* 2(1).

Isoyama, T. (2002). *International Accounting Standards War.* Tokyo: Nikkei BP.

Japan Institute for Labour Policy and Training (2005). "Transforming Human Resource Management and Governance/Corporate Strategies," *JILPT Research Report*, 33, Tokyo.

Jones, Gareth R. and George, Jennifer M. (2011). *Contemporary Management*, 7th edition. McGraw Hill, New York, USA.

Kaifi, B.A. (2008). The power of education in international economic development. *Sitara Magazine*, 1(5), 16-17.

Kaifi, B.A. (2009). A Critical Hermeneutic Approach to Understanding Experiences of Selected Afghan-American Leaders post-9/11 in the Bay Area. ProQuest Dissertation Service. Copyrighted by Belal A. Kaifi. USF: 2130 Fulton Street, San Francisco, CA 94117-1080. (415) 422-5555.

Kaifi, B.A., & Mujtaba, B. G. (2010). Transformational leadership and the impact of socialization in the Afghan culture: A study of behavioral differences based on gender, age, and place of birth. *International Leadership Journal*, 2(2), 33-52.

Kaifi, B.A., Mujtaba, B.G., & Xie, Y. (2009). Future Afghan-American leaders' perception of their role in economic development in Afghanistan: A study of gender differences and willingness to return to the motherland. *Journal of Diversity Management*, 4(3), 35-46.

Kelman, S. (2000). Corruption and government: Causes, consequences, and reform. *Journal of Policy Analysis and Management*, 19(3), 448.

Klein, N. (2007). The Shock Doctrine: The Rise of Disaster Capitalism. New York, NY: Picador.

Knights, D. and Willmott, H., 2007. *Introducing organisational behaviour and management*. London: Cengage Learning EMEA.

Kobayashi, M.K. (1996). Adult Business Education Programmes in Private Educational Institutions in Japan. *Journal of Management Development*, 15(8), 30–37.

Koch, C. G. (2007). *The Science of Success: How Market-Based Management Built the World's Largest Private Company*. Wiley Publications; United States.

Ksenia, G. (2008). Can corruption and economic crime be controlled in developing countries and if so, is it cost-effective? *Journal of Financial Crime*, 15(2), 222-233.

Lewis, A. (1954). Economic Development with Unlimited Supplies of Labor. The Manchester School, 22, 139-191.

Li, D. (2010). *Singapore is most open economy: Report*. Available at: http://www.asiaone.com/Business/News/My+Money/Story/A1Story20100201-195831.html [Accessed 04 September 2012]

Liu, L. A., Friedman, R. A., & Chi, S. C. (2005). "Ren Qing" versus the "Big Five": The role of culturally sensitive measures of individual difference in distributive negotiations. *Management and Organization Review*, 1(2): 225-247

Lim, L. (2005). Hegemony and Political Dominance in Singapore. 2005. Available at: http://www.allacademic.com/meta/p21520_index.Html [Accessed 05 September 2012]

Liñán, F. (2008). Skill and value perceptions: How do they affect entrepreneurial intentions? *International Entrepreneurship Management Journal*, 4(3), 257-272.

Liñán, F., & Chen, Y. (2009). Development and cross cultural application of a specific instrument to measure entrepreneurial intentions. *Entrepreneurship Theory and Practice*, 33(3), 593-617.

Londoño, E. (2012). Afghanistan Sees Rise in 'Dancing Boys' Exploitation. Retrieved from http://www.washingtonpost.com/world/asia_pacific/afganistans-dancing-boys-are-invisible-victims/2012/04/04/gIQAyreSwS_story.html on November 29, 2012.

Lookfah Marketing, (2012). Basic Jamaica Facts. Retrieved from http://www.jamaica-dream-vacation.com/basic-jamaica-facts.html#parishes

Maddison, A. (2003-2012). *Economy Statistics > GDP per capita in 1950 (most recent) by country* . Retrieved December 29, 2012, from NationMaster.com: http://www.nationmaster.com/graph/eco_gdp_per_cap_in_195-economy-gdp-per-capita-1950#source

Martin, H. (2012). A development plan for independent Jamaica. *The Gleaner*, July 29, 2012. Retrieved from http://jamaica-gleaner.com/gleaner/20120729/focus/focus3.html

Maitland, E. (2001). Corruption and the Outsider: Multinational Enterprises in the Transitional Economy of Vietnam. *Singapore Economic Review*, 46(1), 63-82.

Manyak, T. G. and Mujtaba, B. G. (February 2013). Task and Relationship Orientations of Ugandans and Americans. *International Business and Management,* 6(1), 12-20. Website: http://www.cscanada.net/index.php/ibm/article/view/j.ibm.1923842820130601.1010

Maskalyk, J. (2011, August 4). *Paul Farmer's "Haiti: After The Earthquake".* Retrieved from The Washington Post Web site: http://www.washingtonpost.com/entertainment/books/paul-farmers-haiti-after-the-earthquake/2011/07/14/gIQAluTquI_story.html

Mazakazu, Y. (1996). Asia: A civilization in the making. *Foreign Affairs, 75*(4), 106-118.

Mayer, R.C, Davis, J.H, and Schoorman, F.D. 1995. An integrative model of organizational trust. *Academy of Management Review,* 20(3):709-734.

MBM Video (2009). Market Based Management video presentation. Available at Koch Industries Website: http://www.kochind.com/MBM/default.aspx

McGrath, R. G., MacMillan, I. C., Yang, E. A., & Tsai, W. (1992). Does culture endure or is it malleable? Issues for entrepreneurial economic development. *Journal of Business Venturing,* 7(2), 115-35.

Meng Xue, Liu Xuexin. (2007). On the Expression, Cause of Medical Corruption and the Prevention Measure. *Journal of Anhui Vocational College of Police officers,* 6(28):9-12.

Michel, Albert (1993). *Capitalism against Capitalism.* New York: Wiley.

Minister of Finance (1997). About the financial system reform (The Japanese version of the Big Bang), available at http://www.fsa.go.jp/p_mof/english/big-bang/ebb1.htm (accessed on September 19, 2012).

Minister of Finance (1998). About Financial System Reform Act, available at http://www.fsa.go.jp/p_mof/low/1f001.htm (accessed on September 19, 2012).

Minister of Health, Labor and Welfare (2012). Historical data 1 (10): unemployment rate (by age group), whole Japan, monthly data. available at http://www.stat.go.jp/data/roudou/longtime/03roudou.htm (accessed September 23, 2012).

Ministry of Health of People's Republic of China, 2008 and 2006. Survey on doctor-patient relationship. Website: http://www.moh.gov.cn/publicfiles//business/htmlfiles/wsb/index.htm

Morgan, G., (1986). *Images of Organization.* Beverly Hills, CA: Sage Publications

Morris, M. W., Williams, K. Y., Leung, K., Larrick, R., Mendoza, M. T., Bhatnagar, D., Li, J., Kando, M., Luo, J.-L., & Hu, J.-C. (1998). Conflict management style: Accounting for cross-national differences. *Journal of International Business Studies,* 29(4): 729-748.

Mujtaba, B. G. (2014). *Managerial Skills and Practices for Global Leadership.* ILEAD Academy: Florida.

Mujtaba, B. G. (April 2013). Ethnic Diversity, Distrust and Corruption in Afghanistan: Reflections on the Creation of an Inclusive Culture. *Equality, Diversity and Inclusion: An International Journal,* 32(3), 245-261. DOI 10.1108/EDI-12-2012-0113,

Mujtaba, B. G. (2011). Perceptions of bribery and business ethics across Afghanistan: A reflection on reality and crises management. *Journal of Global Business Advancement, 4*(2), 88-117.

Mujtaba, B. G. (2007). Afghanistan: Realities of war and rebuilding (2nd edition). Florida: ILEAD Academy, LLC.

Mujtaba, B. G., Ping, H., and Jieqiong, C. (2013). A Cross-cultural Analysis of Management Skills with Chinese, Iranian, Pakistanis, Thai, and American Managers. *SAM: Advanced Management Journal,* 78(1), 50-67.

Mujtaba, B.G., Afza, T., Byabashaija, W., Cavico, F.J., David, J., Delgado, M.E., Fernandez, N., Habib, N., Isomura, K., Katono, I.W., Manyak, T.G., Masahudu, O., McFarlane, D.A., Mendez, M.I., Nguyen, L.D., Pellet, P.F., Plangmarn, A., Ping, H., Torres, R., and Udechukwu, I. (2013). *Capitalism and Corruption across the African, Asian, and North American Economies.* Professional Development Workshop, Academy of Management Conference, Orlando, Florida. Sunday, August 11, 2013.

Mujtaba, B. G. and Cavico, F. J. (May 2013). A Review of Employee Health and Wellness Programs in the United States. *Public Policy and Administration Research,* 3(4), 01-15.

Mujtaba, B. G. and Cavico, F. J. (May 2013). Corporate Social Responsibility and Sustainability Model for Global Firms. *Journal of Leadership, Accountability and Ethics,* 10(1), 58-76.

Mujtaba, B. G. and Cavico, F. J. (February 2013). Corporate Social Responsibility and Sustainability Model for Global Firms. *Journal of Leadership, Accountability and Ethics,* 10(1), (*in-press*).

Mujtaba, B. G., McClelland, B., Cavico, F. J., Williamson, P. (January 2013). A Study of Bribery and Wealth in the ASEAN Community Based on the Corruption Perception Index Scores and GNP per Capita. *International Journal of Management, IT and Engineering*, 3(1), 576-597.

Mujtaba, B. G., Cavico, F. J., and Plangmarn, A. (2012). Corporate Social Responsibility and Globalization. *Proceedings of the 17th International Conference of Asia Pacific Decision Sciences Institute* (APDSI), pp. 89-109. Chaing Mai, Thailand. July 22 - 26, 2012. ISSN: 1539-1191.

Mujtaba, B.G. and Isomura, K. (2012). Examining the Japanese Leadership Orientations and their Changes. *Leadership & Organization Development Journal*, 33(4), 401–420.

Mujtaba, B. G., Tajaddini, R. and Chen, L. Y. (2011). Business Ethics Perceptions of Public and Private Sector Iranians. *Journal of Business Ethics*, 104(3), 433-447.

Mujtaba, B. G. and McCartney, T. (2010). *Managing Workplace Stress and Conflict amid Change, 2nd edition*. ILEAD Academy: Florida.

Mujtaba, B. G., & Kaifi, B. A. (2010). Business ethics and morality in Afghanistan. *Business and Professional Ethics Journal*, 29(1-4), 32-63.

Mujtaba, B. G., and Cavico, F. J. (2010). *The Aging Workforce: Challenges and Opportunities for Human Resource Professionals*. ILEAD Academy, LLC: Florida.

Munene, J. C., Schwartz, S. S., & Smith, P. B. (2000). Development in sub-Saharan Africa: Cultural influences and managers' decision behavior. *Public Administration and Development, 20*(4), 339-51.

Nakane, C. (1970). *Japanese Society*, Berkeley, CA: University of California Press.

Nguyen, L. D., Mujtaba, B. G., Tran, C. N., and Tran, Q. H. M. (2013). Sustainable Growth and Ethics: A Study of Business Ethics in Vietnam between Business Students and Working Adults. *The South East Asian Journal of Management*, 7(1), 41-56.

Nguyen, L.D. and Mujtaba, B. G. (2013). Entrepreneurship progress and developments in Vietnam: An Interview with the Bureau Chief, Director General of the Ho Chi Minh City Ministerial Office of the Ministry of Industry and Trade. *Journal of Applied Management and Entrepreneurship*, 18(2), 116-122.

Nguyen, Lam D., Mujtaba, Bahaudin G., and T. Boehmer (2012), Stress, Task, and Relationship Orientations across German and Vietnamese Cultures, *International Business and Management, 5*(1), 10-20.

Nigeria: 2 presumed dead after Chevron rig fire. (2012, January). *USATODAY*. Retrieved from http://www.usatoday.com/news/world/story/2012-01-19/nigeria-rig-fire/52676696/1

Northouse, P.G. (2004). *Leadership: Theory and practice* (3rd ed). Thousand Oaks, CA: Sage Publications.

NPR. (2011, July 12). *Paul Farmer Examines Haiti 'After the Earthquake'*. Retrieved from NPR Website: http://www.npr.org/2011/07/12/137762573/paul-farmer-examines-haiti-NY Times. (2012). Ghana. Retrieved from: http://topics.nytimes.com/top/news/international/countriesandterritories/ghana/index.html

O'Higgins, E. R. E. (2006). Corruption, underdevelopment, and extractive resource industries: Addressing the vicious cycle. *Business Ethics Quarterly*, 16(2), 235-254.

Onuejeougwu, M. A. (1995). *Development in Africa: Common cultural values central for effective managerial and administrative training programmes*. A paper presented at a regional seminar on Cultural Dimensions and Appropriate and Effective Management in Africa. Kampala, UG: Makerere University.

OPPapers, 2012. Geert Hofstede Cultural Dimensions. Available at: http://www.oppapers.com/essays/Geert-Hofstede-Cultural-Dimensions/194611Ouchi, W. G. (1978). Markets, Bureaucracies, and Clans. *Administrative Science Quarterly*, 25(1), 129–41.

Ouchi, W. G. (1980). Type Z Organization: Stability in the midst of Mobility, *Academy of Management Review*, 3(2), 305–14.

Ouchi, W. G. (2004). An Interview with William Ouchi, *Academy of Management Executive*, 18 (4), 108–16.

Padgett, T. (2011, January 18). *Baby Doc Charged, but Duvalier Still Has Fans*. Retrieved from Time Web site: http://www.time.com/time/world/article/0,8599,2043133,00.html

Padgett, T. (2011, January 21). *Why Aristide Shouldn't Be Allowed Into Haiti.* Retrieved from Time Magazine Web site: http://www.time.com/time/world/article/0,8599,2043829,00.html

Pakistan Economic Survey. (1996). *Government of Pakistan, Ministry of Finance.* Islamabad: Printing Corporation of Pakistan.

Parks, D., & Vu, A. D. (1994). Social Dilemma Behavior of Individuals from Highly Individualist and Collectivist Cultures. *The Journal of Conflict Resolution, 38*(4), 708-718.

Paul, E. C., 2003. Obstacles to Democratisation in Singapore. *Centre for Southeast Asian Studies,* Working Paper No .78,

Peng, M.(Ed.). (2011). *Global.* Mason, OH: Cengage Learning.

Peng, M. W., Wang, D., & Jiang, Y. (2008). An institution-based view of international business strategy: A focus on emerging economies. *Journal of International Business Studies, 39,* 920-936.

Perraton, J. (2007). Evaluating Marxian contributions to development economies. *Journal of Economic Methodology,* 14(1), 27-46.

Pohlman, Randolph A. & Gardiner, Gareth S. (2000). *Value-Driven Management: How to Create and Maximize Value over Time for Organizational Success.* AMACOM. United States.

Polanyi, K. (1944). *The Great Transformation: The Political and Economic Origins of Our Time.* New York: Farrar & Rinehart.

Polanyi, K. (1977). *The Livelihood of Man.* New York: Academic Press.

Powers, J. L, Brotheridge, C. M, Blenkinsopp, J., Bowes-Sperry. L., Bozionelos, N., Buzady, Z., Chuang, A., Drnevich, D., Garzon-Vico, A., Leighton, C., Madero, S. M., Mak, W., Mathew, R., Monserrat, S. I., Mujtaba, B. G., Olivas-Lujan, M. R., Polychroniou, P., Sprigg, C. A., Axtell, C., Holman, D. Ruiz-Gutierrez, J.A., and Obiajulu Nnedum, A. U. (2013). Acceptability of workplace bullying: A comparative study on six continents. *Journal of Business Research,* 66(1), 374-380.

Prahalad, C. K. (2010). The responsible manager. *Harvard Business Review,* 88(1), 36.

Quinn, M. J., Mujtaba, B. G. and Cavico, F. J. (March 2011). Global tobacco sales dilemmas: the clash of freedom and markets with morality and ethics. *Journal of Business Studies Quarterly,* 2(2), 107-124.

Quang, T. (1997). Conflict Management in Joint-Ventures in Vietnam. *Transitions, 38*(1&2), 282-306.

Quang, T., & Vuong, N. T. (2002). Management Styles and Organisational Effectiveness in Vietnam. *Research and Practice in Human Resource Management, 10*(2), 36-55.

Quinones, E. (2000). What is corruption? *Organization for Economic Cooperation and Development,* 220(1), 23-24.

Ralston, D. A., Nguyen, T. V., & Napier, N. K. (1999). A Comparative Study of the Work Values of North and South Vietnamese Managers. *Journal of International Business Studies, 30*(4), 655-672.

Ralston, D. A., Terpstra-Tong, J., Terpstra, R. H., Wang, X., & Egri, C. (2006). Today's state-owned enterprises of China: Are they dying dinosaurs or dynamic dynamos? *Strategic Management Journal,* 27(9): 825-843.

Rebuild Globally. (2012, October 10). *About Us: Rebuild Globally.* Retrieved from ReBuild Globally Web site: http://www.rebuildglobally.org/

Rivas, D. (2002). *Missionary Capitalist: Nelson Rockefeller in Venezuela.* Chapel Hill, NC: University of North Carolina Press.

Robert J.B.,Cathy S.,Catherine D. (2003). Common concerns amid diverse systems: health care experiences in five countries. *Health Affairs,*3(22):106-120.

Rossier, N. (Director). (2005). *Aristide and the Endless Revolution* [Motion Picture].

Sanyal, R. N. (2006). *International Management: A Strategic Perspective.* Upper Saddle River, NJ: Prentice-Hall.

Savage, V. R. and Yeoh, B. S. A. (2004). *Toponymics: A study of Singapore's Street Names.* Singapore: Eastern University Press.

Schneider, M. L. (2012, September 20). *UN Can't Leave Haiti Until Rule Law Established.* Retrieved from Christian Science Monitor : http://news.yahoo.com/un-cant-leave-haiti-until-rule-law-established-160910773--politics.html

Scott, D., Bishop, J. W., & Chen, X. (2003). An Examination of the Relationship of Employee Involvement with Job Satisfaction, Employee Cooperation and Intention to Quit in U.S.

Invested Enterprise in China. *The International Journal of Organizational Analysis, 11*(1), 3-19.

Sen, Amartya (Spring 2010). Adam Smith and the Contemporary Word. *Erasmus Journal for Philosophy and Economics*, 3(1), 50-67.

Sheckleford, M. (2006). *Jamaica: Debt, Economic Performance and Labour Productivity.* Washington D.C.: Council on Hemispheric Affairs. Retrieved from http://www.coha.org/jamaica-debt-economic-performance-and-labour-productivity/Siddiquee, N. A. (June 2010). Combating Corruption and Managing Integrity in Malaysia: A Critical Overview of Recent Strategies and Initiative. *Public Organization Review*, 10(2), 153-171.

Siddique, K. (*2011) Experiences of Capitalism in India and Pakistan, Research in Applied Economics,* Vol. 3, No. 1: E1, pp. 1-48.

Simonson, S. (2004) Ethnicising Afghanistan?: Inclusion and exclusion in post-Bonn institution building. Third World Quarterly, Vol. 25, No. 4, pp. 707- 729

Singapore Academy of Law (2007). *The Singapore Legal System.* Available at: http://www.singaporelaw.sg/content/LegalSyst1.html [Accessed 04 September 2012]

Singapore Economic Development Board (2012). Facts and Figures. Available at: http://www.edb.gov.sg/edb/sg/en_uk/index/industry_sectors/energy/facts_and_figures.html [Accessed 04 September 2012]

Smith, A. (1776). The Wealth of Nations. New York, NY: Random House, Inc.

Soek-Fang, S., 2001. Asian Values, Authoritarianism and Capitalism in Singapore ' *The Public*, 8(2), pp. 46

Survey Report on doctor-patient relationship, 2006. Website: http://www.91health.org/message.asp?D_ID=323

Svensson, J. (2005). Eight Questions about Corruption. *Journal of Economic Perspectives, 19*(3), 19–42.

Swierczek, E. W. (1994). Culture and Conflicts in Joint-Ventures in Asia. *International Journal of Project Management, 12*(1), 7.

Tang, A. (2008A). Sex trade thrives in Afghanistan. Retrieved on December 2, 2012 from: http://usatoday30.usatoday.com/news/world/2008-06-15-460899821_x.htm?csp=34.

Tang, A. (2008B). Chinese prostitutes work brothels in Afghan capital. Retrieved on November 28, 2012 from: http://articles.latimes.com/2008/jun/15/news/adfg-afghan15.

Tanner, S. (2009). Indomitable Afghanistan. *Military History, August/September issue, 26 -35.*

Teng, C. S., & Foster, M. J. (2006). A flexible response to Gou Qing: Experience of three MNCs entering restricted sectors of the PRC economy. *Asia Business & Management*(5), 315-332.

The United States Department of Justice (2010). Nexus Technologies Inc. and Three Employees Plead Guilty to Paying Bribes to Vietnamese Officials. Retrieved from http://www.justice.gov/opa/pr/2010/March/10-crm-270.html

The Chinese Medical Doctor Association (2011). Investigation of Physician practice condition. Website: http://med.39.net/a/2011811/1775440.html

The EuroCham (2010). *Singapore ranked 7th in the world for innovation.* Available at: http://eurocham.org.sg/index.php?option=com_eurochammobile&view=news&id=289&temp late=ccmobile [Accessed 04 September 2012]

The World Factbook. (2012). Jamaica. Washington, D.C.: Central Intelligence Agency. Retrieved from https://www.cia.gov/library/publications/the-world-factbook/geos/jm.html

Thom, D.H. (1999). Validation of a measure of patients' trust in their physician: the trust in physician scale. *Medical Care*, 5(137):510-517.

Thomson Reuters Foundation. (2011). Vietnam under pressure from international anti-corruption laws to act. Retrieved from http://www.trust.org/trustlaw/news/vietnam-under-pressure-from-international-anti-corruption-laws-to-act/

Transparency International (2011). Corruption Perceptions Index 2011. Retrieved from http://cpi.transparency.org/cpi2011/results/

Triandis, H.C. (1989). The Self and Social Behavior in Differing Cultural Contexts. *Psychological Review, 96*, 606-520.

Udechukwu, I. I, and Mujtaba, B. G., (March 2013). An Institutional and Architecture Based View of Corruption in Nigeria: An Analysis of a Developing Economy's Formal and Informal Structures. *Journal of Business Studies Quarterly*, 4(3), 230-239

UNDP. (2011). *Human Development Report.* United Nations: New York.
UNIDO. (1990). *Pakistan: Towards Industrial Liberalization and Revitalization.* Oxford: Blackwell Publishers.
US Department of State (2008) Bureau of South and Central Asian Affairs. Retrieved from http://www.state.gov/r/pa/ei/bgn/5380.htm on October 2, 2008.
United Nations. (2012, September 17). *News Centre: Despite progress, Haiti facing challenges on justice reform and poverty* . Retrieved from United Nations: http://www.un.org/apps/news/story.asp?NewsID=42916&Cr=haiti&Cr1=
United Nations. (2012, October 9). *Peacekeeping Missions Minustah.* Retrieved from United Nations Web site: http://www.un.org/en/peacekeeping/missions/minustah/
United Stated Census Bureau. (2012). Trade in Goods with Vietnam. Retrieved from http://www.census.gov/foreign-trade/balance/c5520.html
United States Country Review (2010). *Country Watch Inc.* Available at: www.countrywatch.com. [Accessed 04 September 2012]
USAID. (2012, January 9). *US Government Strategy on Haiti.* Retrieved from USAID Web site: http://haiti.usaid.gov/about/our_strategy.php
Vecchio, R., Justin, J., & Pearce, C. (2008). The utility of transactional and transformational leadership for predicting performance and satisfaction within a path-goal theory framework. *Journal of Occupational and Organizational Psychology*, 81 (1), pp. 71-82.
Venezuela Facts and Figures. (2012). Retrieved December 30, 2012, from Organization of the Petroleum Exporting Countries: http://www.opec.org/opec_web/en/about_us/171.htm
Verger, R. (2011, August 7). *Paul Farmer's Fight for Haiti.* Retrieved from The Daily Beast Web site: http://www.thedailybeast.com/articles/2011/08/07/paul-farmer-on-his-new-book-haiti-after-the-earthquake.html
Vietnam News (2011). Corrupt official gets seven years in jail. Retrieved from http://vietnamnews.vnagency.com.vn/politics-laws/law-justice/213064/corrupt-official-gets-seven-years-in-jail.html
Vietnam News (2012a). Corruption probes uncovers 49 cases. Retrieved from http://vietnamnews.vnagency.com.vn/politics-laws/226929/corruption-probes-uncover-49-cases.html
Vietnam News (2012b). More efforts needed in fight against corruption, says PM. Retrieved from http://vietnamnews.vnagency.com.vn/politics-laws/229126/more-effort-needed-in-fight-against-corruption-says-pm.html
Vogel, E.F. (1979). *Japan as Number One: Lessons for America.* Cambridge, MA: Harvard University Press.
Waseem, M. A., Mujtaba, B. G. and Kamal, M. F. (April 2013). Cultural Dimensions and Theories of Public Relations: A Study in the Case of Pakistan. *European Journal of Scientific Research*, 99(3), 452-460.
Watkins, H.S., Liu, R. (1996). Collectivism, individualism and in-group membership: implications for consumer complaining behaviors in multicultural contexts. *Journal of International Consumer Marketing, 8* (3/4) 69-96.
WB Report. (2012). Ghana: Retrieved from: htt://www.worldbank.org/en/country/ghana
Weinberg, M. (2002). A Short History of American Capitalism. Retrieved from: http://www.newhistory.org/CH01.htm on November 28, 2012.
Williamson, C. R. (2009). Informal institutions rule: institutional arrangements and economic performance. *Public Choice, 139*, 371 – 387.
World Bank. (2011). Economy rankings. *Doing Business.* Retrieved from http://www.doingbusiness.org/rankings.
World Bank. (2006). *Pakistan: Growth and Export Competitiveness.* Report No.35499-PK, Washington D.C.
World Bank. (1997). Helping Countries Combat Corruption: The Role of the World Bank, Poverty Reduction and Economic Management. Retrieved from http://www1.worldbank.org/publicsector/anticorrupt/corruptn/corrptn.pdf
World Bank (2010). *Development Indicators: Singapore.* Available at: http ://data.worldbank.org/country/singapore?display=default [Accessed 05 September 2012]

World Economic Forum (2009). *The Global Competitive Index, 2009-2010.* Available at: https://members.weforum.org/pdf/GCR09/GCR20092010fullrankings.pdf [Accessed 04 September 2012]

Xueying, L. (2009). Old and new citizens get equal chance, says MM Lee. Available at: http://www.pmo.gov.sg/content/pmosite/mediacentre/inthenews/ministermentor/2009/April/ol d_and_new_citizensgetequalchancesaysmmlee.html [Accessed 05 September 2012]

Yasmeen, G., Begum, R., and Mujtaba, B. G. (June 2011). Human Development Challenges and Opportunities in Pakistan: Defying Income Inequality and Poverty. *Journal of Business Studies Quarterly,* 2(3), 1-12.

Yoo, B., & Donthu, N. (2005). The effect of personal cultural orientation on consumer ethnocentrism: Evaluation and behaviours of US consumers toward Japanese products. *Journal of International Consumer Marketing,* 18(1/2), 7-44.

Younos, F. (2008). Democratic Imperialism: Democratization vs. Islamization. Bloomington, IN: Authorhouse.

Zhang, C., Cao, L and Vaughn, M. S. (2009). Social support and corruption: Structural determinants of corruption in the world. *The Australian and New Zealand Journal of Criminology,* 42(2), 204-217.

Zuliani, L. (2011). The trouble with the Singapore workplace. Available at: http://www.economywatch.com/economy-business-and-finance-news/the-trouble-with-the-singapore-workplace.21-07.html [Accessed 05 September 2012]

Author Biographies

Talat Afza, Ph.D., is Professor and Dean, Faculty of Business Administration at COMSATS Institute of Information Technology, Pakistan. She has earlier served as the department chair at the same university and National University of Sciences and Technology Pakistan. Ms. Afza has more than twenty five years of teaching experience including the adjunct professor at University of Michigan, Dearborn and Wayne State University Detroit U.SA. Her areas of research interest include efficiency analysis, Women Entrepreneurships and Business Ethics. She can be reached at: talatafza@ciitlahore.edu.pk.

Mahmoud Bodla, Ph.D., is Professor and Director, Faculty of Business Administration at COMSATS Institute of Information Technology, Lahore, Pakistan. He has more than twenty five years of teaching and administration experience including an adjunct professor at University of Michigan, Dearborn and Wayne University Detroit U.SA. Her areas of research interest include leadership, management, entrepreneurships, and operations management.

Warren Byabashaija, Senior Lecturer and Dean of the Faculty of Entrepreneurial Studies, Makerere University Business School, Uganda. He holds a doctoral degree from Louisiana State University. His teaching and research interests are in entrepreneurship, ethical behavior in procurement, and business statistics. His recent publications include articles in the *Journal of Public Procurement* and the *Journal of Developmental Entrepreneurship.*

Frank J. Cavico is a Professor of Business Law and Ethics at the H. Wayne Huizenga School of Business and Entrepreneurship of Nova Southeastern University in Ft. Lauderdale, Florida. He has been involved in an array of teaching responsibilities, at the undergraduate, master's and doctoral levels, encompassing such subject matter areas as business law, government regulation of business, constitutional law, administrative law and ethics, labor law and labor relations, health care law, and business ethics. In 2000, he was awarded the Excellence in Teaching Award by the Huizenga School; and in 2007, he was awarded the Faculty Member of the Year Award by the Huizenga School of Business and Entrepreneurship; and in 2012 he was again honored by the Huizenga School as Faculty Member of the Year. He holds a J.D. from the St. Mary's University School of Law and an LL.M from the University of San Diego, School of Law; and is a member of the Florida and Texas Bar Associations. He is the author and co-author of several books and numerous law review and management journal articles.

Jackson David was born in Leogane, Haiti. He was shot during a robbery and kidnapping and left for dead on July 4, 1998. He lived and was required to relocate to Miami for medical care. He is a recent business graduate from Miami Dade College earning his Bachelor's Degree in Supervision & Management. Jackson is married to Eugenie David and is currently employed as a Disability Advocate with the Center for Independent Living and owns Olympas Corner Enterprises providing immigration and tax services.

Mario E. Delgado, M.A., M.B.A., has been Adjunct Professor of Economics & Business Administration at Edison College in Fort Myers, Florida. He is also a Rural Development Specialist of the United States Department of Agriculture, facilitating access and process/underwrite applications for affordable housing ownership and rehabilitation programs. Professor Delgado conducts Latino outreach activities throughout Area 2 and provides support as needed State wide. He became familiar with Business & Industry, Community Facilities and Farm Services programs to provide a one stop capability in Rural Development Specialist/USDA outreach efforts. He also developed a strategic plan proposal for the State's Latino outreach mandate, successfully implementing it within his immediate area significantly increasing the number of Latino applicants and callers. Participate with SBDC (Small Business Development Center) and TAG (Team Agriculture Georgia) in the design and delivery of seminars to

Latino owned small businesses and Latino farmers and ranchers. He can be reached through email at: medelgado2000@yahoo.com

Noel Fernandes is currently pursuing a Ph.D. at the Institute of International Studies, Ramkhamhaeng University, Bangkok of Thailand. His research topic revolves around understanding motivation in learning a Foreign Language and its implications on the Academia, Industry and policy makers. Noel is the Co-Founder and Managing director of the Kent School of Languages based in Bangkok, Thailand. The company has been created couple of years ago to tap the growing need of the corporate training market in Thailand. Prior to living in Bangkok, Thailand, Mr. Fernandes worked in Asia, Middle East and the Americas in various positions including Marketing, Logistics and Trading of petrochemicals. In the last twenty years, Noel has had the opportunity to travel across Asia, Europe, Middle East and North America which helped him experience and learn from different cultures thus enabling him to easily overcome cultural barriers and facilitate relationship building. He was born in Kerala, India.

Guillermo Gibens was born and raised in Venezuelan. He holds a doctorate degree in communication. Dr. Gibens has taught classes in the United States, Venezuela, United Arab Emeritus, Thailand, and other countries. His areas of research are communication, culture, and education. He can be reached at: ggibens@gmail.com

Naseem Habib is Research Associate at COMSATS Institute of Information Technology, Pakistan. She is a graduate researcher in MS (management) and her areas of interest and research are leadership development, career planning and development and cross cultural management. Email: naseemhabib@ciitlahore.edu.pk

Kazuhito Isomura is Professor of Organizational Behavior at Graduate School of International Accounting, Chuo University, Tokyo, Japan. Prior to joining Chuo University, he was with Faculty of Economics, Fukushima University, as an Associate Professor. He earned a BA, MA and Doctor of Economics at Kyoto University. His areas of research are leadership development, corporate strategy, knowledge management, organization theory, and management history. He can be reached at: kisomura@tamacc.chuo-u.ac.jp.

Belal A. Kaifi is a Faculty Lead and Professor of Business Administration at Trident University. Belal completed a Post-Doctoral program in Business Administration with an emphasis in Management and Marketing at the University of Florida. Belal completed his Doctoral degree in Organization and Leadership at the University of San Francisco. He has published over 30 peer-reviewed articles since 2008 and is the author of several books. Belal spent one month in Afghanistan in 2005, where he would teach English (ESL) in the evenings.

Isaac Wasswa Katono, Associate Dean of the Faculty of Business and Administration, Uganda Christian University. He is presently a doctoral candidate at the University of Capetown, South Africa. His research focus is in entrepreneurship, marketing, and research methodology. Research articles have appeared in the *Journal of Internet Banking and Commerce, International Journal of Emerging Markets, Education & Training, and Strategic Change.*

Yunshan (Victor) Lian has a Doctor of Business Administration degree from Nova Southeastern University. He received his Master of Business Administration from Saint Leo University. Mr. Lian has been working in management positions in the FAW (China First Automobile Group) for over 15 years and has accumulated 30 countries import and export experience. His excellent performance in leadership roles is evidenced by the rewards honored to him and the units that he directed. These include Working Star of FAW in 1997, Distinguished Department of FAW in 2000, and Representative of Chinese Entrepreneur in Sino-African Ministers' Forum in 2000. He could be reached at: victor.lian@hotmail.com

Terrell G. Manyak, Professor of Management at Nova Southeastern University. His doctoral degree is from the University of California, Los Angeles. The focus of his research interests are in leadership and development in African countries. He has published in *African Studies Quarterly, African Conflict and Peacekeeping Review, Gender in Management, International Business and Management, and Critical Perspectives on International Business.*

Osman Masahudu is an online adjunct professor of Finance and Accounting at Colorado State University Global-Campus; Masters of Science in Management. Osman is the chairman and CEO of an online professional development and training company, dedicated to promoting online teaching and learning. Osman is also a financial policy analyst for the United States Department of Agriculture – Forest Service in Washington D.C. Osman has written several financial policy handbooks and manuals for the agency. Osman can be reached through email at: Osman.masahudu@csuglobal.edu

Donovan A. McFarlane is currently a Visiting Professor of Management at the Keller Graduate School of Management and College of Business and Management of DeVry University, where he teaches Leadership and Organizational Behavior across the College's nine masters programs. He also serves as Professor of Business Administration and Business Research at Frederick Taylor University in its MBA and undergraduate programs. Professor McFarlane is an Adjunct Professor in Marketing at the H. Wayne Huizenga School of Business and Entrepreneurship at Nova Southeastern University where he teaches in the MBA program, and an Adjunct Professor of Business Administration at Broward College's North Campus in Florida. He is published in several peer review academic and professional journals and is a National Certified Mediator and member of the National Association of Certified Mediators (NACM). Dr. McFarlane is a native Jamaican and graduate of DeCarteret College in Jamaica, and he also attended Church Teachers' College in Manchester, Jamaica, before moving to the United States. He has earned degrees in several fields including Educational Leadership, International Business, Business Administration, Management, Paralegal Studies, Finance, Marketing, Accounting, Religious Studies, as well as in alternative studies such as Metaphysics, Parapsychology and Holistic Studies. He can be reached at don_anthoni@yahoo.com

Bob McClelland is currently The Reader in Educational Technology at Liverpool Business School, Liverpool John Moores University. He is also Visiting Professor at the Institute of International Studies, Ramkhamhaeng University, Bangkok, Thailand. Initially a Chemist he switched to Statistics lecturing in the late 1980s. He has spent the majority of his career as an academic. His research interests centre around Public and Private Sector evaluations and Business Educational Technology. His subject discipline is Research Methods. He is a research consultant and trainer (SPSS and NVivo) to a number of UK national and international companies. He can be reached at email: b.mcclelland@ljmu.ac.uk

María Isabel Méndez, M.B.A., is Visiting Professor of undergraduate courses in Finance and Management at Ramkhamhaeng University in Bangkok Thailand to students of diverse nationalities such as Thailand, China, Malaysia, Germany and Nigeria. Previously, she taught grades 4th through 8th with focus on exploratory and beginner's Spanish including development of communicative competence and understanding of the culture. Professor Méndez has twenty years of business and management experience in the telecommunications field covering areas such statistical analysis, pricing strategies, financial analysis and forecasting, sales and customer services in a telemarketing environment and international negotiations. She can be reached through email at: marisa.m214@yahoo.com

Bahaudin G. Mujtaba is Professor of Management and Human Resources at the H. Wayne Huizenga School of Business and Entrepreneurship of Nova Southeastern University in Ft. Lauderdale, Florida. Bahaudin is the author and coauthor of twenty professional and academic books dealing with management, diversity, business ethics, and cross-cultural management, as well as over 200 academic journal articles. During the past thirty years he has had the pleasure of working with human resource professionals in the United States, Brazil, Bahamas, Afghanistan, Pakistan, St. Lucia, Grenada, Malaysia, Japan, Vietnam, China, India, Thailand, and Jamaica. This diverse exposure has provided him many insights in ethics, culture, and management from the perspectives of different firms, people groups, and countries. Bahaudin can be reached at: mujtaba@nova.edu

Lam D. Nguyen is an Associate Professor of Management at the AACSB-accredited College of Business at Bloomsburg University of Pennsylvania. He has served as a Visiting Professor at Webster University Thailand and at the University of Economics, Ho Chi Minh City in Vietnam. Lam possesses a solid practitioner experience in business. This includes various managerial and leadership positions that he held in Vietnam as well as in the U.S. Lam has presented his research at many prestigious conferences and published in peer-reviewed journals. His areas of research are job satisfaction, leadership, strategic decision making, ethics, and cross cultural differences. He can be reached through email at: lnguyen@bloomu.edu.

Pedro F. Pellet, Ph.D., is Professor of Economics and Statistics at the H. Wayne Huizenga School of Business and Entrepreneurship. He has been a full-time teacher at Nova Southeastern University since April, 1982. He has attended higher education centers in Cuba, Great Britain, Puerto Rico, Spain and U.S.A. Dr. Pellet currently teaches Undergraduate, Masters and Doctoral courses. He has also supervised close to two-hundred doctoral dissertations and conducts scholarly researches in the area of Applied Economics and related socio-economic fields. He has taught and/or conducted research in five continents and eighteen countries. His doctoral dissertation on Input-Output analysis applied to Cuba, was personally influenced by Professor Wassily W. Leontief (Nobel Prize in Economics, 1973). He was taught by Dr. Amartya Sen (Nobel Prize in Economics, 1998) at the London School of Economics and Political Science. Bahaudin can be reached through email at: He can be reached through email at: pellet@huizenga.nova.edu

Han Ping is an Associate Professor of Organizational Behavior and Human Resource Management at The School of Management in Xi'an JiaoTong University P.R. China. Han Ping has ever been visiting scholar in Alberta University, Harvard Business School and Brigham Young University. Han Ping focused on the research of trust, effective leadership, positive organizational behavior. Han Ping can be reached at: hpca@mail.xjtu.edu.cn.

Acheraporn Plangmarn resides in Lampang, Thailand. She is a lecturer in the Department of Business Administration, Rajamangala University of Technology Lanna. She received a Bachelor of Business Administration degree in Marketing from Yonok College, a Master of Business Administration in Marketing from ChiangMai University and she received a Doctoral Business Administration program at the Institute of International Studies, Ramkhamhaeng University. Her areas of research interests include consumer behavior, cross-cultural consumer behavior and brand management. Email: acheraporn@gmail.com

Ruth Torres was born in Chicago, Illinois. She dropped out of high school in 10th grade. She earned her Bachelor's Degree in Business Administration from Dallas Baptist University, Dallas, Texas and her Master's Degree in Management, Human Resources from Florida International University and holds SPHR Certification. Ruth is the single mother of 3 incredible children ages 18, 16 & 8. She currently owns HR Strategic Consulting and teaches business courses at Miami Dade College, Florida International University & Nova Southeastern University.

Ike Udechukwu is a faculty member at Shorter University where he teaches courses in management. He is published in journals such as Human resource Development Review, Public Personnel Management, and the Journal of Management and Entrepreneurship. His areas of research interest are management, African studies, leadership, productivity management, and employee commitment. E-mail: Udechukwu@hotmail.com

Ramon J Venero is a doctoral student in business administration at the H. Wayne Huizenga School of Business and Entrepreneurship of Nova Southeastern University. His research interests include cross-cultural communications (as they relate to the enterprise); leadership; organizational behavior; business continuity and organizational resilience. His MAHRM is from Marymount University and in undergrad degree from Rutgers with a double major in economics and urban studies. He is a graduate of the Leadership Development Program of the Center for Creative Leadership, the Disney Institute's

WDW approach to HRM and also attended training at Harvard's School of Public Health in pandemic planning. He has presented double blind papers at scholarly conference and has a number of journal articles in process. Ray can be reached at: ramon@rayvenero.com

Peter Williamson is currently a Visiting Professor at the Institute of International Studies, Ramkhamhaeng University, Bangkok, Thailand. Following a spell in the pharmaceutical industry, he spent the majority of his career as head of the Marketing & Strategy faculty at Liverpool Business School, a constituent part of Liverpool John Moores University. His research interests include professional service provision, airline and pharmaceutical marketing. He is a consultant and trainer to a number of UK national and international companies. He can be reached at email: peterwilliamson.ljmu@gmail.com

Index

May you have the hindsight to appropriately diagnose problems and opportunities, the foresight to solve them effectively while capitalizing on the prospects, and the insight to ask for help when appropriate!

www.ingramcontent.com/pod-product-compliance
Lightning Source LLC
Chambersburg PA
CBHW031809190326
41518CB00006B/256